THE MAKING OF

𝕿𝖍𝖊 𝕮𝖑𝖔𝖎𝖘𝖙𝖊𝖗 𝖆𝖓𝖉 𝖙𝖍𝖊 𝕳𝖊𝖆𝖗𝖙𝖍

THE UNIVERSITY OF CHICAGO PRESS · CHICAGO

THE BAKER & TAYLOR COMPANY, NEW YORK; THE CAMBRIDGE UNIVERSITY
PRESS, LONDON; THE MARUZEN-KABUSHIKI-KAISHA, TOKYO, OSAKA,
KYOTO, FUKUOKA, SENDAI; THE COMMERCIAL PRESS, LIMITED, SHANGHAI

THE MAKING OF
The Cloister and the Hearth

By

ALBERT MORTON TURNER

Professor of English and Comparative Literature
The University of Maine

THE UNIVERSITY OF CHICAGO PRESS
CHICAGO · ILLINOIS

To the Memory of My Father

A TRUE LOVER OF BOOKS

WHO MADE A LIFE OF STUDY POSSIBLE FOR ME

I DEDICATE THIS BOOK

Preface

I FIRST read *The Cloister and the Hearth* while crossing the Pacific Ocean from Japan to San Francisco in April, 1924. Gerard, with all his adventures, proved an admirable companion during the many days of the voyage, longer than his, but happily much less eventful. After enjoying the vivid action of the novel and the varied human beings living in its pages, I became interested in the question of whence Reade derived all his information. The result of my studies was an article on "Another Source for *The Cloister and the Hearth*," in the *Publications of the Modern Language Association* in 1925. Thereafter I turned my attention elsewhere, thinking I should have no more to do with the novel. I became interested once more, however, and published another article, "Charles Reade and Montaigne," in *Modern Philology*, 1932–33. Again I bade farewell to *The Cloister and the Hearth*, but for a third time I was attracted to the novel. On this occasion my studies were very much more extensive than previously; the result is the present volume.

This book, then, embodies everything I have been able to discover about Reade's borrowings for his great novel. The only aspect I have not investigated is his occasional archaic or dialectal language. All the content of my two previous articles, I should add, is included in this more extensive study. In addition to tracing all the sources I could find, however, I have considered Reade's treatment of the points borrowed and thus have thrown much light upon his art. Moreover, since *The Cloister and the Hearth* has many friends, I have thought that some of them—even though not professional students of literature—might be led by their love of the novel to read at least parts of my book. If such should be the case, in order to make the perusal easier, I have, in those instances where Reade drew from French or Latin books, given the passages in translation instead of the original, even though this is contrary to the procedure of most American scholars. When a satisfactory translation was available, I have quoted

vii

from that. In other cases, though my references are to the pages of the original, I have rendered it into English myself.

I am under very great obligations to the officers of the library of Harvard University for permitting me to use its resources. In particular I feel especial gratitude to Mr. Walter B. Briggs and Mr. Robert H. Haynes for their unfailing helpfulness and kindness. I am likewise much indebted to the officers of the Boston Public Library, in which I have done much reading, and to those of the library of the University of Maine. To the librarians of Columbia University, the American Geographical Society of New York, the Library of Congress, and the Bodleian at Oxford I am grateful for answering my queries or allowing me to read books in their collections.

I am under obligation to Mr. M. L. Parrish, of Philadelphia, for placing at my disposal several notebooks of Reade in his possession and permitting me to make use of information therein. To Mr. Malcolm Elwin, author of the recent biography of Reade, and to Mr. M. H. Spielmann of Folkestone, England, I am indebted for their kind answers to my requests for information. Again, I am grateful to Professor Clyde K. Hyder of the University of Kansas for allowing me to include in this study one case of influence upon Reade which he himself had noticed. Finally, I wish to express my special thanks to Professor Emerson Grant Sutcliffe of Purdue University. He has been extremely helpful to me, answering various questions and generously drawing upon his ample fund of information about all of Reade's work.

The editors of *PMLA* and *Modern Philology* have permitted me to include in this volume all the facts in my two articles published in these journals. Miss A. F. Rowe, of Cambridge, has kindly looked up several points for me. Certain undergraduates of the University of Maine—especially Miss Priscilla D. Haskell, Miss Lillian R. Herrick, and Miss Edna P. Adams—have typed my manuscript for me. To all these I render my thanks.

Finally, I wish to express my particular gratitude to my wife. She has given me numerous good bits of advice, has helped me in the preparation of the final copy for the printer, and has encouraged me throughout.

Table of Contents

Chapter One
READE AT WORK

CHARLES READE'S masterpiece is unquestionably *The Cloister and the Hearth*. This fact is obvious now and indeed has been admitted for years. Even in 1887 the writers of the official *Memoir* declared that Reade

never regarded the book as his master-piece, proving thereby that the maker is seldom the best judge of his own work. Yet the verdict has long since been unanimous, that this same painfully evolved monument of fiction is not only his best, but, further, one of the rarest gems of English literature.[1]

The Cloister and the Hearth originally began its public appearance under the title "A Good Fight" in the magazine *Once a Week*. The editor proved "very annoying, tampering" with the text. Reade remonstrated, but the editor persisted. The disagreement grew, and the editor requested that the author end the story as soon as possible. Reade at length acceded by giving the story an unsuitable happy outcome at a most unexpected moment. As Reade himself puts it:

I have—"Away with melancholy!"—reversed the catastrophe; made Gerard and his sweetheart happy; sent Kate to Heaven, and they [the editors] and their weekly may go to the other place. Any way the story is finished, and they are rid of me, and I of them—*for ever!*[2]

"A Good Fight" with the hasty ending was indeed grotesque. The general course of the story is like the early part of *The Cloister and the Hearth*. Gerard was forced to leave Holland, and the wicked brothers sent a false letter after him. Then in three short final chapters the story changed its course and completely thwarted the reader's expectations. Gerard, finding printing in Germany, went to Florence. Here he happened to examine the deed

[1] Charles L. Reade and Compton Reade, *Charles Reade, Dramatist, Novelist, Journalist: A Memoir Compiled Chiefly from His Literary Remains* (2 vols.; London, 1887), II, 85. This work I cite as *Memoir*.

[2] *Ibid.*, pp. 93–95.

brought from Holland and, in consequence, started his return. Indeed, so opportune was his departure that Memling with the false letter just missed him. Gerard, on reaching home, married Margaret. Kate died; Cornelis, Sybrandt, and Giles fared as in the longer novel. The burgomaster, punished by the Duke, opportunely gave up the ghost, leaving everyone who deserved to be, happy. Such a makeshift could not satisfy Reade, genuinely interested as he was in the novel. The upshot was that in 1861 appeared *The Cloister and the Hearth*, far longer than "A Good Fight" and with the present tragic conclusion.

The plot of *The Cloister and the Hearth*, as is well known, is based on the life of Erasmus' father, and the source from which Reade drew his central facts, as he declares on the first page of the novel, is "a musty chronicle." But more of this later. The reason for Reade's tremendous interest in poor Gerard—unable to marry Margaret because he was a priest—was that his own case was similar. As the writers of the *Memoir* put it:

> Celibacy also with its cruel claw held Charles Reade prisoner. Had Gerard married, he would, on the lines of his belief, have lost his soul. Had Charles Reade married, he would have starved. Two-thirds of his life had passed before he could dream of dispensing with what he often termed his prop, viz., his Fellowship at Magdalen.[3]

Elsewhere the same authors imply that this financial dependence on Magdalen thwarted a love affair.

> As a matter of plain fact, the alliance he may secretly have coveted was, for pecuniary reasons, an impossibility. . . . . His dependence on the College was perhaps his misfortune, since it interposed a barrier between him and the one lady whom in the best days of his manhood he idealized, and never forgot, even in his dying moments.[4]

We nowhere learn from the *Memoir* who the lady was, but the authors state that in depicting Margaret in *The Cloister and the Hearth*, Reade did not have in mind Mrs. Seymour, who kept house for him and gave him her sympathy for years.[5]

John Coleman, in his *Charles Reade as I Knew Him*—an unreliable biography—declares that Reade fell deeply in love with a girl in Scotland, that a difference arose between them, and that

[3] II, 99.   [4] *Memoir*, I, 271.   [5] *Ibid.*, II, 100.

some years later he returned only to find the maiden had died.[6] This romance, moreover, Coleman says was the basis of the novel *Christie Johnstone*. Mr. Malcolm Elwin, in his sympathetic *Charles Reade: A Biography*, while recognizing Coleman's great inaccuracy, feels that in this case he may be near the truth. To be more exact, Mr. Elwin believes that about 1840 Charles Reade probably fell in love with a girl and desired to marry her, but his dependence on the Magdalen fellowship, aided perhaps by opposition of his family, rendered the match impossible. In support of this view Mr. Elwin cites some words written by Reade in 1876:

> In my medieval romance *The Cloister and the Hearth* I use this expression celibacy of the clergy, an invention truly devilish. A French critic is surprized at this violence in me since the rest of my work in general deals benevolently and benignly with Pope, Priests, Convents, and the unreformed Church in general. . . . . The opinion I uttered in 1860 [while writing the novel] was even then twenty years old in me: it is now thirty-six.[7]

Now the story of Gerard's misfortune, most appealing to Reade, almost surely came to his attention about 1856. "The idea of a book to be called 'Heroes and Martyrs,'" we read in Mr. Elwin's volume, "originated in the late, 'fifties, when he was collecting biographies as the best foundation for characters in fiction."[8] I noticed this fact myself, but Professor Emerson Grant Sutcliffe of Purdue University, an authority on Reade's novels, has informed me that this book *Heroes and Martyrs* was intended to glorify obscure men and women who performed noble deeds but were soon forgotten. Thus, when in his biographical reading for this purpose the father of Erasmus came to the novelist's attention, he was supremely attracted, for here was an obscure man who had lived heroically and, moreover, a man who had suffered from the same enforced celibacy as Reade. What wonder, then, that with such a hero the author produced his masterpiece![9]

[6] *Charles Reade as I Knew Him* (London, 1903), pp. 49, 60.

[7] *Charles Reade: A Biography* (London, 1931), pp. 44–45. (The expression in the novel, about celibacy, occurs in a footnote in the next to the last chapter.)

[8] *Ibid.*, p. 276.

[9] Another example of Reade's interest in the "underdog" may be the play *The First Printer*, written in 1856 in collaboration with Tom Taylor. Costar of Harlem is the hero, and Gutenberg steals from him the secret of printing.

Once embarked on a historical novel, Reade obviously had no end of research before him, especially since he liked to have his novels well documented. "He read," says the *Memoir*, "not only volumes, but bookshelves and libraries, with patience, if not with avidity."[10] Reade's usual system of notebooks must have flourished with such study. So did other methods, for he writes "I found such a wealth of material about hermits in the Magdalen College Library that I have filled three more of those gigantic cards." Moreover, during this study he was tossed by doubt: "Sometimes I say, it must be dangerous to overload fiction with facts. At others, I think fiction has succeeded in proportion to the amount of fact in it."[11] And, once more, "I will never attempt an old world story again. Good Heavens! How often have I been stuck!"[12]

It is noteworthy, however, that in spite of all these protestations Reade had part of the necessary study done for him by other men. Thus he writes in a notebook:

Having wasted too many years to be learned I must use cunning. Think of some way to make young active fellows run and collect materials for me. Think of a Machinery . . . . German hacks good for this. University hacks ditto. Pay them well and keep them dark.[13]

The books and cards used in the preparation of *The Cloister and the Hearth* are not known to exist. Professor Sutcliffe informs me that the thirty-two volumes of Reade's notebooks in the London Library, St. James's Square, London—volumes which he has studied carefully—do not bear upon the sources of *The Cloister and the Hearth*, except for rare indirect references which he has transcribed in his article on "Charles Reade's Notebooks."[14] The other group of Reade notebooks, which is now in the possession of the author, Mr. Michael Sadleir, similarly is not concerned with the sources of *The Cloister and the Hearth*, as I am told by Mr. Malcolm Elwin, who has gone through them in preparation for writing his biography of Reade; in fact, they date mostly from a period subsequent to the writing of this novel (i.e., 1869–80).

[10] II, 88.

[11] *Memoir*, II, 104–5.

[12] *Ibid.*, p. 109.

[13] Elwin, p. 150.

[14] *Studies in Philology*, XXVII, 64–109.

There is, however, a most important letter printed in the *Century Magazine* for November, 1884.[15] The article in which it appears, entitled "An Acquaintance with Charles Reade," is by Annie Fields and was obviously prompted by the novelist's recent death on April 11, 1884. For our purposes the letter is significant because it enumerates a large number of works read in preparation for writing *The Cloister and the Hearth*. It runs as follows:

You may well be surprised that I am so long over "Good Fight," but the fact is, it is not the writing but the reading which makes me slow. It may perhaps give you an idea of the system in which I write fiction, if I get down the list of books I have read, skimmed, or studied to write this little misery.

The great work, 1. "Lacroix and Sire on the Middle Ages"; 5 thick quartos. 2. "Du Sommerard," do.; the plates only. 5. "Strutt's Works," and 9. "Hone's Day-books, Table-books," etc. 10. "Leland's Itinerary." 11. Fynes' Moryson's do. 12. "Bouyer's History of the Popes." 13. Ranke's ditto. 14. "Erasm. Colloquia." 15. "Erasm. Parabola." 16. Munster's "Cosmographia." 17. Luther's "Table Talk." 18. Wanley's "Little World." 19. Victor Hugo's "Hunchback." Scott's "Quentin D.," "Monastery." 22. "Abbot." 23. Fosbrooke's "British Monachism." 24. Newcome's "Abbey of St. Albans." 25. "Fox on Monasteries." 26. M. H. Bloxam on ditto. 27. "Monumenta Franciscana." 28. "Epistolae Obscurorum Virorum." 29. Mosheim. 30. Jamieson's "Legends of the Monastic Orders," ditto. 31. "Sacred and Legendary Art." 32. Vasari. 33. Bryant. 34. Mrs. Merrifield's "History of Painting." 35. "Mores Catholici." 36. 3 vols. Southey's "Common-Place Book." 37. "History of the Dominicans," Marchese. 38. Hallam's "Middle Ages." 39. Lit. Europe. 41. Humphrie's two works on do. 42. Shaw's "Dresses and Decorations." 43. Maitland's "Dark Ages." 44. Pugin and Smith, "Ecclesiastical Vest." 45. Warton's "Early English Poetry." 46. "The Harleian Miscellany." 47. "The Paston Letters." 48. "Correspondence, Henry and Wolsey," Government Publication. 49. Grove's "Antiquarian Repository." 50. Index "Gentleman's Magazine." 51. Do. "Archaeological Journal." 52. Labarti's "Handbook of the Middle Ages." 53. "Les Voyages de Montaigne." 54. Coryat's "Crudities." 55. Monteil's "Vie Privée des Français." 56. "Le Grand d'Aupy," ditto. 57. "Dutch Geography," Reynolds G. Van Reschied. 58. Knight's "Life of Erasmus." 59. Jortin's. 60. Bayle's in Dict. 61. "Chronique de Flandres." 62. Henry's "History Great Britain." 63. Sharon Turner's ditto. 64. Froissart. 65. Monstrelet. 66. Philippe de Comines. 67. Barante's "Dukes of Burgundy." 68. Brandt's "History of the Reformation." 69. Liber Vagatorum. 70. Hecker's "Epidemics of the Middle Ages." 71. Welars de Honecort's "Sketch-book." 72. Norica. 73. John Guttenberg. 75. Ben Jonson's "Alchemist" and "Volpone," the old plays in Dodsley, and especially 76. "The Four P's." 77. "Le Livre d'Or des Meteors,"

[15] XXIX, 73.

by Michel & Fournier. 78. Pugin's "Contrasts." 79. Monuments Français inedits, etc., etc.

Reade declared at the beginning of this long list that he had "read, skimmed, or studied" these books. One must, of course, take this statement freely, for in all probability some were "read by deputy, and extracts made of them" by Reade's assistants. Moreover, as the "etc., etc." at the end indicates, the list does not purport to be a complete list of all books which were consulted for writing *The Cloister and the Hearth*. On the other hand, hasty as this list is, the chances are that it contains most of the important sources of the novel. In any case, where an author has been careful enough to draw up a long list of sources for a great novel, it behooves us to scrutinize these works carefully. Indeed, so worth while has seemed the study of just what Reade took from these various books and of how he used his borrowings in the novel that I too have "read, skimmed, or studied" all the volumes in this long list. This study forms the base of the present book.

Reade's actual writing of the list is hasty enough. The numbering is often erratic, the spelling is erroneous, and, in particular, the titles are frequently inexact. (Some of these mistakes, it is true, may come from the misreading of Reade's rather difficult penmanship.) Certain ones of the books have been decidedly hard to identify, but I have eventually succeeded in all but one case. To simplify matters I shall give the authors and titles in correct form, arranging them in classes, and adding, in some cases, significant information.

I. ERASMUS AND HIS WORKS

BAYLE, PIERRE. Article on Erasmus in his *Dictionaire historique et critique*.

ERASMUS. *Colloquia*.

———— *Parabolae sive similia*. Aphorisms, making ordinary objects or happenings symbolic of moral truths. It may be found in the first volume of his complete works, Leiden, 1703–6.

JORTIN, JOHN. *The Life of Erasmus*.

KNIGHT, SAMUEL. *The Life of Erasmus*.

II. LITERARY WORKS

DODSLEY. *Collection of Old Plays*. The first three editions of this collection were published before *The Cloister and the Hearth*. The third was in twelve volumes.

HEYWOOD, JOHN. *The Foure PP.* An old play.

HUGO, VICTOR. *Notre-Dame de Paris.*

JONSON, BEN. *The Alchemist.*

———. *Volpone.*

SCOTT, WALTER. *The Abbot.*

———. *The Monastery.*

———. *Quentin Durward.*

III. BOOKS ON LITERATURE

HALLAM, HENRY. *Introduction to the Literature of Europe in the Fifteenth, Sixteenth, and Seventeenth Centuries.*

WARTON, THOMAS. *The History of English Poetry.*

IV. THE FINE ARTS

BLOXAM, MATTHEW HOLBECHE. *The Principles of Gothic Ecclesiastical Architecture.* An account of Gothic architecture in England. (This must be Reade's "M. H. Bloxam on ditto," though I have also looked through Bloxam's *Fragmenta sepulchralia.*) Reade knew Bloxam personally at Oxford.

BRYAN, MICHAEL. *A Biographical and Critical Dictionary of Painters and Engravers.* (Reade's "Bryant.")

HUMPHREYS, HENRY NOEL, must be the man intended in Reade's "Humphrie's two works on do" ("do" being either the literature of Europe or the literature of the Middle Ages). Of Humphreys, I have looked over the following books published before 1861 (the date of Reade's novel): *Illuminated Illustrations of Froissart,* from manuscrip s in the British Museum; another similar volume from the Bibliothèque Royale, Paris; *The Origin and Progress of the Art of Writing; Stories by an Archaeologist and His Friends; The Illuminated Books of the Middle Ages; A Record of the Black Prince; Ten Centuries of Art.* Most of these books are connected with medieval manuscripts, and many are handsomely illustrated.

JAMESON, MRS. *Legends of the Monastic Orders* and

———. *Sacred and Legendary Art.* Both of these works concern the lives of saints and paintings depicting them.

LABARTE, JULES. *Handbook of the Arts of the Middle Ages and Renaissance.* (Reade's "Labarti.")

MARCHESE, VINCENZO FORTUNATO. *Lives of the Most Eminent Painters, Sculptors, and Architects of the Order of S. Dominic.* An English translation from Italian appeared in 1852. (Reade's " 'History of the Dominicans,' Marchese.")

MERRIFIELD, MARY P. *The Art of Fresco Painting* and *Original Treatises Dating from the XIIth to XVIIIth Centuries on the Arts of Painting, etc.* Both books are accounts of the technique of these arts; either might be Reade's "Mrs. Merrifield's 'History of Painting.' "

Monuments français inédits pour servir à l'histoire des arts. Two folio volumes handsomely illustrated with plates of manuscript illuminations, sculptures, furniture, arms, etc.; its list of subscribers include "le Roi des français," the Emperor of Austria, the King of Prussia, and the Empress Josephine.

PUGIN, A. WELBY. *Contrasts: Or, a Parallel between the Noble Edifices of the Middle Ages, and Corresponding Buildings of the Present Day.*

———. *A Glossary of Ecclesiastical Ornament and Costume.* Revised by BERNARD SMITH. A glossary of church terms, with many fine illustrations of church robes, etc. (Reade's "Pugin and Smith 'Ecclesiastical Vest.' ")

SHAW, HENRY. *Dresses and Decorations of the Middle Ages.* Two folio volumes with handsome plates.

SOMMERARD, ALEXANDRE DU. *Les Arts au Moyen Age.* Reade says he examined only the plates; there are three large volumes of these.

VASARI, GIORGIO. *Lives of the Most Eminent Painters, Sculptors, and Architects.* A complete English translation was in existence,—by Mrs. Jonathan Foster.

Wilars de Honecort, Facsimile of the Sketch-Book of. An English edition of this medieval architect's sketchbook, with notes by Robert Willis, appeared in London in 1859. (Reade's "Welars de Honecort 'Sketch-book.' ") A French edition called *Album* and spelling the author's name "Villard de Honnecourt" was likewise in existence.

V. ECCLESIASTICAL WORKS

BOWER, ARCHIBALD (Reade's "Bouyer"). *The History of the Popes.* 7 vols. 1750–66.

BRANDT, GERARD. *The History of the Reformation . . . . in and about the Low-Countries.* Translated from the Dutch. 4 vols. 1720–23.

FOSBROKE, THOMAS DUDLEY. *British Monachism: Or, Manners and Customs of the Monks and Nuns of England.*

FOX, SAMUEL. *Monks and Monasteries.* On English monasticism.

Monumenta Franciscana. Edited by J. S. BREWER. 1858. (The second volume was published after *The Cloister and the Hearth.*) A collection of Latin documents about the Franciscans in England.

Mores Catholici: Or, Ages of Faith. The anonymous author is KENELM HENRY DIGBY. A huge modern work—twenty-two hundred large, double-columned pages in the edition I used—ardently celebrating the Middle Ages and their religion.

MOSHEIM, JOHANN LORENZ VON. *An Ecclesiastical History.* An English translation from the Latin was available.

NEWCOME, PETER. *The History of the Ancient and Royal Foundation, Called the Abbey of St. Alban.*

RANKE, LEOPOLD. *The Popes of Rome.* An English translation was available.

VI. POLITICAL HISTORY
A. MEDIEVAL AUTHORS

Chronique de Flandre. I have examined all the works I could find with anything like this title. By far the most important and almost surely the one intended by Reade is *Recueil des chroniques de Flandre* publié ... par J. J. DE SMET, Brussels: Vol. I, 1837; Vol. II, 1841; Vol. III, 1856; Vol. IV, after Reade's novel. Reade, in this *Century* list, has a penchant for bulky works; these volumes of Smet, qualifying admirably in this respect, contain medieval chronicles mostly in Latin.

FROISSART, SIR JOHN. *Chronicles.*

Memoirs of Philip de Commines, The.

MONSTRELET, ENGUERRAND DE. *Chronicles.* English translations of this and the two previous old chronicles were available.

B. MODERN AUTHORS

BARANTE, A. G. P. B. DE. *Histoire des ducs de Bourgogne de la maison de Valois.* 12 vols.

HALLAM, HENRY. *View of the State of Europe during the Middle Ages.*

HENRY, ROBERT. *The History of Great Britain.* 12 vols.

TURNER, SHARON. *The History of England.* 12 vols.

VII. SOCIAL HISTORY, ETC.

AUSSY, LE GRAND D'. *Histoire de la vie privée des françois* (Reade's "Le Grand d'Aupy"). This antiquarian book treats the history of French food, and the allied subjects of hunting and banquets. Its author intended to treat other aspects of French life but failed to do so.

HECKER, J. F. C. *The Epidemics of the Middle Ages.* An English translation appeared in 1844.

LACROIX, PAUL (literary ed.) and FERDINAND SERÉ (artistic ed.). *Le Moyen Age et la Renaissance.* Five large volumes treating some twenty-five different aspects of medieval life, the articles being written by various authors. (Reade's "Lacroix and Sire.")

Liber vagatorum. A book in German about the habits of beggars; published *ca.* 1509. J. C. Hotten published an English version in 1860: *The Book of Vagabonds and Beggars with a Vocabulary of Their Language and a Preface by Martin Luther.*

MAITLAND, S. R. *The Dark Ages: A Series of Essays.*

MICHEL, FRANCISQUE and FOURNIER, EDOUARD. *Le Livre d'or des métiers: histoire des hôtelleries.* An episodic account of French inns of the past.

MONTEIL, AMANS ALEXIS. *Histoire des français des divers états.* This work treats, in as graphic a way as possible, the social history of France from the fourteenth to the eighteenth century. (Reade's "Monteil's 'Vie Privée des Français.'")

"Strutt's Works" (Reade). These include *The Sports and Pastimes of the People of England; A Compleat View of the Manners, Customs, Arms, Habits, &c of the Inhabitants of England; The Regal and Ecclesiastical Antiquities of England; A Supplement* to this last; and *A Complete View of the Dress and Habits of the People of England.* I have gone through all these.

VIII. HISTORY OR BIOGRAPHY, IN THE FORM OF FICTION

Norica or Tales of Nürnberg from the Olden Time. Translated from the German of AUGUST HAGEN, London, 1851. Though a modern work, it is supposed to be the diary of a sixteenth-century traveler visiting Nuremberg; it glorifies the city and its art.

"John Guttenberg" (Reade's entry), coming directly after "Norica" in the list, is surely, I think, a biography of Gutenberg in the form of fiction, by Franz Ferdinand Friedrich Dingelstedt. A French translation, *Jean Gutenberg, premier maître imprimeur*, appeared in 1858; an English one, *John Gutenberg, First Master Printer*, in 1860. I believe Reade used the French version.

IX. TRAVELS AND GEOGRAPHY

CORYAT(E), THOMAS. *Crudities.* Coryate (1577?–1617) traveled extensively on the Continent and published his book in 1611.

Itinerary of John Leland, the Antiquary, The. A Renaissance account of England and Wales.

Montaigne, Les Voyages de. The travels of the great sixteenth-century essayist through Germany and Italy as recounted by himself. Published in the original in 1774. Its authenticity is sometimes questioned.

MORYSON, FYNES. *An Itinerary.* First published in 1617. Moryson (1566–1629) traveled extensively on the Continent and in Ireland. Book I tells of his trips on the Continent; Book II recounts his Irish sojourn; Book III contains his generalizations as to food, dress, inns, etc., of different countries.

MÜNSTER, SEBASTIAN. *Cosmographia universalis.* A weighty Renaissance tome on geography, in Latin.

RESCHIED, REYNOLDS S. VAN. *Dutch Geography.* This is the only book in Reade's list which I cannot identify. Nothing like it is in the libraries of Harvard or Columbia, in the Boston Public or New York Public Library, or in the Library of Congress. Moreover, the officials of the Library of Congress, the library of the American Geographical Society in New York, and the Bodleian Library at Oxford (where Reade might have found it) can tell me nothing of such a work. It must have been a book of little importance, or the author's name must be badly garbled.

X. LETTERS AND DISCOURSES

Epistolae obscurorum virorum. A satirical work of the Renaissance in Latin; the authorship is dubious. It is made up of letters supposed to be written to a German scholar by his admiring former students. There was no English translation in Reade's day, though there is one now.

"LUTHER's 'Table Talk' " of Reade would seem to be *The Table Talk or Familiar Discourse of Martin Luther*, translated by WILLIAM HAZLITT, London, 1848, and not CAPTAIN BELL's translation entitled *Dris Martini Lutheri col-*

loquia mensalia: Or, Dr. Martin Luther's Divine Discourses at his Table, London, 1652.

Paston Letters, The: Original Letters, Written during the Reigns of Henry VI, Edward IV, and Richard III. Received by members of the Paston family. 5 vols. 1787–1823.

State Papers Published under the Authority of His Majesty's Commission, Vol. I: *King Henry the Eighth,* Parts I and II. 1830. Part I contains letters interchanged by Henry and Wolsey.

XI. COLLECTIONS AND INDEXES

Antiquarian Repertory, The. Chiefly compiled by FRANCIS GROSE, THOMAS ASTLE, and other eminent antiquaries. 4 vols. London, 1807–9. Various documents and pictures, both old and modern, descriptive of past times. (Reade's "Grove's 'Antiquarian Repository.' ")

Harleian Miscellany, The. Ten volumes of documents from the library of Edward Harley, second Earl of Oxford. They usually concern English politics and religion, and mostly date from the seventeenth century.

"HONE's Day-books, Table-books, etc.," comprise: *The Every-day Book,* 2 vols., London, 1826–27; *The Table Book,* 2 vols., London, 1827–28; *The Year Book of Daily Recreation and Information,* London, 1841. These compilations often go through the year, telling the significance of each day; they contain miscellaneous information, including essays, stories, poems, and quotations from plays. I have gone through all these and also the same author's *Ancient Mysteries Described,* London, 1823.

SOUTHEY. *Common-Place Book.* First, second, and third series, London, 1850. Reade apparently did not use the fourth volume. Voluminous quotations recorded by the industrious poet Southey in his extensive reading.

WANLEY, NATHANIEL. *The Wonders of the Little World: Or, a General History of Man in Six Books, wherein by many thousands of examples is shewed what man hath been from the First Ages of the World to these Times, in respect of his Body, Senses, Passions, Affections: his Virtues and Perfections, his Vices and Defects, his Quality, Vocation, and Profession,* London, 1678. This entertaining folio, as extensive in content as in title, gathers unusual anecdotes and occurrences from all times and places, arranging them in classes: e.g., examples of great eating, examples of great cruelty. Being much in the manner of Reade's notebooks, it must have appealed to him strongly.

"Index 'Gentleman's Magazine' " and

"D[itt]o 'Archaeological Journal' " must mean that Reade looked over general indexes of these magazines in existence, or the tables of contents of other individual volumes, reading any articles which attracted him. I have looked over the essay index of the *Gentleman's Magazine* for the years 1731–86 and 1787–1818, the tables of contents of individual volumes of both magazines down to 1861, and read any articles that seemed near Reade's subject. Both magazines were printed in London.

This list of Reade's contains seventy-four entries. Of these, six are works that he must have read in Latin. At least nine others he must have read in French, and perhaps as many as thirteen. All the others were in English. In no case, it should be observed, does Reade mention a work in any other foreign language which had to be read in the original. Finally, Reade has a deeply ingrained affection for large works, whether those in big tomes or those in many volumes. In fact, in reading or skimming just the works in Reade's list I have, in the editions I used, gone through two hundred and six volumes, and this, too, without any assistants in Reade's manner.

Though I have made no systematic or prolonged search beyond the *Century* list, I have followed up several clues given me. In particular, Mr. Elwin informed me that the only material he had met with which might be of service to me was in one or two notebooks of Reade's in the possession of Mr. M. H. Spielmann, of Folkestone, Kent. I wrote to this gentleman and was informed that the notebooks were now owned by Mr. M. L. Parrish, of Philadelphia, a collector whose library possesses many Readeana. When I applied to Mr. Parrish, he very kindly allowed me to inspect his four Reade notebooks and from two of them I was able to glean some useful information.

On the basis of the *Century* list, then, together with some other hints, I have made a study of the sources of *The Cloister and the Hearth*. I do not, of course, maintain for a moment that I have discovered all the sources from which Reade drew; such a claim of necessity would be absurd. The novelist must have taken points from books not in the *Century* list or among the other works I have hit upon. Again, even in the volumes in the *Century* there is so huge a mass of material that I must have overlooked some resemblances; I have, however, been as thorough as I could be. In addition, I have made a special point to consider how Reade has treated his sources, borrowing some points and omitting others, changing the order in which they were presented, and mingling the facts with his own imagination.

As regards previous work on the sources of this novel, the indebtedness to Erasmus—acknowledged in general terms by

Reade at the end of the novel—has been universally recognized in such scenes as the shipwreck and various inns.[16] The identity of the "musty chronicle" mentioned on the first page has also been discovered, as will be brought out soon. Again, in the excellent edition of *The Cloister and the Hearth* prepared by Mr. C. B. Wheeler (Oxford University Press, 1915), this gentleman, going beyond the necessary tasks of an editor, investigated the sources of the novel. Aside from the generally known Erasmus borrowings, he did good work on the important influences exercised by Coryate, Moryson, and the *Liber vagatorum*. Indeed, besides mentioning the specific passages in these authors, he at times quotes from them but does not take the space necessary to discuss Reade's handling of the borrowed facts. Obviously a large number of passages from these books influencing *The Cloister and the Hearth*, mentioned by Mr. Wheeler, have to appear again in my book. In the cases of these three sources, however, I have detected a good number of borrowings which Mr. Wheeler, not being primarily concerned with influences, overlooked; again I have quoted the passages more fully; and, finally, I have had the space to consider Reade's treatment of the facts which he borrowed. However, in order to be wholly fair, I have in the case of every borrowing from Coryate, Moryson, and the *Liber vagatorum* specified in my footnote whether Mr. Wheeler has noted the borrowing before me. A third previous treatment of sources is embodied in two articles of my own.[17] All the facts contained in these two essays I have included in this volume, distributing them in the proper places. The present study, however, is more extensive than anything previously attempted, for no one has yet made a study of all the books in Reade's list.

I have taken Mr. Wheeler's Oxford edition, the best edition of *The Cloister and the Hearth*, as the basic text for my study; but, since copies of the "Everyman edition" are frequently in the

[16] A list of passages in Reade's novel showing the influence of Erasmus is given in *Notes and Queries* (10th ser., 1905), IV, 313.

[17] "Another Source for *The Cloister and the Hearth*," *PMLA*, XL (1925), 898–909, and "Charles Reade and Montaigne," *Modern Philology*, XXX (1932–33), 297–308.

hands of admirers of the novel, I have also specified the corresponding pages in this.

In the present treatment I have arranged my material according to the position in the novel of the incident upon which it bears. That is, I begin at page 1 of the novel and go through to the end, discussing, in order, the sources of all the passages for which I have found an origin. The book is thus arranged so that a reader may find the source of any episode he desires, provided I know it. On the other hand, if a person wishes to know the influences exercised by a particular book on all portions of *The Cloister and the Hearth*, he should look up that book in my Index and then consult all the references under it.

Chapter Two

AT HOME IN HOLLAND

READE begins his novel by two paragraphs on persons who have lived remarkable lives but who have been undeservedly forgotten: "Not a day passes over the earth, but men and women of no note do great deeds, speak great words, and suffer noble sorrows. . . . ."[1] This exordium, characteristic of the sympathetic author, proclaims, as we have seen, one of his favorite ideas at the time. Moreover, this idea, as Professor Sutcliffe informs me, was cherished by Reade in opposition to the views of Carlyle, whose perpetual championing of "heroes" irritated him. Most of such humble great men, Reade continues, are forgotten absolutely, but the deeds of a few are recorded in brief and dry annals. These narratives, however, may be enlivened by the imagination of the writer of fiction and be made to appeal to mankind.

And thus the novelist happily leads us to the old record of the life of Gerard and Margaret—"a musty chronicle, written in tolerable Latin, and in it a chapter where every sentence holds a fact." This bald series of events will once more become living in the pages of *The Cloister and the Hearth*.

The identity of this "musty chronicle" was first pointed out by Andrew Lang in his Introduction to a reprint of "A Good Fight" in 1910. Lang made the discovery hestitatingly,[2] but everyone since then has been convinced of his correctness. The facts are as follows.

In the year 1524, Erasmus, being in fear of dying, wrote in

---

[1] *The Cloister and the Hearth*, ed. C. B. Wheeler (Oxford University Press, 1915), p. 1; *ibid.*, (Everyman ed.; London, Toronto, and New York, 1906), p. 15. In future I cite them as Oxf. and Ev.

[2] Charles Reade, *A Good Fight*, with an Introduction by Andrew Lang (London, 1910), pp. v–xi.

Latin a compendium of his life and sent it with an accompanying letter to a friend. This *Compendium vitae* was first printed in Leiden in 1607, at the end of Erasmus' letter to his friend, under the title *Vita Des. Erasmi Roterodami ex ipsius manu fideliter repraesentata*, by Paul Merula, professor of history in the University of Leiden. The *Compendium* was printed again at Leiden in 1615 by Peter Scriverius, professor of jurisprudence. The original manuscript was in existence as late as 1649 but has since perished.[3] The early part of the *Compendium* dealing with Erasmus' parents is the "chapter" of the "musty chronicle" from which Reade drew the theme of *The Cloister and the Hearth*.

It should be remarked, in passing, that the authenticity of the *Compendium* has sometimes been questioned. P. S. Allen, a great authority on Erasmus and editor of his letters, nevertheless, believes it to be genuine. To be sure, Erasmus had an elder brother, of whom the *Compendium* makes no mention. This omission however, Allen thinks, is partly because Erasmus grew to disapprove of his brother, and partly because the suppression of the brother put the relationship between the parents in a better light.[4] Reade of course wholly follows the story as given in the *Compendium*. Even if he knew about the brother, he had of necessity to leave him out of the novel; failing to do so would have ruined all the pathos and poetry of the tale.

The beginning of the *Compendium*—the only part from which Reade drew—runs as follows (I translate the choppy Latin literally):

He was born in Rotterdam on the eve of Simon and Jude. He computes about 57 years ago. His mother was called Margaret, daughter of a certain doctor named Peter. She came from Septimontium, in the common tongue Zevenberge; he saw two of her brothers at Dordrecht, almost nonagenarians. His father was named Gerard. He secretly had an affair with the said Margaret, hoping for marriage. And there are those who say they were betrothed. Both the parents and brothers of Gerard were incensed at this happening. His father was Elias, his mother Catharine; each of them attained extreme old age, Catharine wellnigh her ninety-fifth year. There were ten brothers but no sister; all

---

[3] P. S. Allen, *Opus epistolarum Des. Erasmi Roterodami* (8 vols.; Oxford, 1906–34), I, 46, 575–78.

[4] *Ibid.*, pp. 575–78.

born of the same father and mother; all married. Gerard was the youngest, except one. It seemed best to them all that from so great a number one should be consecrated to God. You know old people's moods. The brothers, too, were unwilling that the property should be diminished and liked to have someone with whom they might live. Gerard, seeing he was shut off, in every way, from matrimony by general agreement, did what desperate men are wont to do; he secretly took flight and, while on his journey, sent to his parents and brothers a letter with a hand clasping a hand and one sentence added, "Farewell; I shall never see you again."

In the mean time, his intended wife was left with child. The boy was brought up in his grandmother's home. Gerard betook himself to Rome. There by writing he did a fair business, for the printer's art had not yet arrived. Moreover, he was deft with his hands. And he lived as youths do. Soon he applied his mind to honest studies. He became well versed in Greek and Latin. In jurisprudence, too, he gained more than common skill. For Rome was then most rich in learned men. He heard Guarinus lecture. He copied all authors with his hand. His parents, when they learned he was in Rome, wrote him that the girl whom he had sought to marry was dead. Believing this, he became a priest for grief and turned his whole mind to religion. Returning home, he discovered the trick. Nevertheless she would never marry afterward, nor did he ever lay hand on her.

He had the boy well educated, however, and put him to study his letters when he was barely four. But in his early years, the boy derived but little profit from his unpleasant studies, for which he did not seem to be born. When he was in his ninth year, Gerard sent him to Deventer; his mother came with him, the protector and guardian of his tender youth. The school was still barbarous then (the *Pater meus* was read aloud; the tenses were called for; Ebrardus and Joannes de Garlandia were read aloud); save that Alexander Hegius and Zinthius had begun to introduce something of good literature. At length, from those of his playmates who were older and listened to Zinthius he first got the taste of better learning; afterward, now and then, he listened to Hegius, but only on those holidays when he read to all the boys. He reached the third class; then a pestilence, raging violently there, carried off his mother, leaving the boy now in his thirteenth year. When the disease grew daily more terrible, all the household in which he had been living having been stricken, he returned to his home. Gerard, upon receiving the sad news, began to languish and shortly afterward died. Both parents died not much after their fortieth year.[5]

Though the resemblance between this and the plot of *The Cloister and the Hearth* is clear enough in itself to show borrowing, we may derive some external evidence as to the identity of the

[5] The original Latin is found in *ibid.*, pp. 47–52.

"musty chronicle," by turning again to the article in the *Century* already mentioned. Here we read:

I can recall his [Reade's] taking down the "Autobiography of Erasmus" from the shelf in the great library at Oxford, and showing us a brief description (only a line or two) of the father and mother of Erasmus, with a few dates concerning them, saying, "There is all the foundation for my story, 'A Good Fight.' "[6]

The family of Gerard in Reade's novel are residents of the town of Tergou. Though there is no place mentioned in the *Compendium*, the biographies of Erasmus by Bayle, Knight, and Jortin—all of them in the *Century* list—mention Tergou as their home, though Knight spells it Ter Gou.[7] The children, moreover, have been reduced from ten in the *Compendium* to nine in Reade. A much more important change, however, is the introduction of one girl among eight brothers. Contrast always makes for interest; hence it is more dramatic to have one girl in this large family than to have all boys. To sharpen the contrast, moreover, Reade has made this one daughter—against a background of admirably healthy brothers—a suffering cripple, yet possessed of as much sweetness of character as weakness of body. Kate is just the sort of figure that a sympathetic novelist like Reade would wish to introduce, and the sort that would appeal immensely to a Victorian audience, rich in sentiment. She usually appeals even today, though I venture to believe less strongly than in Reade's time.

The seven boys in the family, aside from the hero, present a problem to the novelist, as they did, in the matter of food, to their parents. They cannot be left a mere group like the chorus in an opera, nor does space permit them to be all individualized. Reade solves the problem by sharply marking off three sons. Two of these are Cornelis the eldest and Sybrandt the youngest (a pleasant balance being thus secured in age). Both are lazy, and both are eager to gain much with no effort on their own part. The *Compendium* said that Gerard's brothers "were unwilling that the property should be diminished." This feeling reaches its apogee in Cornelis and Sybrandt. They form the opposing wing

---

[6] XXIX (November, 1884), 73.

[7] Pierre Bayle, *Dictionaire historique et critique* (4 vols.; Rotterdam, 1720), II, 1091; John Jortin, *The Life of Erasmus* (3 vols.; London, 1808), I, 1; Samuel Knight, *The Life of Erasmus* (Cambridge, 1726), p. 4.

of the family to little Kate—she is all sweetness and love, they are all selfishness and greed; she is favorably disposed to Gerard, never going back on him, they are persistently hostile to him, stopping at no injury if they may secure benefit for themselves. Gerard's family in the *Compendium* does not impress us favorably. However, by creating Cornelis and Sybrandt, Reade has, as it were, cleansed the others. The family must, in accordance with the *Compendium*, treat Gerard shabbily. With two villainous brothers as leaders in the oppression, the rest of the group may be painted as more agreeable and thus keep the sympathy of the reader much better.

The third brother distinguished by Reade is, except perhaps for the hero, the most interesting member of the family. More highly individualized than Kate, Cornelis, and Sybrandt, the dwarf Giles always impresses readers of the novel and remains in their memories. Now Giles, I feel sure, is strongly influenced by a famous character in one of the books in Reade's list—namely, Quasimodo in Hugo's *Notre-Dame*.

In the first place, no one reading Hugo's romance can fail to be impressed with Quasimodo; he of course dominates the book. Then there are many similarities between the two. Most noticeable of course is their physical deformity. Giles is "a dwarf, of the wrong sort . . . . all head and claws and voice, run from by dogs and unprejudiced females," and his face is called "hideous."[8] Quasimodo is a hunchback, and his ugliness is stressed markedly. Thus Victor Hugo, fond of extremes, writes:

We will not try to give the reader any idea of that tetrahedron-like nose; of that horseshoe-shaped mouth; of that small left eye overhung by a bushy red eyebrow, while the right eye was completely hidden by a monstrous wart; of those uneven, broken teeth, with sad gaps here and there like the battlements of a fortress.[9]

Both men were monsters. Indeed, the epithet "monster" is often applied to Quasimodo. When he is exposed as a child, an old woman exclaims, "This foundling, as they call it, is a regular monster of abomination." Again, when Quasimodo on being

[8] Oxf., pp. 4, 420; Ev., pp. 19, 424.

[9] *Notre-Dame de Paris* (2 vols.; Boston: Estes & Lauriat n.d.), I, 74.

placed in the pillory is jeered at, one man cries, "Oh, you deaf man! you blind man! you hunchback! you monster!"[10] (In both these examples, the word in the original French also is *monstre*.) In at least one notable case, and perhaps more, Giles is called "a monster."[11]

Another point of similarity is the great gymnastic ability of both men. Quasimodo, when the bells of Notre-Dame swing, catches hold of them and swings too. He clambers with ease over the façade of the church; and when the edifice is besieged by a mob, he is long able to beat off the assailants, pushing their scaling ladders from the wall and casting down on their heads a massive beam.[12] Giles, too, is athletic. He can swing by his teeth from the edge of the table, and he finds running up and down a rope hanging from a high tower a most delightful prank.[13]

Finally both men are mischievous and somewhat malicious. In the case of Quasimodo:

The second effect of his misfortune [i.e., his deformity] was to make him mischievous. He was mischievous because he was an untrained savage. . . . . His strength, wonderfully developed as it was, was the cause of still greater mischief. . . . . As he grew up, he encountered nothing but hate. He caught the infection. He acquired the universal malevolence.

Similarly, Giles is called "half stupidity, half malice"; his method of mounting a horse is climbing up his tail; and he plays several pretty tricks on a giant.[14]

It must not be supposed, however, that the two characters are alike in all respects. Quasimodo, though unreal, is intense, uncomprehending, hated, and hating; Giles, especially as the novel progresses, is playful, warm-hearted, and true to his family. Quasimodo is tragedy personified; Giles, comedy. But though their spirit is quite different, many of their traits are the same.[15]

One notable detail about Giles, his big voice, may come from

[10] *Ibid.*, pp. 211, 350.

[11] Oxf., p. 342; Ev., p. 450 (the passage in this text is shifted to a different part of the volume).

[12] Hugo, I, 225, 230.   [13] Oxf., pp. 35, 79; Ev., pp. 47, 88.

[14] Hugo, I, 227; Oxf., pp. 4, 341, 604–5; Ev., pp. 19, 449, 612.

[15] One might also remark that, as Quasimodo attains a new life through love for Esmeralda, Giles suddenly has new "intellectual powers unchained" (Oxf., p. 603; Ev., p. 611).

Wanley's *Wonders of the Little World*. In this we read: "Augustus Caesar exhibited in his plays one Lucius, a young man, born of honest parents: he was not full two foot high, saith Ravisius, he weighed but seventeen pounds, yet he had a great and strong voice."[16]

Gerard, intended by his whole family for the church, practiced calligraphy and, to a less extent, the illumination of manuscripts. In the second activity he became acquainted with Margaret van Eyck, painter and sister of the two famous artists. Now this lady really existed, but, whereas her brothers, Hubert and Jan, are known to every student of art, she herself is obscure. How did Reade happen upon this woman whom he has made prominent in his novel? It seems entirely probable that he became acquainted with her from Lacroix and Seré's large book on the Middle Ages. In the section on painting in this long work are reproduced two full-page plates of pictures by Margaret van Eyck. One is in color, and the other in black and white; the latter is said to be an episode from the life of St. Catherine, and the former, though without title, is obviously the same. The colored plate depicts St. Catherine with her crown, sword, and broken wheel, sitting in a small garden with another lady. The background is composed of town houses with adjacent fields, woods, and a mountain. Both women have yellow hair, and the usual weak chins of Flemish religious paintings. The uncolored plate is similar. Reade borrowed numerous details from Lacroix and Seré, and nothing could be more natural than for him to notice these two paintings and become interested in Margaret van Eyck—partly because of her family and partly because of women painters' being uncommon. Searching the text of the book, he would then have come upon the following information: "The sister of the famous citizens of Limburg [i.e., the van Eyck brothers], Margaret, who likewise wielded the brush, having ceased to live soon after [her brother Hubert's death], was interred in the same vault." (Jan survived both.)[17]

[16] (London, 1678), p. 37. Conceivably, on the same page, another example may have had some influence on Giles, the example of "a Man called Rodomas, of little stature, but so strong, that he brake a cable as big as a man's arm."

[17] Lacroix and Seré, *Le Moyen Age et la Renaissance*, V, "Peinture sur bois, sur cuivre, etc.," xxxviii. Plates IV and V after this section are Margaret's. (The arrangement

His interest being stimulated in this woman painter, Reade decided to introduce her as a character. If she were portrayed in the company of either of her famous brothers, she would be notably cast into the shade. Thus Reade changed the facts and made her, and not Jan, the survivor of the trio. Margaret is an appealing character to anyone, but Reade must have been especially interested in her personality as he depicted her; for she, too, is celibate. In her youth she had "scorned love, preferring art." In her age she bitterly regretted the choice: "Behold me here a barren stock, while the women of my youth have a troop of children at their side, and grandchildren at their knee."[18]

Gerard's troubles as an illuminator are briefly mentioned by Reade: "He could not afford the gold, the blue, and the red, but only the cheap earths" (i.e., paints).[19] It seems likely that these facts are taken from Mrs. Merrifield's *Original Treatises . . . . on the Arts of Painting, etc.,* where, in a long Introduction, she indicates the cost of these three colors.[20]

Gerard set out for Rotterdam to be present at the announcement of the prizes for which he had contended. On the way he met by the roadside Margaret and her old father Peter, both of them weary and hungry. Taking pity on their misery, he lighted a fire and warmed some *soupe au vin.* Peter was so refreshed that, like a typical old scholar, he launched into a quaint, learned, and decidedly long discourse in praise of this beverage. His daughter tried to check him, but he kept on, merely remarking, "I will be brief, unreasonably and unseasonably brief." This long-windedness, joined to protestations of brevity, surely indicates the influence of Polonius, in *Hamlet,* on this scene.[21]

Two important points in his talk are drawn from Le Grand

---

of this book is most irritating. Each volume is divided into several sections—each with its own title—and each section has its leaves, not pages, numbered with Roman numerals.)

[18] Oxf., p. 61; Ev., p. 71. This particular speech seems an echo of Queen Elizabeth's: "The Queen of Scots is lighter of a fair son, and I am but a barren stock."

[19] Oxf., p. 7; Ev., p. 20.

[20] (2 vols.; London, 1849), Vol. I: gold, p. xcviii; blue, p. ccxiii; red, p. clxxxv.

[21] Oxf., pp. 13–15; Ev., pp. 26–28; *Hamlet,* II, ii, 85–92.

d'Aussy's *Histoire de la vie privée des françois*. The first—of particular significance—is the mention of *soupe au vin*. "When Duguesclin, defied by Guillaume de Blancbourg," we read, "went forth to fight this Englishman, he first swallowed three of these soups in honor of the three persons of the Holy Trinity." Moreover, in a note at the bottom of the page, three lines from an Old French *fabliau* are quoted, in which a man requests some *soupe au vin* because he is going to set forth on a journey. Now this mention of *soupe au vin* and the addition of the most picturesque detail about Duguesclin were enough to suggest to Reade's fertile imagination the whole episode and the content of Peter's speech. The old man runs on for over a page, citing Hector and the Romans, both of whom unfortunately lacked this restorative, and thereafter passing to "Duguesclin, a French knight, being about to join battle with the English—masters, at that time, of half France, and sturdy strikers by sea and land—drank, not one, but three, 'Soupes au vin,' in honor of the Blessed Trinity." The discourse is quite in harmony with the character of a Renaissance scholar and creates a really charming scene. The idea, too, of having Gerard carry *soupe au vin* with him on a journey may have come from the three lines quoted from the *fabliau*.[22]

The second point of indebtedness to Le Grand d'Aussy in Peter's tirade is in the old man's protestation that "for the last few hundred years physicians have been idiots, with their chicken broth and their decoction of gold, whereby they attribute the highest qualities to that meat which has the least juice of any meat . . . . mountebanks! dunces! homicides!" This comes from the Frenchman's discussion (a few pages after that on *soupe au vin*) concerning chicken broth being given as a "divine restorer" to the sick. An old author, Palissy, in a book on *The Abuses of Doctors*, objects to the practice.

Take an excellent bird . . . . cook it in its juice; you will discern in this juice a good odor, if you smell it, and a good flavor, if you taste it; so much so, indeed, that you will consider it admirable as a restorative. Boil it, on the contrary;

[22] Le Grand d'Aussy, II, 229–30. The source might also be Lacroix and Seré's book, I, "Nourriture et cuisine," xxix, which has exactly the same information, having obviously copied Le Grand d'Aussy (who is listed among the authorities drawn from).

then take some of the water and taste it; you will find it insipid, and without taste or smell except that of burning. Then you well know that your restorative is no good and can not give any nourishment to an enfeebled body.

Old Peter, then, is only voicing Palissy's objection to such soup and extending it also to the "decoction of gold."[23]

Gerard, arriving at Rotterdam, attended the duke's festival in the course of which the prize-winners were to be announced. The festival gives Reade an admirable opportunity to introduce a wealth of medieval local color. It is possible that the idea of placing much pomp and circumstance near the beginning of the novel was suggested by Hugo's *Notre-Dame*, which very effectively opens with the celebration at Paris of the Epiphany and the Feast of Fools.

Gerard, with Margaret and old Peter, was brought into a banquet at which Duke Philip the Good himself was present—a banquet conducted with all the luxury of the Burgundian court. Reade takes great pains to describe carefully the setting and all the courses. Since naturally such details must be drawn from some authority, we may well examine his sources in detail. Reade's setting runs:

> The court-yard was laid out in tables loaded with rich meats, and piled with gorgeous plate. Guests in rich and various costumes sat beneath a leafy canopy of fresh-cut branches fastened tastefully to golden, silver, and blue silken cords that traversed the area; and fruits of many hues, including some artificial ones of gold, silver, and wax, hung pendent, or peeped like fair eyes among the green leaves of plane-trees and lime-trees. The duke's minstrels swept their lutes at intervals, and a fountain played red Burgundy in six jets that met and battled in the air.[24]

Le Grand d'Aussy observes that in the Middle Ages the walls and chimneys of medieval dining-rooms were often decorated with green boughs, but he makes no mention of fruits. Thus it is more likely that Reade took these facts from Monteil's *Histoire des français des divers états*, a work from which he borrowed heavily. In this a hotel-keeper describes his customary preparation for a feast: "I took great pains to strew the table with flowers and to

[23] Le Grand d'Aussy, II, 235. Lacroix and Seré follow him in these facts (I, "Nourriture et cuisine," xxxi).

[24] Oxf., pp. 19–20; Ev., pp. 32–33.

adorn *the ceiling with branches of trees from which fruits hung*" (the italics are mine).[25]

The fountain spouting Burgundy at a feast may be from Le Grand d'Aussy or from either of two places in Lacroix and Seré; the details in the novel are not specific enough for us to determine.[26]

The duke, from a distance, now bade Gerard and his two companions welcome, and they sat down to the feast. The detailed account of the banquet comes, much condensed, from Monteil, where the hotel-keeper, for twenty pages, holds forth on the various courses that are served, one after another, on fine occasions.[27] His first course was composed of lemons, cherries, and salads to excite the appetite, but Reade made Gerard and his friends enter in the middle of the banquet; that is, after this course had finished. Seven of the duke's servants

seated them at a table, and put fifteen many-coloured soups before them, in little silver bowls, and as many wines in crystal vases . . . . the soup was tasted, and vanished in a twirl of fourteen hands, and fish came on the table in a dozen forms, with patties of lobster and almonds mixed, and of almonds and cream, and an immense variety of "brouets," known to us as "rissoles."[28]

Now according to Monteil's hotel-keeper, the second course is "composed of pâtés, brouets, and soups. The pâtés . . . . of lobster and almonds, pâtés of chicken, pâtés of almonds with cream, brouets" necessitate skill on the part of the cook but much less than the soups. He enumerates, according to the difficulty in preparation, various soups, and they number just fifteen, as in Reade. Moreover, since soups must delight the eyes as well as the

[25] Le Grand d'Aussy, III, 161; A. A. Monteil, *Histoire des français des divers états* (5 vols.; Paris, 1853), II, 245. Monteil devotes a volume to the social life of each century from the fourteenth to the eighteenth; Vol. II treats the fifteenth, that of Reade's novel. To make his description vivid the author has, in this volume, representatives of all professions appear before the assembled magistrates and each describe his business, maintaining that it is attended by the most trouble.

[26] Le Grand d'Aussy, III, 195; Lacroix and Seré, I, "Nourriture et cuisine," xlvii; IV, "Ameublement," iii.

[27] II, 235–56. In the books in Reade's list are a good many banquets resembling this one in Reade's novel in some respects, but the account of Monteil is the most similar altogether.

[28] Oxf., p. 20; Ev., p. 33.

taste, "one must then color them, according to their varieties, each with a different color."[29] Hence it follows that Gerard enjoyed "fifteen many-colored soups." This account, it should be noted, had been previously given to the hotel-keeper by a cook in the service of the duke of Burgundy; hence it is particularly suitable in this banquet in *The Cloister and the Hearth*. Reade has followed Monteil closely, except that he seems to have made two courses out of this second course of Monteil, although it is also possible to understand Reade as meaning the soup and patties were two dishes in the same course.

Reade's "little silver bowls" for soup and "crystal vases" for wine may be from Le Grand d'Aussy, who discusses the use of both silver and crystal utensils for many pages.[30]

The third course, in Monteil, is roast. In *The Cloister and the Hearth*, Reade centers our attention on two things—a wild boar and "beef-stuffing." When Margaret shrieks with terror on seeing the boar, the duke sends her a delicacy of which he was very fond:

> The beef-stuffing was his own private dish. On these grand occasions an ox was roasted whole, and reserved for the poor. But this wise as well as charitable prince had discovered, that whatever venison, hares, lamb, poultry, etc., you skewered into that beef cavern, got cooked to perfection, retaining their own juices and receiving those of the reeking ox. These he called his beef-stuffing, and took delight therein, as did now our trio; for, at his word, seven of his people went headlong, and drove silver tridents into the steaming cave at random, and speared a kid, a cygnet, and a flock of wild fowl.[31]

The source of this is, I think surely, an example in the chapter called "Of the Prodigious Luxury of Some Men in Their Feasting" in Wanley's *Wonders of the Little World:*

> . . . . At the very entry into the Hall, where the Feast was appointed, lay spread upon a curious board, a great Beef with his head cut off, and his entrails taken out, having in his belly a whole Hart or Deer of the like dressing, stuffed full of little Birds, as Quailes, Partridges, Larks, Pheasants and other like, the same being so cunningly conjoyned in the belly of the second beast, that it seemed some excellent Mathematician had been the Workman thereof.[32]

[29] Monteil, II, 240–41.

[30] Vol. III: silver, pp. 236–59; crystal, pp. 219–26.

[31] Oxf., p. 21; Ev., p. 34.   [32] P. 387.

The arrangement of meat within meat is similar, though Reade has simplified it from birds within a deer, which, in turn, is within an ox—to deer, etc., within an ox. Moreover, the words "beef" and "stuff" occur in Wanley, giving Reade's "beef-stuffing." The presence of the example under the heading "Of the Prodigious Luxury of Some Men in Their Feasting" would attract Reade, when he was meditating the account of a splendid banquet.

Reade omits Monteil's fourth course—likewise roast—probably since it is too much like the previous one; then he continues (the italics are mine):

After this [the beef-stuffing], *twenty different tarts of fruits and herbs*, and last of all, *confectionery on Titanic scale—cathedrals of sugar*, all gilt and painted in the interstices of the bas-reliefs; castles with their moats, and ditches, imitated to the life; elephants, camels, toads; knights on horseback jousting; kings and princesses looking on; trumpeters blowing; and all these personages delicious eating, and their veins filled with sweet-scented juices: works of art made to be destroyed. *The guests breached a bastion, crunched a* crusader and his horse and lance, or cracked a bishop, cope, chasuble, crosier and all, as remorselessly as we do a carraway comfit; sipping meanwhile *hippocras* and other spiced drinks and *Greek and Corsican wines*, while every now and then *little Turkish boys*, turbaned, spangled, jewelled, and gilt, *came offering* on bended knee golden *troughs of rose-water and orange-water to keep the guests' hands cool and perfumed.*[33]

The basis of this is drawn from the fifth and last course of Monteil's hotel-keeper.[34] "The pastry of tarts, as everyone is aware, distinguishes the fifth or last course," he declares. Thereafter he enumerates many varieties, ending with "tarts made with every sort of *herbs*, flowers, grains, vegetables, *fruits* [cf. Reade's 'twenty different tarts of fruit and herbs']." Moreover, at more important banquets, "I had to vary the ornaments of the pastry, fashioning sometimes scales, hands of justice, sometimes *churches* [cf. Reade's 'cathedrals of sugar'], monasteries; sometimes donjons, towers, *castles*, coats of arms." In high society were served, usually after the company adjourned to another room, "sweetmeats which represent fleurs de lis, crowns, sometimes more or less large figures of *men* or *animals*, of which *each person breaks and takes the part most* pleasing to him." Reade runs the pastry and sweet-

[33] Oxf., pp. 21–22; Ev., pp. 34–35.   [34] Monteil, II, 246–47.

meats together; he makes *men* and *animals* more specific and effective; and, from the idea of breaking the sugar images, he develops the humorous fancy "the guests breached a bastion, crunched a crusader, etc."[35] Moreover, the guests in the novel were too numerous to move to another room. Monteil then continues: "In addition *there are served at the same time Corsican wines* with honey, *hypocras* made of excellent sugared wine. . . . . Finally rose water or orange water is brought *for washing the hands*."

This is obviously the basis of Reade, but he probably made additions from Le Grand d'Aussy. At any rate, this latter French author has Reade's spelling "hippocras," he praises Greek wine, and he says that in washing the hands at banquets "the napkin and basin were offered to ladies by squires or young pages,"[36] a suggestion from which Reade developed the colorful touch of the "little Turkish boys."

After enjoying the feast, Gerard was conducted to an interview with the Countess of Charolois and her daughter Marie, called the heir apparent by Reade. Gerard was led

into a room where sat or lolloped eleven ladies, chattering like magpies. Two, more industrious than the rest, were playing cat's cradle with fingers as nimble as their tongues. At the sight of a stranger all the tongues stopped like one piece of complicated machinery, and all the eyes turned on Gerard, as if the same string that checked the tongues had turned the eyes on. Gerard was ill at ease before, but this battery of eyes discountenanced him, and down went *his* eyes on the ground. Then the cowards finding, like the hare who ran by the pond and the frogs scuttled into the water, that there was a creature they could frighten, giggled and enjoyed their prowess. Then a duenna said, severely, "Mesdames!" and they were all abashed at once as though a modesty string had been pulled. This same duenna took Gerard, and marched before him in solemn silence.[37]

This lively little passage, I feel sure, is built out from a short suggestion in Monteil. The courtier is speaking:

A lady of my acquaintance was much bored also by being governess or, as the expression runs, mother of the queen's maids of honor. . . . . "If you only

[35] There are several accounts of sweet figures to eat, in Le Grand d'Aussy, Lacroix and Seré, etc.

[36] Vol. III: hippocras, pp. 67–68 (epicures may be interested in a receipt on p. 71 for making hippocras); Greek wine, pp. 48–50; squires and pages, pp. 312–13.

[37] Oxf., p. 28; Ev., p. 41.

knew," she said to me, "what a task it is to watch over twenty-six pairs of eyes which are always eager to wage war with those of young archers and young sentinels . . . . you'd soon get enough: I've had enough now."[38]

The similarity is obvious enough, and, when one considers that Reade borrowed from this volume of Monteil time and again, the influence becomes sure. The whole scene is a good example of the novelist's taking a mere suggestion from another book and working it up with lively details so that the resulting scene moves as easily and quickly as one that is wholly original.

Gerard was well received by the countess and her daughter. In fact, little Marie was for making him a bishop on the spot and recalled how splendid the Bishop of Liége had appeared to her: "He had on a crown, a high one, and it was cut in the middle, and it was full of oh! such beautiful jewels: and his gown stiff with gold; and his mantle, too; and it had a broad border, all pictures: but, above all, his gloves; you have no such gloves, mamma. They were embroidered and covered with jewels, and scented with such lovely scent."[39]

These details about the bishop are probably drawn from the text and plates of Pugin and Smith's *Glossary of Ecclesiastical Ornament and Costume*. Thus we read: "Gloves, worn by Bishops and others in ecclesiastical functions, were usually made of silk, and richly embroidered." And thereafter we read of the gifts of a certain bishop to St. Paul's Cathedral, among them: "Also two gloves of like workmanship, the gift of the same, in which many stones are wanting. Also two pair of gloves, ornamented with silver plates gilt, set with stones."[40] As for the bishop's "crown," we learn from Pugin and Smith:

The early double-pointed Mitres were very low. . . . . In the fourteenth century they became more pointed and enriched . . . . and the enrichments were of the most costly and elegant description, the edges being crocketed, and the points terminating in jeweled crosses. . . . . From the latter part of the fifteenth century, the Mitres increased in bulk and height.[41]

[38] Monteil, II, 356.   [39] Oxf., p. 31; Ev., pp. 43–44.

[40] Pp. 148–49. The third edition, which I used, is dated London, 1868.

[41] Miters, pp. 173–74 (see also pp. 175–77); gorgeous robes (text), pp. 62–71, 78–83, 111–14; plates, pp. 7, 41, 42, 43, 44.

Various plates show bishops in highly ornate miters. The gorgeousness of episcopal robes is brought out somewhat in the text but, even more, in numerous colored plates.

At the end of his interview with the noble ladies Gerard left the palace and happened upon a mystery play. Reade may have received the idea of putting in this spectacle from the beginning of *Notre-Dame*, where such a medieval drama occupies an important place during the celebration of Epiphany. The mystery in *The Cloister and the Hearth* is thus described (the italics are mine):

> In this representation *divine personages, too sacred for me to name here*, came clumsily down from heaven to talk sophistry with the *cardinal Virtues*, the nine Muses, and *the seven deadly Sins*, all present in human shape, and not unlike one another. To enliven which weary stuff in rattled the *Prince of the power of the air* [the devil], and an imp that *kept molesting him and buffeting him with a bladder*, at *each thwack of which the crowd were in ecstasies*. When the Vices had uttered *good store of obscenity* and the Virtues twaddle, the celestials, including the nine Muses, went gingerly back to heaven one by one; for there was but *one cloud;* and two artisans worked it up with its supernatural freight, and worked it down with a winch, in full sight of the audience. These disposed of, *the bottomless pit opened and flamed in the centre of the stage;* the carpenters and Virtues *shoved the Vices in*, and the Virtues and *Beelzebub and his tormentor* danced merrily round the place of eternal torture to the fife and tabor. This *entertainment was writ by the Bishop of Ghent, for the diffusion of religious sentiment.*[42]

This account of the mystery is freely written by Reade, with elements probably drawn from several sources. Many details, however, seem to have come from Lacroix and Seré's account of the medieval theater. For example, the main theme would appear to be from the following (the italics, again, are mine): "In 1437, at the entry of Charles VII was enacted the *combat of the seven deadly Sins* with the *three theological Virtues and the four cardinal Virtues*. The seven Sins rode upon different beasts, and the whole was enhanced by *representations of* Purgatory and *Hell*. . . . ."[43]

As for the form of hell, "In a mystery played at Metz in 1437, the entrance of hell was represented by the gaping mouth of a dragon . . . . : it was through this mouth that devils entered and went off." In another mystery where hell also appeared:

> Paradise . . . . was represented by *another machine*, eight feet broad and twelve feet long surrounded by open thrones painted *like clouds*. . . . . In the middle

[42] Oxf., p. 33; Ev., pp. 45–46.   [43] IV, "Théâtre," xii.

was a seat made like a rainbow, on which were seated *the Divinity—Father, Son, and Holy Spirit* [Reade's "divine personages, too sacred for me to name"] . . . . at the four corners [of paradise] were *two benches on which were the four virtues, Justice, Peace, Truth, and Mercy*, richly dressed.[44]

As to the obscenity of the Vices, Lacroix and Seré say that the comic plays of the Middle Ages "are too often disfigured by grossness and obscenity." As for the authorship of the Bishop of Ghent, we learn from the French that "with rare exceptions, miracle and mystery plays were, in the beginning composed by priests or monks," one reason being that "in sacred dramas the clergy found an indirect means of instructing the faithful and attaching them still more strongly to the church."[45]

The part about the devil in Reade's description may well be from Joseph Strutt's *Sports and Pastimes of the People of England:* "Beelzebub seems to have been the principal comic actor, assisted by his merry troop of under-devils, who, with variety of noises, strange gesture, and contortions of the body, excited the laughter of the populace."[46] The subordinate fiend, the uncontrolled laughter, and especially the use of the word "Beelzebub" in Reade all incline us to accept this borrowing.

Gerard, arriving home again, announced that he had won a prize and generously distributed some of the money to Kate and his brothers. Thereafter:

The first time the bishop came that way, he applied to be admitted "exorcist," the third step in holy orders. The bishop questioned him, and ordained him at once. He had to kneel, and, after a short prayer, the bishop delivered to him a little MS. full of exorcisms, and said: "Take this, Gerard, and have power to lay hands on the possessed, whether baptized or catechumens!"[47]

This passage is derived from Pugin and Smith's *Glossary of Ecclesiastical Ornament and Costume*, the information being given under the heading "Exorcist." After learning that an exorcist is "the third of the minor orders," we read: "When an exorcist is ordained, let the Bishop deliver to him a book of exorcisms, saying, 'Take this, and commit it to memory, and have power to lay hands on the possessed, whether baptized or catechumens.' "[48]

[44] *Ibid.*, leaf vi (both quotations).

[45] *Ibid.*, leaves iv, x.   [47] Oxf., p. 38; Ev., pp. 50–51.

[46] (London, 1801), p. 118.   [48] P. 130.

Gerard was happy in meeting Margaret once more, for she lived—as did the real Margaret of the *Compendium*—in Sevenbergen, not far distant.

Now one day it happened that a good number of the duke's retainers passed through the streets of Tergou. Among them were, first, a huntsman with the duke's leopard and, second, the duke's giant. Let us first consider the giant.

The duke's giant, a Hungarian seven feet four inches high, brought up the rear. This enormous creature had, like some other giants, a treble, fluty voice of little power. He was a vain fellow, and not conscious of this nor any defect. Now it happened he caught sight of Giles sitting on the top of the balcony; so he stopped and began to make fun of him.

"Hallo! brother!" squeaked he, "I had nearly passed without seeing thee."

"*You* are plain enough to see," bellowed Giles, in his bass tones.

"Come on my shoulder, brother," squeaked Titan, and held out a shoulder-of-mutton fist to help him down.

"If I do I'll cuff your ears," roared the dwarf.

The giant saw the homuncule was irascible, and played upon him, being encouraged thereto by the shouts of laughter. For he did not see that the people were laughing not at his wit, but at the ridiculous incongruity of the two voices —*the gigantic feeble fife*, and the *petty deep, loud drum.*[49]

Irritated by the giant's teasing, the fearless Giles dropped on the giant's neck and began punching his head. The giant, in pain, tried to bump the dwarf against a balcony, but the latter leaped off in time, leaving the angry giant to get the full force of the blow on his own head. The people cheered, and the big man strode off defeated by a dwarf.

Now this lively scene is made interesting, first, by the sharp contrast in height between the giant and Giles, and, second, by their differing in voice, each having the sort of voice the reader would expect in the other. The suggestion for the scene, I believe, surely came from *Norica*, the idealized tale of Renaissance Nuremberg. In this book the narrator, going to a country estate to visit a friend, saw a giant and a dwarf who were retainers of the owner.

The one might be as much above three ells in height as the other was under one, and both were clad in the same party-coloured garments, only that the dwarf had a bald head, and the giant, on the other hand, was adorned with a

[49] Oxf., p. 45; Ev., pp. 56–57. (Italics are mine.)

high turban. The tall man appeared to be twenty years of age, but the little one had wrinkles like a sexagenarian. . . . . [The narrator next made a mistake.] Then the tall and the short man burst into a ringing laugh, and the two voices *united like the shrill note of a fife with the roll of a drum.*[50]

The German story has created an effective contrast between the two men—a contrast in height, the appearance of their heads, their age, and their voices, the big man having evidently the loud voice and the little one the shrill voice. When he perused the story Reade must have been struck with the effectiveness of placing a giant and dwarf together. Moreover, the contrast in voices suggested a new idea: he would exchange their voices, giving each one the unexpected sort of voice. With this happy thought he proceeded to write his own scene, original and much superior to that in the German book. The influence is proved by the fife and drum comparison in both authors.

One cannot, of course, be sure in what order the influences worked. It is conceivable that, before reading *Norica*, Reade had had no idea of having a dwarf in his novel and that he was so much pleased with this passage that he decided upon both a giant and a dwarf, the latter of whom he thereupon made a spiritual son of Quasimodo. It seems more natural to suppose, however, that Quasimodo first engendered Giles in Reade's imagination. Thereafter he might have met this scene and created Giles's voice at the same time he did the giant with the little voice, or he might have drawn Giles's voice from the Wanley passage and then, happening on *Norica*, have determined on a giant with a little voice.

And now for the leopard in Reade's novel:

Towards the rear of the pageant rode one that excited more attention [than had a tumbler]—the duke's leopard. A huntsman, mounted on a Flemish horse of prodigious size and power, carried a long box fastened to the rider's loins by straps curiously contrived, and on this box sat a bright leopard crouching. She was chained to the huntsman. The people admired her glossy hide and spots, and pressed near, and one or two were for feeling her, and pulling her tail; then the huntsman shouted in a terrible voice, "Beware! At Antwerp, one did but throw a handful of dust at her, and the duke made dust of him."[51]

[50] *Norica*, translated from the German of August Hagen (London, 1851), pp. 120–21.

[51] Oxf., p. 45; Ev., p. 56.

We meet the leopard again in the passage where old Martin was out hunting deer. A buck dashed by, and after it the duke's leopard. Martin followed and soon found the leopard tearing the struggling buck. Anxious for meat, the old man shot the buck, and the leopard sprang upon him. Being a gallant old soldier, Martin gripped the beast by the throat and finally succeeded in strangling it. Thereafter, badly wounded, but dragging the buck, he entered the house where were Margaret and Gerard. In a few moments they looked up and saw shining through the window the green eyes of the leopard looking hungrily at the meat; moreover, the duke's huntsmen and hounds, as they could hear, were approaching. Then the quick-witted Margaret ended the tense situation by cutting off a piece of the buck and tossing it to the leopard, who dashed off, followed by the huntsmen.[52]

These passages come from Lacroix and Seré. To be sure, Le Grand d'Aussy also treats the custom of hunting with leopards, but Lacroix and Seré are closer to Reade, although he, of course, might have read both. (This part of their book is not copied from Le Grand d'Aussy.) Lacroix and Seré run thus:

> The leopard itself was brought to France and trained to catch game for the benefit of man. Hunters on horseback carried behind them a box placed like a portmanteau; upon this box was seated the leopard. These hunters scoured the plain and woods, preceded by dogs to stir up the game. At the moment the wild animal broke cover, the leopard bounded after it and in three leaps captured it. Then the hunters, dismounting, offered the leopard a piece of fresh meat in a bowl full of blood and the animal left them his prey.[53]

Unlike Le Grand d'Aussy, moreover, Lacroix and Seré have a picture of the hunter and the leopard on horseback, a picture reproduced at this point in this volume. The method of carriage with the straps to the hunter's loins is clearly brought out in this plate, and the sturdiness of the horse corresponds with Reade's account. All we learn from Le Grand d'Aussy is that the leopard was carried on the horse behind the rider (*en croupe*). Moreover, the way the leopard's tail hangs down in the picture

[52] Oxf., pp. 54–57; Ev., pp. 65–68.

[53] I, "Chasse," vii. Le Grand d'Aussy's treatment is I, 421–23.

Chasse au léopard (XVIe siècle), d'après une estampe de Jean Stradan.

Lacroix and Seré

HUNTSMAN AND LEOPARD

fairly invites anyone to pull it. Finally, the method in Lacroix and Seré of making the creature quit his prey by offering him a piece of meat, I believe, suggested Margaret's clever idea of getting rid of the duke's leopard in *The Cloister and the Hearth*.

Gerard's family made life difficult for him by insisting, as in the *Compendium*, that he should become a priest. Dame van Eyck, however, came to his rescue. She told him decisively that he must marry Margaret and take her with him to Italy, for Italy was the land where "painters are honoured like princes." In order to make a sojourn in that country possible, she intrusted to him the artistic secrets of her great brother Jan, by means of which he might gain his livelihood. Thus ran her advice:

Note my brother Jan's pictures: time, which fades all other paintings, leaves his colours bright as the day they left the easel. The reason is, he did nothing blindly, nothing in a hurry. He trusted to no hireling to grind his colours; he did it himself, or saw it done. His panel was prepared, and prepared again— I will show you how—a year before he laid his colour on. Most of them are quite content to have their work sucked up and lost, sooner than not be in a hurry. Bad painters are always in a hurry. Above all, Gerard, I warn you use but little oil, and never boil it; boiling it melts that vegetable dross into its very heart, which it is our business to clear away; for impure oil is death to colour. No; take your oil and pour it into a bottle with water. In a day or two the water will turn muddy: that is muck from the oil. Pour the dirty water carefully away, and add fresh. When that is poured away you will fancy the oil is clear. You are mistaken. "Reicht [her maid], fetch me *that!*" Reicht brought a glass trough with a glass lid fitting tight. "When your oil has been washed in bottle, put it into this trough with water, and put the trough in the sun all day. You will soon see the water turbid again. But mark, you must not carry this game too far, or the sun will turn your oil to varnish. When it is as clear as crystal, and not too luscious, drain carefully, and cork it up tight. Grind your own prime colours, and lay them on with this oil, and they shall live. Hubert would put sand or salt in the water to clear the oil quicker. But Jan used to say, "Water will do it best, give water time." Jan Van Eyck was never in a hurry, and that is why the world will not forget *him* in a hurry.[54]

This passage is a free rendering of material drawn from Mrs. Merrifield's *Original Treatises, Dating from the XIIth to XVIIIth Centuries on the Arts of Painting, etc.*—from her very long Introduction, to be exact. The part of Dame Margaret's advice where the

[54] Oxf., p. 63; Ev., p. 74.

borrowing is most obvious is her recommendations about purify-
ing oil, these being drawn from Mrs. Merrifield (the italics are
mine):

A bottle was filled, about one third with oil, another third with water; it was then
corked and shaken until the water and oil were mixed like an emulsion. . . . .
The oil was shaken every day . . . . for a few days, and then suffered to clear.
In about a week the oil was removed from the water into another bottle, and the process
was repeated for several weeks until the water below the oil ceased to appear
milky, and *the oil itself was clear and colourless.* . . . . *The addition of salt or sand ac-
celerates the clarification of the oil.* [This method Reade assigns to Hubert van
Eyck.] Many weeks are necessary to complete the process of bleaching and
purification. If the oil is intended to remain fluid, *it should be preserved in bottles
well stopped.*[55]

A neighboring passage in Mrs. Merrifield (quoted from another
artist) also provides its bit for the talk on oil:

Pour on to this water the oil which is to be clarified and bleached, and then
put the vase, with water and supernatant oil, into a place free from dust, and
exposed to the hottest rays of the sun in summer for a few days; in a short time *the oil
will deposit all its impurities,* and be *wonderfully clarified and bleached* by this process.[56]

Mrs. Merrifield likewise gives details as to carefulness in the
grinding of colors. She then adds, "This is in accordance with
the old Italian practice . . . . and with the example of *Michael
Angelo, who is said to have ground his own colours,* and also with
the practice of the Flemish school."[57] Reade attributes to Jan van
Eyck Michael Angelo's habit of grinding his own colors and the
general carefulness approved of here.

With regard to the deliberate preparation of panels that suck
up paint, Mrs. Merrifield declares:

*There is nothing, perhaps, on which the durability of a picture so much depends as on the
goodness of the ground;* and at the same time there is, perhaps, no part of a picture
on which the opinions of artists have been so much divided as on the manner of
preparing the grounds; . . . . some *electing to paint on absorbent grounds,* others on
non-absorbent grounds. . . . . The subject of the *preparation of panels and canvass
forms an important part* of most of the old treatises.[58]

All these borrowings from Mrs. Merrifield, Reade has worked
into a passage that sounds smooth and true to life. In particular
Jan's remark, "Water will do it best, give water time," which is
apparently Reade's own contribution, appears eminently natural.

[55] I, ccxxxv.   [56] I, ccxxxiv.   [57] I, ccxxx.   [58] I, cclxxxi.

In spite of family opposition, aided by the collusion of the meddling burgomaster, Gerard and Margaret prepared for their marriage, and the curé read the banns thrice within twenty-four hours. On the third occasion, however, there was trouble:

> The next morning they were both there palpitating with anxiety, when, to their horror, a stranger stood up and forbade the banns, on the score that the parties were not of age, and their parents not consenting. Outside the church door, Margaret and Gerard held a trembling and almost despairing consultation; but, before they could settle anything, the man who had done them so ill a turn approached, and gave them to understand that he was very sorry to interfere; that his inclination was to further the happiness of the young! but that in point of fact his only means of getting a living was by forbidding banns! what then? "The young people give me a crown, and I undo my work handsomely; tell the curé I was misinformed; and all goes smoothly." "A crown? I will give you a golden angel to do this," said Gerard, eagerly. The man consented as eagerly, and went with Gerard to the curé, and told him he had made a ridiculous mistake, which a sight of the parties had rectified. On this the curé agreed to marry the young couple next day at ten.[59]

This incident comes from Monteil, being taken from that part of the hotel-keeper's talk in which he tells of his marriage:

> When the banns were read, they were forbidden. The opposer was a poor fellow who lived by thus impeding marriage, and who pretended that I had been god-father at the confirmation of a child to whom Paulette had stood godmother. We soon discerned that the man wanted a few coins. We gave them to him and he at once desisted.[60]

The episode is picturesque in itself, but the best thing about Reade's use of it is the way he weaves it into the plot. The man who forbade the banns resorted to an inn at Tergou, and, getting drunk there on the money he had gained, proceeded to boast of his exploit. One of Gerard's knavish brothers, Sybrandt, who was fond of frequenting the hostelry, heard the whole story. Since his father was away from home, he and the other envious brother informed the burgomaster, an enemy of Gerard's, and the next day when the curé tried to marry the lovers the burgomaster's emissaries interrupted the wedding. This is a skilful use of cause and effect on Reade's part.

Gerard was imprisoned by the burgomaster in a tower but

[59] Oxf., pp. 65–66; Ev., p. 76.   [60] Monteil, II, 243.

escaped by means of a rope. Thereafter his brother Giles went up the rope for the mere pleasure of climbing and brought down a quantity of parchment—Gerard being in the habit of buying this material from him for writing and painting. One of the pieces procured by Giles was a deed which proved that the burgomaster had long been defrauding Margaret's father of his rightful property.

Gerard, on escaping, went to Margaret's home, whither the burgomaster, missing the precious deed, sent his retainers. Searching for Gerard, they went through the house thoroughly. Among other things "they ran their knives into an alligator he [Margaret's father, Peter] had nailed to his wall."[61] This same specimen of Peter's is mentioned twice later in the novel and in both places is called a crocodile. The association of such a beast with a room devoted to medicine is derived from a passage in a book from which Reade borrowed heavily, the *Crudities* of the famous Renaissance traveler Thomas Coryate:

Also I saw two goodly faire roomes within the Monastery abundantly furnished with passing variety of pleasant fine waters and Apothecary drugges that serve onely for the Monkes. In the first of these roomes I saw the skin of a great crocodile hanged up at the roofe, and another skinne of a crocodile in the inner roome. This crocodile is a beast of a most terrible shape, fashioned something like a Dragon with wonderfull hard scales upon his backe. I observed that he hath no tongue at all.[62]

Margaret had concealed the fugitive in an old chest, on top of which she appeared to be sleeping. Thus his pursuers failed in their search for him and departed to an inn named The Three Kings. Coryate, it should be noted, mentions an inn of this name at Lyons; hence Reade probably derived it from him.[63] Margaret now found Gerard almost stifled in the chest and with difficulty revived him. After this the lovers, strongly moved by the

---

[61] Oxf., p. 91; Ev., p. 100. The other occurrences are: Oxf., pp. 348, 351; Ev., pp. 351, 354.

[62] (2 vols.; Glasgow, 1905), I, 290. Fynes Moryson (*An Itinerary Containing His Ten Years Travell through the Twelve Dominions* [4 vols.; Glasgow, 1907–8], I, 415), mentions a crocodile in the courts of justice at Paris; but Coryate, since he is speaking of a medical room, is a better source. (Mr. Wheeler notices neither of these.)

[63] Oxf., p. 97; Ev., p. 106; Coryate, I, 211. (Not observed by Mr.Wheeler.)

perils they had been through and passionately devoted to each other, spent the night together. The next day the burgomaster instigated another pursuit of Gerard, this time with the help of bloodhounds. The lovers escaped in an exciting chase, wherein Martin shot the bloodhounds and Gerard knocked down the burgomaster with a cudgel. Thereafter, compelled to flight by the hot pursuit, Gerard said goodbye to Margaret and left Holland.

Chapter Three

ON THE ROAD IN GERMANY

THE wanderings of Gerard are treated at great length in *The Cloister and the Hearth* and contribute some of the most interesting scenes of the novel. It will be observed, however, that the *Compendium* says nothing about what happened to the hero between his leaving home and his arriving in Rome, except that he sent a brief letter to his family. All the wandering and adventures, then, were put in by Reade of his own accord.

One reason for his doing this, of course, is that he liked to provide thrills for his audience, and adventures during a journey are one of the best ways yet discovered of effecting this end. I suspect, however, that the influence of Sir Walter Scott also had something to do with Reade's stressing this part of the plot. Scott, as the father of the historical novel, could not but occur to anyone writing this sort of novel in Victorian times. More important, three of Scott's novels are found in the *Century* list of books: *The Monastery*, *The Abbot*, and *Quentin Durward*. The first two were obviously consulted by Reade because they treat of the church in a period not too remote from that of *The Cloister and the Hearth*. *Quentin Durward*, on the other hand, was chosen because it concerns the very century of Reade's novel and because part of it happens in Flanders and deals with the court of the Duke of Burgundy. Though, with one possible exception, I have not found any influence of these three novels on specific passages of Reade's, Scott's fondness for adventure instead of psychology may well have encouraged Reade to stress this element in *The Cloister and the Hearth*. In particular, the journey of Quentin Durward, escorting the ladies of Croye from the court of France to that of Burgundy, with many hazards by the way, is the part of these Scott novels which would be most likely to stimulate the element of adventure in Reade's book.

After a mention of Gerard's "little dial," of which I shall speak later, the novel takes the hero into Germany. The first episode, that of the drunken count on the ground, is drawn from the following passage in Fynes Moryson's book of travels (the italics are mine):

Only I did once see, not without astonishment, *a man of honorable condition*, as it seemed by his apparrell, of Velvet, and many rings on his fingers, *who lay groveling on the ground, close by the carte rutt of the high-way, with two servants* distending *his cloake* betweene the Sun and him, and when wee lighted from our waggon, *to behold more neerely this spectacle, thinking the man to be killed or sore wounded, his servants* made signes unto us, *that wee would not trouble him, who was onely drunken, and would be well assoone as he had slept a little.* At this we much wondred, and went on our journey.[1]

This episode as narrated by Moryson has great possibilities, but it becomes animated only when Reade takes it in hand:

Not far on this road, he came upon a little group. Two men in sober suits stood leaning lazily on each side of a horse, talking to one another. The rider, in a silk doublet and bright green jerkin and hose, both of English cloth, glossy as a mole, lay flat on his stomach in the afternoon sun, and looked an enormous lizard. His velvet cloak (flaming yellow) was carefully spread over the horse's loins.

"Is aught amiss?" inquired Gerard.

"Not that I wot of," replied one of the servants.

"But your master, he lies like a corpse. Are ye not ashamed to let him grovel on the ground?"

"Go to; the bare ground is the best cure for his disorder. If you get sober in bed, it gives you a headache; but you leap up from the hard ground like a lark in spring. Eh, Ulric?"

"He speaks sooth, young man," said Ulric, warmly.

"What, is the gentleman drunk?"

The servants burst into a hoarse laugh at the simplicity of Gerard's question.[2]

The passage is ably handled: the description of the count is made more specific; the dialogue is natural and lively; the cloak, held over the sleeper in the original, has been placed over the horse, adding another note of the incongruous. Then we proceed. The servants were half scornful, half suspicious that Gerard

[1] *An Itinerary Containing His Ten Yeeres Travell through the Twelve Dominions* (4 vols.; Glasgow, 1907–8), IV, 63. (This borrowing is noted by Mr. Wheeler.)

[2] Oxf., pp. 118–19; Ev., pp. 126–27.

did not know the count was always intoxicated at this time of day. Before giving them *trinkgeld*, Gerard ventured to ask why the horse was covered up and the nobleman was not. Each servant propounded a grotesque answer, and, being somewhat tipsy themselves, they began to dispute over the question. Then they proceeded to cuff each other; the horse as a result grew restive; he stepped on the nobleman; the latter came to his senses and rose up, tugging at his sword. Away went the horse; after him dashed the servants; and in pursuit stumbled the count, furious at his men, but wobbling badly in his course. The growing tensity of this humorous scene and its climax of sharp action show the hand of the practiced dramatist.

Gerard next reached the first of the German inns in the novel. Both Moryson, and Erasmus in his *Colloquies*, gave many racy details about German inns. Reade, had, of necessity to betake himself to authorities, since no modern writer can invent details of the life in a past epoch. Here, however, he found so abundant a supply that, feeling he wished to dispense with but little of it, he actually described three different German inns. The first one is mostly Moryson, with a touch of Erasmus.

The borrowings from Moryson in this first hostelry are from several different passages and are skilfully woven together by Reade. The framework of Gerard's visit is taken from an account by Moryson of one of his own experiences. He arrived in a coach at a German inn at eight in the evening and found that no food was being served. When he asked whether he might have an egg,

The servant answered that the old woman was in bed, and that he knew not the mystery, whether any eggs were in the house or no. . . . . To be brief, the women [who had arrived in the same coach with him] took compassion on me, and I without blushing was content to eat of free cost.

As a matter of fact, he had previously hoped he would get some "dried puddings" at the inn. During the night,

the Women, Virgins, Men and Maids, servants, all of us lay in one roome, and my selfe was lodged furthest from the stove, which they did not for any favour, though contrary to their opinion I was glad of it, delighting more in sweete aire, then the smoke of a dunghill.[3]

[3] Moryson, I, 27.

Similarly, Gerard arrived after eight and found nothing to eat. The landlady, who was plucking goose quills, remarked, "Supper is over this hour and more." Thus the wayfarer prepared to lie down supperless but was finally given a "dried pudding" by a kindly matron. Because of the unpleasant smells, Gerard chose to lie far away from the stove, being hence "on the shore of odour and stifling heat, instead of in mid-ocean" and sheathing his nose in clean straw. "And soon they were all asleep: men, maids, wives, and children, all lying higgledy-piggledy, and snoring in a dozen keys like an orchestra slowly tuning."[4]

Of the other bits from Moryson drawn upon for this passage, the most important is one about the bad air of German inns:

They use hot stoves . . . . , which are certaine chambers or roomes, having an earthen oven cast into them. . . . . And as well to keepe out cold as to retaine the heate, they keepe the dores and windowes closely shut; so as they using not only to receive Gentlemen into these stoves, but even to permit rammish clownes to stand by the oven till their wet clothes be dried, and themselves sweat . . . . , it must needes be, that these ill smelles, never purged by the admitting of any fresh ayre, should dull the braine, and almost choke the spirits of those who frequent the stoves. When my selfe first entred into one of them, this unwonted heate did so winde about my legges, as if a Snake had twined about them, and made my head dull and heavy.[5]

Reade uses these details, making them more vivid, and he adopts some of the actual phrases. The low room of his inn had a "clay-oven" with wet clothes drying around it, whether on lines or on "what another foot traveller [i.e., Moryson] in these parts calls 'rammish clowns.' " The windows were closed and the stench, which Reade enlarges upon, was intolerable. In fact, Gerard detected three different smells: "rammish clowns," dirty children, and garlic. As a result he "found something like a cold snake wind about his legs, and his head turn to a great lump of lead."[6]

[4] Oxf., pp. 120–25; Ev., pp. 128–32. (These borrowings are not mentioned by Wheeler.)

[5] IV, 15. This traveler adds that, when he once got used to German inns, he never enjoyed better health elsewhere.

[6] Oxf., pp. 120–21; Ev., pp. 128–29. Wheeler notes the borrowing of "rammish clowns" and the cold snake.

Again, Moryson observes, "The Innes of Germany hang out no signes at their gates, but they are vulgarly knowne, and so may be easilie found out."[7] In *The Cloister and the Hearth*, Gerard asked whether the building was a hostelry:

"Whence come you, who know not 'The Star of the Forest'?" was the reply.

"I am a stranger; and in my country inns have aye a sign."

"Droll country yours! What need of a sign to a public-house—a place that every soul knows?"[8]

Whenever Gerard betrayed ignorance of German ways at the inn, all the other guests stared at him. On one such occasion his interlocutor,

turning to his mates, let them know what an outlandish animal was in the room. Thereat the loud voices stopped, one by one, as the information penetrated the mass; and each eye turned, as on a pivot, following Gerard, and his every movement, silently and zoologically.[9]

This detail is borrowed from Erasmus' account of inns in his *Colloquies*: "And if they see any Body of another Country, who by his Habit looks like a Man of Quality, they all stare at him so wistfully, as if he was a Sort of strange Animal brought out of Africa."[10]

The landlady's picking goose feathers is drawn from a remark made elsewhere by Moryson "every winter night the servants are called into the warme stove [i.e., room], whereof such fethers as are reserved, they pull the fethers from the quill, using onely the softest of them for making of beds."[11]

Gerard helped the landlady gather up the feathers and, to repay him, she later sent him a mug of beer by her servant. Reade tells the episode vividly enough. The servant remorselessly awakened guest after guest until he found Gerard.

"Oh, it was you, was it?" said the other . . . . "here's your night-cap"; and he thrust a great oaken mug under Gerard's nose.

---

[7] IV, 33. (Noted by Wheeler.)   [8] Oxf., p. 121; Ev., p. 129.

[9] Oxf., p. 122; Ev., p. 129.

[10] *The Colloquies of Desiderius Erasmus*, trans. N. Bailey; ed. Rev. E. Johnson (3 vols.; London, 1900), II, 22. (Reade used the Latin original.)

[11] IV, 31. (Not noted by Wheeler.)

"I thank her, and bless her; here goes—ugh!" and his gratitude ended in a wry face; for the beer was muddy, and had a strange, medicinal twang new to the Hollander.

"Trinke aus!" shouted the hind reproachfully.

"Enow is as good as a feast," said the youth Jesuitically.

The hind cast a look of pity on this stranger who left liquor in his mug. "Ich brings euch," said he and drained it to the bottom.[12]

This taking episode is, I believe, prompted by Moryson's mention of "the pot of Schlaffdruncke, (or sleeping cup)."[13] One detail, moreover, surely comes from his statement that the Germans drink "commonly Beere, and that so thicke and ill smelling, and sometimes medicinall, as a stranger would think it more fit to be eaten (or cast into the sinke), then to be drunke."[14] The hind's exclamations, again, are from Moryson's remark that the Germans in tippling cry, "Drinke aus, Drinke out, and as — every Psalme ends in Gloria, so every speech of theirs, ends in Ich brings euch, I drinke to you."[15]

The next morning when Gerard left the inn the servant

demanded trinkgeld, and getting a trifle more than usual, and seeing Gerard eye a foaming milkpail he had just brought from the cow, hoisted it up bodily to his lips. "Drink your fill, man," said he, and on Gerard offering to pay for the delicious draught, told him in broad patois, that a man might swallow a skinful of milk, or a breakfast of air, without putting hand to pouch.[16]

This little episode is prompted by Moryson's remark:

These servants in Innes expect as it were of duty drinking money from all passengers, and boldly demand it, as if it were their right whether the passenger will or no, which they doe rudely in the lower parts of Germany, by offering them a pot to drinke at parting.[17]

It is notable, however, that Reade improves his borrowing by having the drink come after the tip, instead of before.

Gerard paid the landlady's bill, which amounted to "two pfenning," and he offered a creutzer to the woman who gave him the pudding. In this connection it should be remarked that most of the coins mentioned in *The Cloister and the Hearth* seem to come from Moryson, though sometimes with modernized spelling.

[12] Oxf., pp. 124–25; Ev., p. 132.

[13] IV, 34. (Not noted by Wheeler.)

[14] IV, 36. (Not noted by Wheeler.)

[15] IV, 37. (Not noted by Wheeler.)

[16] Oxf., p. 125; Ev., pp. 132–33.

[17] IV, 32. (Not noted by Wheeler.)

This old traveler is exceedingly interested in money, always specifying just how much he paid on all occasions; in addition, he gives a table of coins arranged according to countries.[18]

The pudding-giver refused the money, but her "hulking husband" interposed, "Give the vixen a kiss for her pudding, and cry quits"—a suggestion followed by Gerard to everyone's satisfaction.[19] This passage is drawn from Moryson's remark that men drinking to women must likewise kiss them. "A stranger would at first sight marvell at this custome, and more specially that their very husbands should take it for a disgrace, and be apt to quarrell with a man for omitting this ceremony towards their wives."[20]

The next evening Gerard put up at a monastery. I have met several accounts of monastic hospitality, but none closely resembling this one in details. The night after this the wanderer stayed at his second German inn. The account of this[21] is drawn mostly from Erasmus' *Colloquy on Inns* (*Diversoria*), with some borrowings from Moryson.

This second German inn had no signboard, but its walls, as Gerard noticed on first seeing it, were decorated with the coats-of-arms of distinguished guests. The use by hostelries of the escutcheons of former visitors is mentioned in several books in the *Century* list: Moryson, Montaigne's *Journey*, Michel and Fournier's *Livre d'or des métiers*, and Coryate. Reade might have derived the detail from any one of them.[22]

The indebtedness to Erasmus of the inn description has long been known. In the last paragraph of *The Cloister and the Hearth*, Reade in his praise of Erasmus "the heaven-born dramatist of his century," declares, "Some of the best scenes in this new book are from his mediaeval pen." With this statement it is not strange that various readers hit upon specific passages wherein borrowing was evident. One contributor to *Notes and Queries*, for instance, found the close similarity between Erasmus and Reade

---

[18] I, xxiii–xxv. (Not noted by Wheeler.)

[19] Oxf., p. 125; Ev., p. 133.   [20] IV, 62. (Not noted by Wheeler.)

[21] Reade's long account covers Oxf., pp. 126–31; Ev., pp. 134–39.

[22] Mr. Wheeler notes the Moryson passage (IV, 33).

in their descriptions of inns and was dreadfully shocked at what he considered Reade's plagiarism.[23] This pronouncement drew other communications on both sides, and one gentleman observed, "Nobody but an antiquary really wants chapter and verse for every detail in an historical novel." But the first contributor, in a second notice, insisted on continuing to be shocked. Perhaps it is just as well that he never saw the present book. In any case, it should be observed, the similarity of Reade's to Erasmus' inn is very close; indeed, this account is the second most detailed borrowing from the *Colloquies*.

In Erasmus, Bertulph is describing a German inn to his friend William:

> When you have called a good While at the Gate, at Length, one puts his Head out of the Stove [i.e., room] window . . . . like a Tortoise from under his Shell: Him you must ask if you can have any Lodging there; if he does not say no, you may take it for granted, that there is Room for you. When you ask where the Stable is, he points to it. . . . . If you find Fault with any Thing, they tell you presently, if you don't like [it], look for another Inn.[24]

Reade adapts this in vivid fashion:

> Gerard hammered on the great oak door: no answer. He hallooed: no reply. After a while he hallooed louder, and at last a little round window, or rather hole in the wall, opened, a man's head protruded cautiously, like a tortoise's from its shell, and eyed Gerard stolidly, but never uttered a syllable.
>
> "Is this an inn?" asked Gerard, with a covert sneer.
>
> The head seemed to fall into a brown study; eventually it nodded, but lazily.
>
> "Can I have entertainment here?"
>
> Again the head pondered and ended by nodding, but sullenly, and seemed a skull overburdened with catch-penny interrogatories.
>
> "How am I to get within, an't please you?"
>
> At this the head popped in, as if the last question had shot it; and a hand popped out, pointed round the corner of the building, and slammed the window.

Reade has made the action even more vivid by using additional specific details and natural dialogue. Moreover, since Gerard had no horse, the rude pointing was to the door of the hostelry, not the stable.

[23] *Notes and Queries* (7th ser.), XI, 348–49. The other articles are pp. 398–99, 438, 496, in the same volume, and p. 56 in Vol. XII.

[24] My various citations from this *Colloquy* are found in II, 21–26.

Both authors vividly describe the squalor of the interior, with its assembled guests. Reade, like Erasmus, has men scrape mud off their shoes and comb out their hair (adding the words "inmates included"). Erasmus declares, "There's Water provided for you to wash your Hands, if you will; but as for the Cleanness of it, it is for the most Part such that you will want another Water to wash that off." A similar happening in Reade prompted Gerard's "Wash you first your water, and then a man may wash his hands withal." To this the servant replied, "An it likes you not, seek another inn," the reply found in Erasmus, and here put in a dramatic position. Gerard inquired and ascertained that the nearest inn was distant four leagues.

Next in Erasmus, the gray-bearded servant, "having cast his Eyes about, counts to himself, how many there are in the Stove; the more he sees there, the more Fire he makes." Reade's passage is similar, except that he makes it more specific—"a log for every six" guests. In both cases the room became scorchingly hot. "By and by," continues Erasmus, "in comes our bearded Ganymede again, and lays on the Table as many Napkins as there are Guests: But, good God! not Damask ones, but such as you'd take to have been made out of old Sails." Reade applies the epithet "Ganymede" to the ancient servitor in his description, and says of the table accouterments, "They seemed like sacks that had been worn out in agriculture and come down to this, or like shreds from the mainsail of some worn-out ship."

Here, to break up his long description, Reade introduces the French soldier Denys, to whom I shall return later.

Erasmus then proceeds (with Reade very similar):

Out comes the sour-look'd Ganymede again, and counts his Company over again; by and by he comes in again, and brings every Man a Wooden Dish, and a Spoon of the same Silver, and then a Glass; and then a little after he brings Bread, which the Guests may chip every one for themselves at Leisure, while the Porridge is boiling. For sometimes they sit thus for near an Hour. . . . . And by and by follow the Dishes in great Pomp; commonly the first has Sippits of Bread in Flesh Broth. [Reade adds that this, though unpalatable, served to fill the guest up.]—After that comes in another Soup [omitted by Reade because of sameness], and then a Service of Butcher's Meat, that has been twice boil'd, or salt Meats warm'd again, and then Pulse again, and by and by something of more solid Food [Reade is more specific with "hashed meat highly peppered"], until their Stomachs being pretty well staid, they bring roast Meat or stewed Fish [Reade is again more specific: "roasted kids, most excellent, and carp and trout fresh from the stream"].

The Englishman likewise adds the humorous touch that the French and Dutch were too full to eat of these dainties, whereas the "canny natives had kept an internal corner for contingencies, and polished the kid's very bones."

At this point Reade inserts a description of cheese based on one by Moryson, which is more graphic than that in Erasmus. Moryson runs:

These Cheeses they [the Germans] compasse round with thred or twigges, and the beginne them in the midst of the broade side, making a round hole there, into which hole, when the cheese is to be set up, they put some few drops of wine, that it may putrifie against the next time, when they eate the mouldy peeces and very creeping maggots for dainety morsels, and at last the cheese becomes so rotten and so full of these wormes, that if the said binding that compasseth it chance to break, the cheese fals into a million of crums no bigger than moates.[25]

Reade follows this closely. Moreover, he enlivens the passage by having the cheese put directly in front of the sensitive Gerard, who recoiled from it, much to the disapproval of the natives. They continued drinking "garausses," as Moryson related of Germans.

The feast being ended, the aged servant, in both Erasmus and Reade, grimly entered with a trencher bearing many circles and semicircles drawn on it in chalk; he resembled Charon, as both authors declare. Thereupon the diners all paid their dues. Questioned whether anybody finds fault with the reckoning, Erasmus' chief speaker replies: "No Body that is wise. For they will say, what Sort of a Fellow are you? You pay no more than the rest." This suggestion is admirably developed by Reade, who makes Gerard get a scolding from the old man for wanting to pay less than the average on account of drinking little, and Denys a scolding for trying to pay more.

The account of Gerard's sleep that night utilizes the dirty sheets

[25] IV, 26; Reade: Oxf., pp. 129–30; Ev., p. 137. (Noted by Wheeler.) The "garausses" mentioned are from Moryson, IV, 36. (Noted by Wheeler.)

mentioned by Erasmus, but is dependent mostly on Moryson, whose account runs thus:

> They leade the guests into a chamber of many beds, and if any man have no companion, they give him a bed-fellow. . . . . Through all Germany they lodge betweene two fetherbeds. . . . . This kind of lodging were not incommodious in Winter, if a man did lie alone: but since by the high way they force men to have bedfellowes, one side lies open to the cold, by reason that the upper bed is narrow, so as it cannot fall round about the two, but leaves one side of them both open to the wind and weather.[26]

Reade, starting with this suggestion, imagines the entertaining scene of Gerard being made to sleep with a drunkard. Long kept awake by the fellow's babbling, Gerard finally went to sleep, only to awake and find that his companion had all the upper feather bed. Only by a clever ruse was Gerard able to twitch it away from the man and sleep warm the rest of the night.

But to return to Denys, who is first introduced in this German inn.[27] That Gerard should have a companion on his journey is but in harmony with the tradition of the picaresque novel, from which this wandering part of *The Cloister and the Hearth* is descended. Denys, however, is a most charming companion and remains long in the reader's memory. Indeed, to my own way of thinking, he is the best-drawn male character in the novel. In connection with Denys the following passage from Coryate is significant:

> There rod in our company a merry Italian one Antonio, that vaunted he was lineally descended from the famous Marcus Antonius of Rome the Triumvir, and would oftentimes cheer us with his sociable conceit: Courage, courage, le Diable est mort. That is, be merry, for the Devill is dead.[28]

In the first paragraph in which Denys appears in *The Cloister and the Hearth*, this French countersign occurs, and it forever remains characteristic of him. In fact, in these few lines of Coryate, especially in "Courage, le Diable est mort," lies Denys's whole character. Just as Tennyson imagined his entire poem

---

[26] IV, 31. (Wheeler quotes from this passage apropos of feather beds, but does not remark that from it Reade has imagined his episode.)

[27] Oxf., p. 128; Ev., p. 136.

[28] *Crudities* (2 vols.; Glasgow, 1905), I, 228. (Wheeler notes this passage but does not bring out what seems to me its full significance.)

"The Northern Farmer Old Style" from a single expression of an actual old farmer who lay dying, I am inclined to believe that the inventive mind of Charles Reade developed all of Denys's character from this brief passage of Coryate's, the only addition, perhaps, being that he was a soldier. We have already seen the novelist's imagination evolving a scene from a mere hint in much the same manner. Antonio, we learn in Coryate, was "merry" and was inclined to "cheer us with his sociable conceit." And those few words, "Courage, le Diable est mort"—words, by the way, that Reade would be inclined to put into a Frenchman's, rather than an Italian's, mouth—are suggestive of many qualities: of swagger, profanity, gallantry, good fellowship, and charm—all of them possessed by Denys.

Gerard and his new comrade now journeyed on and put up for the night at a third German inn. This, described in less detail than the other two, is based on two passages in Moryson. Reade says:

Our travellers towards nightfall reached a village; it was a very small one, but contained a place of entertainment. They searched for it, and found a small house with barn and stables. . . . . Gerard asked for supper.

"Supper? We have no time to cook for travellers; we only provide lodging, good lodging for man and beast. . . . . You can buy what you like in the village, and cook it in our oven."[29]

This situation, I believe, is borrowed by Reade from Moryson's remarks about inns in small Polish towns. There are some differences in detail, to be sure, but Reade's habit of borrowing facts about inns from Moryson makes the influence here probable. Moryson says:

For the Innes in such places are poore naked houses, having nothing to sell, but close by them are the shambles, the Bakers and Brewers houses, where the passengers buy beere and such meat as they like, and bring it to the Inne, which a poore Hostesse will dresse, affoording them onely fier, and a course Table-cloth.[30]

The sleeping accommodations at this third inn are drawn from another passage in Moryson, this time about travelers in Saxony:

. . . . all without exception, rich and poore, drunken and sober, take up their lodging among the Cowes in straw, where sometimes it happens, that hee who

[29] Oxf., p. 133; Ev., p. 141.   [30] IV, 72. (Not noted by Wheeler.)

lying downe had a pillow of straw under his head, when hee awaketh finds the same either scattered or eaten by Cowes.[31]

Reade embroiders this suggestion delightfully.[32] The old man who showed the travelers to the cowhouse misunderstood the shocked Gerard's "What, do you set Christian men to lie among cattle?" and replied, "Well, it is hard upon the poor beasts. They have scarce room to turn." As the two friends burrowed in the straw, Denys described how less comfortable it was to lie wounded on a battlefield. They slept soundly in the straw and, the next morning, the playful Denys awoke Gerard by squirting cow's milk in his eye. The cow had eaten the soldier's straw pillow, but Denys bore no grudge and drank the cow's health with her own milk: "A votre santé, madame; et sans rancune."

As they fared onward now, Denys, when he passed a woman, was likely to take off his cap to her; the invariable result was that "she suddenly drew herself up quite stiff like a soldier on parade." This circumstance is taken from a remark about German women made by Montaigne in his *Journey:* "If in passing you make them a bow and doff your hat, most of them will be stuck there without any movement."[33]

Gerard and Denys next visited a German shoe store, an episode of which the germ is from Moryson:

I have formerly advised English travellers, first to passe by [visit] Germany, that they may there learne patience by serving themselves. For if you come to a shop to buy shoes, the Master bids you to find out your selfe those that will fit you, and then to put them on your selfe, which done, he askes the price, whereof he will not bate one halfe penny, and when you have paid his asking, then the Prentices challenge drinking money as of duty.[34]

From this suggestion Reade builds out his scene. The German shoe-store owner was sitting in his doorway asleep, blocking the entrance; the friends discussed how to get past him, and Denys was for prodding his ribs with a crossbow bolt; the apprentice

---

[31] IV, 31–32. (Noted by Wheeler.)

[32] Oxf., pp. 134–36; Ev., pp. 141–44.

[33] Oxf. 136–37; Ev. 144. *The Diary of Montaigne's Journey to Italy in 1580 and 1581,* trans. E. J. Trechmann (London, 1929), p. 29.

[34] IV, 32. (Noted by Wheeler.) Reade's corresponding scene is Oxf., pp. 137–39; Ev., pp. 145–47.

(suggested by Moryson's mention of apprentices) was aggrieved at their disturbing him at dinner; a customer and her maid, arriving, waked the dealer, who then fled, in surly fashion, to a neighboring store; Denys, admiring all women, fitted the customer with two pairs of yellow and one pair of red shoes; and the shop-owner only grumbled that all his colored shoes were now gone.

Reade describes the dress of both the lady and her maid carefully, and all the details come from Moryson's account of women's attire in Germany.[35] The original account, which need not be quoted here, is straggling; but Reade condenses it and makes his description easy and natural. Among other points, Moryson specifies that women wear both yellow and red shoes, a hint used in the narrative previously discussed.

The two travelers proceeded toward the Rhine through many threatening forests.

Every clown they met, carried, whether for offence or defence, a most formidable weapon; a light axe, with a short pike at the head, and a longer slender handle of ash or yew, well seasoned. These the natives could all throw with singular precision, so as to make the point strike an object at several yards' distance. . . . . Gerard bought one and practised with it.[36]

This account is prompted by Moryson's remark: "The Saxons in stead of Swords, carry Hatchets in their hands; being very skilfull in the use of them, so as they will hit any small marke therewith."[37]

And now, as the friends proceeded through a forest near Düsseldorf, there occurred a thrilling adventure with a bear—an adventure that forms one of the most exciting episodes in the whole novel. They encountered a bear cub and killed it. Denys carried its carcass, and Gerard, bearing Denys's crossbow, practiced with it, while the soldier celebrated its great superiority over longbows and over firearms. Then suddenly they saw the mother-bear coming at them. She made for Denys, who dropped the cub and went up a tree, since Gerard was too frightened to shoot. The

[35] IV, 210–11. (Noted by Wheeler.) The maid's linen coif is from IV, 212–13, about Swiss women. (Not noted by Wheeler.)

[36] Oxf., p. 140; Ev., p. 148.   [37] IV, 208. (Not noted by Wheeler.)

bear followed Denys in a rage. Gerard, who likewise had gone up a tree, came down and, picking up the crossbow, fired several bolts into the bear. The creature now came down from Denys's tree and made for Gerard. He at once climbed a tree again, followed by the bear. Denys thereupon descended and, resuming the crossbow, began shooting once more at the monster. Just as she reached Gerard in his tree and was about to kill him, Denys finished her and she fell to the ground.[38]

The passage which, in my opinion, started Reade's imagination going on this adventure is found in Le Grand d'Aussy. Speaking of bear-hunting, he says:

Cross-bows, nets, and even mere boar-spears were used. Nevertheless no single man could venture alone on such hunting with so weak a weapon as the last. He would have risked his life. Since a bear always is accustomed to attack the man who has struck him, he would have strangled the hunter with his paws or would have crushed the man's head with his teeth. "But two very determined men may carry the adventure through successfully," says the Count [a four-teenth-century authority on hunting], "if they are willing to act in concert and especially not abandon each other. The first shoots at the animal; and, by this means, brings the beast at himself; the second hunter then shoots at the creature. The furious bear stops pursuing his first enemy, to run at the second. The first man strikes him again; and soon, by this double attack, they succeed in killing him."[39]

This passage of Le Grand d'Aussy, though it does not attempt to be vivid, is striking. It mentions the crossbow at the beginning; it stresses the great danger of bear-hunting; and it proposes a spectacular method whereby two determined men may attack the bear turn and turn about and, by making the monster go from one to the other, may eventually kill him. This is exactly what happens in *The Cloister and the Hearth*. The two friends are determined and do not abandon each other; the bear goes first for Denys; next, when shot by Gerard, she turns upon him, and finally is shot fatally by Denys. Someone may declare that, in strict adherence to Le Grand d'Aussy's account, the process of going from one hunter to the other should continue longer, but such a

[38] Oxf., pp. 140–45; Ev., pp. 148–53.

[39] I, 379–80. Lacroix and Seré, who sometimes copy Le Grand d'Aussy, have nothing like this.

narrative would soon be tedious and a better dramatic effect is secured by having the change of attack from one hunter to the other be brief, and by developing the action with much vivid detail. It is this latter method that is followed in the episode in *The Cloister and the Hearth*. Moreover, such development of a good scene from a striking hint is exactly the sort of thing that Reade does time and again in this novel. It seems certain to me, therefore, that this passage of Le Grand d'Aussy is the source of the bear episode.[40]

The praises of the crossbow and its superiority over the long-bow and firearms, as celebrated by Denys between the killing of the cub and the coming of the mother, may also be from Le Grand d'Aussy. At any rate, this author discusses in succession the bow, the arbalest, and firearms—all of them in the same general part of his book where the bear passage occurs (that "On Hunting"). Moreover, his second sentence about firearms runs, "Habit, or rather the imperfect state in which fire arms still were, made for the continued use of bow and arbalest." Such a remark may have prompted Denys's words, "Petronel nor harquebuss shall ever put down Sir Arbalest. Why, we can shoot ten times while they are putting their charcoal and their lead into their leathern smoke belchers, and then kindling their matches."[41]

After the bear adventure there followed an experience with robbers. Gerard, wounded by the bear and left alone for a time by Denys, heard a conflict take place near him in the forest. Thereafter he and Denys slept a while, until hunger drove them to walk farther. Soon in the blackness of the wood they beheld men apparently walking on air, but they soon found that what they saw was a gallows laden with dead malefactors. Underneath was one of the gang still alive. They joined him and ate a meal in this ghastly place. The robber, animated by wine, told

[40] It is possible, but unlikely, that the following sentence from Erasmus' *Parabolae* may have fused with the passage from Le Grand d'Aussy: "A man who has stolen the cubs of a tigress thinks he has been successful if he manages to get safely away with one from the pursuing mother" (*Opera omnia* [10 vols.; Leiden, 1703–6], Vol. I, col. 607). But a mishap to a cub would naturally suggest itself to Reade as a means of maddening an animal.

[41] Oxf., p. 142; Ev., p. 150; Le Grand d'Aussy, I, 430.

them how some soldiers of the Archbishop of Cologne, disguised as merchants, had captured his fellow-robbers—this was the battle heard by Gerard—and placed them where they were now hanging on the gallows. After a time the two friends proceeded toward Düsseldorf, making the desperado support Gerard, while the miscreant complained that the laws, by punishing theft with death, thus drove a robber to kill his victim, since murder entailed no greater punishment.[42]

This whole narrative was, I feel sure, suggested to Reade by a passage in Coryate, an author from whom he drew much. The italics are mine.

I observed in a great many places, on both sides of the Rhene [he is descending it], *more gallowes and wheeles betwixt Mentz and Colen, then ever I saw in so short a space in all my life,* especially *within a few miles of Colen,* by reason that the rusticall Corydons of the country, which are commonly called the Boores and the Freebooters . . . . *do commit many notorious robberies neer the Rhene,* who are such cruell and bloody horse-leaches . . . . that they *seldome robbe any man but forthwith they cut his throat.* And some of them doe afterward escape, *by reason of the woodes neere at hand in which they shelter themselves* free from danger. Yet others are sometimes taken, and most cruelly excarnificated and tortured upon these wheels. . . . . And upon those gallowes in divers places *I sawe murderers hang,* partly in chaines, and partly without chaines. . . . . I have heard that *the Free-booters doe make themselves so strong, that they are not to be* taken by the country. . . . . [A great troop of them actually plundered a whole town.] The like they did to a goodly Palace hard by it called the Praepositura, by reason that it belongeth to an Ecclesiastical Praepositus, a man of great authority, that doth sometimes make his residence in that place.[43]

This passage concerns the Rhenish country where the two friends now were (Düsseldorf is on the Rhine only twenty-five miles from Cologne), and one can see how its details worked on Reade's invention. The great frequency of the robbers and the mention of forests prompted Reade to bring both into his novel, and the omnipresence of the gallows led to his imagining the lurid meal beneath it, for Reade of course always loved the sensational. The great strength of the freebooters—too powerful to be overcome by individuals—suggested a group of soldiers as the logical means of overpowering them. The capture of a palace be-

[42] Oxf., pp. 148–56; Ev., pp. 156–64.
[43] II, 308–9. (Not noted by Wheeler.)

longing to "an Ecclesiastical Praepositus" near Cologne naturally
made Reade think of the archbishop of that city, who, if an edifice of his were captured, would be inclined to punish the robbers. Finally, Coryate's expression, "They seldome robbe any
man but forthwith they cut his throat," could easily lead to the
malefactor's excuse for usually adding murder to the theft. In
some such way, I believe, the influence took place, and Reade's
episode gradually arose.

A few descriptive details about the robber sitting under the
gallows, it should be added, come from Moryson. He is armed
with the sort of Saxon ax already described. Moreover, he wore
"the hat of the district, a three-cornered hat called a Brunswicker,
stiff enough to turn a sword-cut. . . . . The weight of the whole
thing had turned his ears entirely down, like a fancy rabbit's in
our century." This comes from Moryson's passage: "Many of
the Saxons weare thrummed hats, which are called Brunswicke
hats . . . . being so stiffe as a sword will hardly pierce them, and being so heavie as they lie upon the eares, and make them hang
downe with small comelinesse."[44]

Reaching Düsseldorf, the two comrades went to an inn and
Gerard was put to bed ill with his wound. The next day he was
visited by an old German doctor. In this connection we should
observe that Reade himself once set out to be a physician, but
that he recoiled from the horrors he had to witness, especially
from seeing a patient bled—a proceeding to which he retained
a strong antipathy.[45] A whole chapter is devoted to the doctor's
visit,[46] and possesses much medieval coloring because of all the
information about the medicine of the time. On the other hand,
the chapter is not a mere collection of dry facts; it is entertaining
reading, and the old physician himself is alive and possessed of a
decided personality. To be specific, his leading traits are lo-
quacity, fondness for showing off, and choler—a bad combination for the sick room. The old fellow at once decided he must
bleed Gerard and recounted how he had bled many other pa-

[44] Oxf., p. 151; Ev., p. 159; Moryson, IV, 207. (Not noted by Wheeler.)

[45] Malcolm Elwin, *Charles Reade: A Biography*, pp. 34–35.

[46] Oxf., pp. 157–68; Ev., pp. 165–76.

tients, curing some and killing others. Thereafter he launched
forth into the praise of the Greek school of physicians, to which
he himself belonged, and into a stinging tirade against the Arabian school, which he hated. Denys now arrived and strongly op-
posed bleeding, declaring doctors killed more people than did
soldiers. The doctor became irritated; he celebrated his medical
education vociferously and continued to show off his learning and
to boast of his skill. The dispute grew louder, as Reade increased
the tensity of the scene. Gerard finally decided against bleeding,
and the doctor broke out into vituperative menaces. Gerard
threw a pillow at him, knocking him down, and the old fellow
tumbled onto the burning coals which were to have been used to
cauterize Gerard, and burned himself terribly. This ending obviously provides a vivid climax.

The main source of the chapter is Monteil's account of a doctor, but a few points come from elsewhere. Thus the old man's
costume is taken from Moryson. Reade's doctor wears "a sword
by his side in a morocco scabbard, a ruff round his neck not only
starched severely, but treacherously stiffened in furrows by rebatoes, or a little hidden framework of wood; and on his head a
four-cornered cap with a fur border."[47] These details come from
two adjacent passages in Moryson: "Onely in Prussia I observed them to weare long ruffes, with rebatoes of wire to beare
them up" and "the scabbards [of German swords] . . . . are al-
waies of leather. Many of the Germans in steede of hats, weare
caps lined with furre."[48]

The main idea of Reade's scene, I believe, is suggested by the
following passage from Monteil, in which the physician tells of a
consultation of doctors over the case of a young archer:

> Then the consultation began. Since the young archer understood Latin a
> little, he wanted it to take place in his presence. The senior doctor held forth
> with much erudition and dignity. After having sung the praises of medicine,
> which even animals practise according to Pliny, having enumerated the Four
> Humors and the diseases that come from them, having proved that, in the opin-
> ion of St. Augustine, the duration of life was formerly longer than now, having

[47] Oxf., p. 158; Ev., pp. 165–66.

[48] IV, 206, 208. (Neither is noted by Wheeler.)

demonstrated that, with all due respect to Aristotle, any man who marries ought not to be twenty years older than his wife and that too long a celibacy has disastrous results, having quoted the finest passages of Plato on the faculties of body and soul and the good use one should make of them at all times of life, he made a thousand other weighty remarks, but not without being often interrupted by the young patient, who cried out time and again: "That hasn't anything to do with my trouble! Come to my trouble!" . . . . [This made the old doctor progress to the archer's particular malady, and he pronounced it without cure.] The views of the other doctors were then pooled; the opinion of the oldest was unanimously supported, a circumstance that infuriated the young archer to such a degree that he jumped up and broke out into abuse. "How splendid medicine is," he cried, "how splendid! And doctors what wonderful fellows!"[49]

Here are many elements that reappear in the English account: the long-windedness of the doctor, his showing off, his talking on matters not closely related to the case, the irritating effect on the patient, and the latter's eventually rising out of bed. Reade drew heavily on Monteil for medical details in this scene, as we shall presently note—a circumstance that strengthens the likelihood of his having derived its main idea from this passage. And, though he might have taken some of the traits of his doctor from other remarks of Monteil, here they are shown graphically and displayed actually at a sick man's bedside. In other words, Reade seems clearly to have got the conception of his scene from this passage and developed it with a different set of pedantries on the part of the physician, and, when the patient arose, a more animated conclusion.

A good number of details in the rambling talk of Reade's doctor come from Monteil. For example, on two occasions the old German told how he bled people in different parts of the body to cure different ailments. Both passages come from a single long one of Monteil,[50] but Reade has divided it into two—probably to avoid monotony—and he has made some alterations. Monteil's doctor, complaining of bleeding by barbers, declares:

Always ready to draw blood, as they have been in recent centuries, they are ignorant in which vein bleeding cures of one malady, in which vein it cures of

[49] *Histoire des français des divers états* (5 vols.; Paris, 1853), II, 302–3.
[50] *Ibid.*, p. 306.

another. A man came to be bled for earache; the barbers didn't know where to bleed him. I boldly bled him in the veins of his thighs, and his ears no longer hurt him.

Reade's doctor is similar.

"But think not," said he, warmly, "that it suffices to bleed: any paltry barber can open a vein (though not all can close it again). The art is to know what vein to empty for what disease. T'other day they brought me one tormented with earache. I let him blood in the right thigh, and away flew his earache."[51]

Then follow a few alterations. The second man—in both books —had a toothache but was bled in the ankle in Monteil and behind the ear in Reade. The third man in both was bled between the thumb and forefinger to cure him of a headache in the French book and of rheumatism in the English one. In both cases he returned later with another malady and was cured: in Monteil, of the itch by bleeding between the thumb and forefinger again, and, in Reade, of the headache by bleeding in the ankle.

The rest of Monteil's passage Reade uses five pages later. In the French work one man is cured of quartan fever by bleeding in the finger; a second man, of leprosy by bleeding at the end of the nose. The English novel is the same except that the order of the two cases is changed. Monteil then proceeds: "By another letting of blood I cleared a man's brain and gave him back his memory. By still another I clarified the mind and gave some intelligence to a young boy belonging to a family composed all of blockheads."

Reade renders the same cases in more vigorous and specific terms: "Our curé lost his memory. I brought it him back on the point of my lance; I bled him behind the ear. I bled a dolt of a boy, and now he is the only one who can tell his right hand from his left in a whole family of idiots."[52] Here Monteil ends, but Reade continues: "When the plague was here years ago—the good honest Byzantine pest, I blooded an alderman freely, and cauterized the symptomatic buboes, and so pulled him out of the grave: Whereas our then chirurgeon, a most pernicious Arabist, caught it himself, and died of it."

[51] Oxf., p. 159; Ev., p. 167.   [52] Oxf., p. 164; Ev., p. 172.

This last example of Reade's is taken from a different passage of Monteil's: "I cured of this terrible malady [the plague] an alderman, either by bleeding or by cauterization of buboes, almost at the very time when the town doctor died, an old Arabist in secret."[53] Monteil says nothing about the plague's being from Byzantium, but Hecker, in his *Epidemics of the Middle Ages*, tells how this disease was likely to spread to the West from this city.[54]

Reade's doctor hated the Arabian school of medicine and denied its powers of curing. The father of Monteil's doctor, "although a physician, hated one thing more than fever: he said that Arabism alone had done more evil than all the diseases of the world together; he likewise declared that the Greek School did as much good as Arabism did harm." Moreover, both Monteil and Reade's doctor spoke of the Arabian school's scorn of anatomy—a likely borrowing.[55]

The physician in the novel listed various famous doctors: the Arabians—Avicenna, Rhazes, Albucazis (as written in the first edition and Everyman, but corrected to Abulcazis in Oxford), Chauliac, and Lanfranc; and the modern champions of the Greek school—Bessarion, Platinus, and Marsilius Ficinus. All these are found in Monteil.[56]

Reade's doctor, moreover, boasted of his education:

I studied at Montpelier; the first school in France, and by consequence in Europe. There learned I Dririmancy, Scatomancy, Pathology, Therapeusis, and, greater than them all, Anatomy. For there we disciples of Hippocrates and Galen had opportunities those great ancients never knew. Good-bye quadrupeds and apes . . . . ; we bought of the church-wardens, we shook the gallows; we undid the sexton's work o' dark nights. . . . . The gracious King assisted us; he sent us twice a year a living criminal condemned to die, and said, "Deal ye with him as science asks! dissect him alive, if ye think fit."[57]

[53] II, 298.

[54] J. F. C. Hecker, *The Epidemics of the Middle Ages*, trans. B. G. Babington (London, 1844), pp. 19–20.

[55] I, 179–80; II, 296; Oxf., p. 161; Ev., p. 169.

[56] Oxf., p. 159; Ev., p. 167; Monteil, I, 177 (Avicène and Rhazès), 180 (Albucassis, Chauliac, Lanfranc); II, 299 (Platine, Bessarion, Marsile Fiscin). The error "Albucassis," instead of the correct form "Abulcasis," indicates that Reade got the name from Monteil.

[57] Oxf., pp. 162–63; Ev., pp. 170–71.

Monteil's doctor had studied at Montpellier (the correct spelling), which his father considered "the most celebrated school in France." Here he gained a passion for anatomy. He studied dririmancy and scatomancy, pathology, and therapeutics (*la thérapeutique* in French and rendered *therapeusis* by Reade).[58] These borrowings are sure.

Certain other details in this passage of Reade's seem to be from Henry Hallam:

> A superstitious prejudice against human dissection had restrained the ancient anatomists, in general, to pigs and apes. . . . . [The students of anatomy in the Renaissance, however, acted differently.] They prowled by night in charnel-houses; they dug up the dead from the grave; they climbed the gibbet, in fear and silence, to steal the mouldering carcass of the murderer.[59]

The last statement in Reade about two living criminals being sent by the king yearly for dissection may be suggested by Monteil's mention of an "archer condemned to death, whom the King in 1474 handed over to surgeons and who was successfully cut [for the stone] and cured."[60]

Once more, the application of the French word *sangsues* ("leeches") to doctors for their frequent bloodletting is probably occasioned by its occurrence in Monteil, where the use of these animals in bleeding is discussed.[61] The maxim *"Cuilibet in sua arte credendum est,"* quoted by the old German, may well have been encountered by Reade in *Mores Catholici*, where it is cited.[62] Finally, the list of threatening symptoms thundered by the now furious doctor at the recalcitrant Gerard may be taken from various parts of Hecker's *Epidemics*.

After the experience with the doctor, Gerard and Denys, fearing his vengeance, left Düsseldorf by boat on the Rhine. Once aboard, Gerard entertained his friend with an account of the sights of Cologne. Reade draws all the details from Coryate, but

[58] All these occur in II, 297 or the top of 298.

[59] *Introduction to the Literature of Europe in the Fifteenth, Sixteenth, and Seventeenth Centuries* (2 vols.; New York, 1868), I, 238–39.

[60] II, 305.

[61] Oxf., p. 165; Ev., p. 173; Monteil, II, 306.

[62] (3 vols.; London, 1845–47), I, 160.

condenses them greatly, putting into two pages[63] what the old traveler, garrulous and with a great penchant for recording Latin inscriptions, took thirty-seven to describe. However, Reade keeps the same order: Cologne itself, the shrine of the Three Kings in the Cathedral, St. Ursula's Church, the church of the Maccabees, and the senate house. It is significant that in the earlier part of his passage Reade has solid description, whereas in the latter part (beginning with St. Ursula's Church), fearing the reader may become tired, he introduces sallies by Denys, singularly characteristic of this soldier and entertaining.

There is no space to quote Coryate and Reade in full, but a comparison will show that Reade systematically borrows and condenses.[64] In the case of the church of the Maccabees, Coryate outdoes himself and records sixteen different inscriptions. Thereafter he passes from the ecclesiastical to secular buildings with the words: "The histories of sacred and religious matters being ended, I will now descend to civill and secular matters." A quotation from Reade will show the brevity of his treatment, the lively comments of Denys, and an admirable transition to the secular edifices of the city:

"And then there is the church of the Maccabees, and the caldron, in which they and their mother Solomona were boiled by a wicked King for refusing to eat swine's flesh."

"O peremptory King! and pig-headed Maccabees! I had eaten bacon with my pork liever than change places at the fire with my meat."

"What scurvy words are these! it was their faith."

"Nay, bridle thy choler, and tell me, are there nought but churches in thy so-vaunted city? For I affect rather Sir Knight than Sir Priest."

In the last words, as Mr. Wheeler points out, there may be an echo of *Twelfth Night* (III, iv, 258–59): "I am one that had rather go with sir priest than sir knight."

Next, Gerard described the market place and the senate house

[63] Oxf., pp. 170–72; Ev., pp. 178–80. (Wheeler noted the borrowing from Coryate.)

[64] For the sources of Reade's description see the following places in Vol. II of Coryate: the founder of the city, p. 312; Attila and Lothaire, p. 348; many churches, p. 314; the shrine of the Three Kings, pp. 316–17; St. Ursula and her church, pp. 336–38; the Maccabees, pp. 340 ff.; the senate house with its sculptures and the university, pp. 343–48.

with its sculptures. In particular, he told of the image of Herman Gryn, who slew a lion with the help of only a cloak and a short sword, an event both appealing to the soldier Denys after so many churches and picturesque for the readers of the English novel. All these details come from Coryate, and it is interesting to observe that, whereas Coryate lists six other men who have killed a lion thus, Reade cuts them down to three, omitting even Richard Cœur de Lion in whom Gerard would probably be less interested than was Coryate.

The voyage of Gerard and Denys was ended by the boat's sinking. Gerard, however, swam ashore with Denys, and they continued on their journey, now spending the nights at monasteries. In consequence, Reade gives considerable information about such institutions, but information for which one cannot usually find a specific source.

On one occasion, while the comrades were walking forward, Denys launched into a tirade against monasteries:

. . . . Nobody is a man here, but all are slaves, and of what? of a peevish, tinkling bell, that never sleeps. . . . . Tinkle, tinkle, tinkle, and you must sit to meat with maybe no stomach for food. Ere your meat settles in your stomach, tinkle, tinkle, and ye must to church with maybe no stomach for devotion: I am not a hog at prayers, for one. Tinkle, tinkle! and now you must to bed with your eyes open. Well, by then you have contrived to shut them, some uneasy imp of darkness has got to the bell-rope, and tinkle, tinkle, it behoves you say a prayer in the dark, whether you know one or not. . . . . Well, you drop off again and get about an eyeful of sleep: lo, it is tinkle, tinkle, for matins.[65]

This entertaining passage, I believe, is prompted by one in Sharon Turner's *History of England*. To be sure, there are twelve volumes of the work, but this account comes from a section dealing with the medieval church, a section which Reade accordingly would be likely to consult.

They [the monks] are to comb themselves: and when the great bell sounds, they must enter the church to receive the holy water. On the signal of another bell, they are to pray; and of another bell, to sing; and afterwards to proceed to the altar, to say or hear mass. They were again to dress themselves, and to return to the choir, to sit there till the bell summoned them to the chapter-house. On another signal, they were to resort to the refectory. After a certain hour, no one was to speak till the children left the monastery; then, when the bell sound-

[65] Oxf., p. 185; Ev., p. 193.

ed again, their shoes were to be taken off, their hands to be washed, and they were to enter the church, to repeat the litany, and to hear high mass. At another signal, they were to go in procession. When the bell vibrated again, they were to pray, and afterwards to revisit the refectory. Some were then to sit in the choir, and they, who liked, might read. At a fresh signal, the nones were to be sung. Similar tasks were to succeed again in allotted order, till they were dismissed to their bed.[66]

The basic idea of the two passages is identical—the regulation of everything by bells. And this punctuating of the whole day with bells—more than the similar details of church, refectory, and prayer—makes influence, I believe, very probable.

Then Denys proceeds in his complaint:

And then to be always checked. If I do but put my finger in the salt-cellar, straightway I hear, "Have you no knife that you finger the salt?" And if I but wipe my knife on the cloth to save time, then 'tis, "Wipe thy knife dirty on the bread, and clean upon the cloth!" Oh small of soul! these peevish pedantries fall chill upon good fellowship like wee icicles a-melting down from strawen eaves.[67]

This is taken from Fosbroke's *British Monachism* or Fox's *Monks and Monasteries,* for identical words appear in both, the second author having copied the first: "No one wiped his knife with the cloth, unless he had first used his bread for this purpose. They took salt with their knives."[68]

At one monastery at which the companions stayed, the prior, because of Gerard's fine calligraphy, sent him in the refectory "a silver grace cup full of rich pimentum. This latter Gerard took, and bowing low, first to the distant prior, then to his own company, quaffed, and circulated the cup." These may have been taken from Fosbroke or Fox, since both mention circulating the grace cup at meals and bowing to the prior when he sent one a present, though Reade does not adhere to all the circumstances mentioned by these authors.[69]

At this convent Denys took part in much carousing. Several of

[66] (London, 1839), VIII, 88–89.   [67] Oxf., pp. 185–86; Ev., p. 193.

[68] T. D. Fosbroke (3d ed.; London, 1843), p. 220; Samuel Fox (London, 1845), p. 171.

[69] Oxf., p. 188; Ev., pp. 195–96; Fosbroke, pp. 216, 220; Fox, pp. 169, 171. (Fox again helps himself to Fosbroke's material.)

the monks and he drank, played cards, and flirted with some women over the monastery wall. The next night the same men had a luxurious party in a crypt beneath a chapel, with wines and splendid foods. Women—some of them novices—took part in the banquet, and indelicate songs were sung.[70]

Any one of three passages—or more than one of them—may have prompted this episode. Of course, Reade may have invented it wholly himself, but since we have time and again seen how a suggestion from a book has started his mind working, the chance of influence, if there is similarity, is good.

The first is the scene in *Quentin Durward* where the hero, his guide, and the two ladies of Croye spent a night at a monastery. At the table the guide, Hayraddin, added strong liquor to the monks' evening drink, making some of them intoxicated, and talked so loosely that eventually he was thrown out of the building.[71]

The second passage—from Fosbroke—appears the closest to the scene in *The Cloister and the Hearth:*

It seems, that in certain solemnities, the Convent was in the habit of retiring with the Abbot, leaving a few in the Refectory, in order to eat meat elsewhere; and that they frequently dined in apartments, where they used to bring women to talk, eat, and drink with them. On the feast of the dedications of the churches of the order they used to eat and drink very intemperately.[72]

Some details may perhaps have been added from the third passage also, though it concerns a rather different subject— namely, two nuns who were absent from their convent visiting relatives. It occurs in Erasmus' *Colloquy* entitled Ἰχθυοφαγία:

At Supper the Nuns begin to grow merry with Wine; they laugh'd, and jok'd, and kiss'd, and not over-modestly neither, till you could hardly hear what was said for the Noise they made; but no Body used more Freedom than those two Virgins. . . . . After Supper there was dancing, singing of lascivious Songs, and such Doings I am asham'd to speak of.[73]

All three of the passages concern the overconviviality of celibates. That from *Quentin Durward* is like Reade's in that both

[70] Oxf., pp. 189–91; Ev., pp. 197–99.

[71] (Dryburgh ed., London, 1894), pp. 188–89.

[72] P. 219.   [73] II, 294.

Hayraddin and Denys are outsiders who, on arriving at a monastery, take a prominent part in revelry. The third—from Erasmus—may possibly have suggested the occasional free ways of certain nuns and the indelicate songs. The second, that from Fosbroke, however, is especially like Reade's episode, for both involve an unusual eating apartment, intemperate feasting and drinking, and the introduction of women. Whether or not the first and third contributed anything, it seems likely that Fosbroke's account had an influence on Reade.

Having left the monastery, Gerard and Denys continued their journey and crossed into Burgundy, where they put up at an inn called Les Trois Poissons.[74] The name is taken from Michel and Fournier's book on inns, for they declare it was a favorite one for French hostelries.[75] Reade closes a chapter with the inscription across the front of the building: "On ne loge céans à crédit: ce bonhomme est mort, les mauvais paieurs l'ont tué," This sign is that found by Coryate at an inn at Lyons,[76] except that Reade has changed "car il est mort" into the livelier "ce bonhomme est mort."

[74] Oxf., p. 192; Ev., p. 200.

[75] F. Michel and E. Fournier, *Le Livre d'or des métiers: histoire des hôtelleries* (2 vols.; Paris, 1851), II, 44.

[76] I, 213. (Noted by Wheeler.)

Chapter Four

THE BURGUNDIAN ADVENTURES

TO THE Burgundian inn where Gerard and Denys spent the night are devoted ten pages.[1] The main thread of the account, as has been known for some time,[2] is drawn from the colloquy of Erasmus about hostelries from which Reade has borrowed previously. The Dutch scholar described this agreeable French inn rather briefly, and then, by way of contrast, turned to his more detailed account of the German one. Reade thus does not have so many specific facts as for his German hotels, but he builds out the briefer statements of the colloquy into characteristic action and sparkling dialogue. Let us follow the Erasmus colloquy, with occasional attention to Reade's treatment of his borrowings:

WILLIAM: There's a Woman always waiting at Table, which makes the Entertainment pleasant with Railleries, and pleasant jests. And the Women are very handsome there. [By way of contrast, Reade invented the landlord, who wandered about aimlessly, doing nothing but taking his cap off to guests.] First the Mistress of the House came and bad us Welcome, and to accept kindly what Fare we should have; after her, comes her Daughter, a very fine Woman, of so handsome a Carriage, and so pleasant in Discourse, that she would make even Cato himself merry, were he there. [Reade adds the appealing note of having her sympathize with the youthful Gerard, far from home.] And they don't talk to you as if you were perfect Strangers, but as those they have been a long Time acquainted with, and familiar Friends. [Reade makes them act thus throughout the whole episode.]

BERTULPH: O, I know the French Way of Civility very well. [Reade for this speech felicitously substitutes a rejoinder by Denys to Gerard's wondering admiration of the inn: " 'qui fit François il fit courtois,' " said Denys, bursting with gratified pride—the French words being a quotation from Moryson.[3]

[1] Oxf., pp. 193–202; Ev., pp. 200–209.

[2] A writer in *Notes and Queries* (10th ser., 1905), IV, 313, mentions it as one of the borrowings from Erasmus.

[3] *An Itinerary Containing His Ten Yeeres Travell through the Twelve Dominions*, III, 461. (The Moryson quotation is noted by Wheeler.)

WILLIAM: And because they can't be always with you, by Reason of the other Affairs of the House, and the welcoming of other Guests, there comes a Lass, that supplies the Place of the Daughter, till she is at Leisure to return again. This Lass is so well instructed in the Knack of Repartees, that she has a Word ready for every Body, and no Conceit comes amiss to her. [Reade builds this bare suggestion into Marion, the serving maid with the ready wit, who is the central figure of this very agreeable episode and one of the most successful lesser characters in the novel.] . . . . Why, there was every where some pretty Lass or other, giggling and playing wanton Tricks. [From this Reade imagines Marion conducting Gerard to his room and insisting on his kissing her good-night, under threat of taking away the clean sheets and replacing them with "the pair the drunken miller slept in last night."] They ask'd us if we had any foul Linnen to wash; which they wash and bring to us again. [Reade has Marion take away their linen to launder it, so that they could not get up in the morning until she brought it back clean to them.] . . . . When you go away, they embrace ye, and part with you with as much Affection, as if you were their own Brothers, or near Kinsfolks. [Gerard and Denys, on leaving, exchanged kisses with the three chief women and even with the spineless landlord.][4]

This account of Reade's, then, is an admirable example of his expanding, as the handling of Coryate's material on Cologne was an excellent one of his condensing. One should note, in passing, that the habit of writing the accounts of guests on the smoky ceiling in this inn probably came from the mention of this practice in Michel and Fournier.[5]

As the two friends wandered on their way they happened upon a group of human beings—both men and women and varying in age—being driven along by soldiers. All except the soldiers were melancholy. Gerard, curious about the circumstance, approached an officer and courteously asked what was being done. The soldiers chuckled that anyone could be so ignorant as not to know what they were about. Then, the officer, finding a single word to express the activity, replied "*Nous transvasons*" ("We are decanting"). Thereafter he politely explained that one town was "sore thinned by a pestilence, whole houses emptied and trades short of hands." Learning this fact, the duke inquired and found another town too full of people; in consequence, he was

[4] *Colloquies*, II, 19 f.

[5] Oxf., p. 196; Ev., p. 203; Michel and Fournier, *Le Livre d'or des métiers*, II, 123.

deporting this group of men and women from the full to the empty town. Was not this a fatherly action in the good duke, he asked. And then he roared, "Long live the duke," at the top of his lungs, whereat "the decanted ones" raised the same cry very feebly. Thereafter their real feelings burst forth in piercing wails from the women and deep groans from the men.[6]

This spectacle appeals greatly to Charles Reade, the writer of humanitarian novels. He has developed it from an abstract account, in Monteil, of the king of France's action, improving the narrative with realistic dialogue and affecting specific details. Monteil runs as follows:

It is, first of all, unnecessary to remind you that our age, mighty and strong in every respect, has so much wanted to put the population of cities in equilibrium that it has sometimes, so to speak, decanted [*transvasé*—the very French word taken over by Reade] the overfullness of some into the emptiness of others. Thus if one city has been devastated by wars or sickness [cf. Reade's "sore thinned by pestilence, whole houses emptied"], if it has houses that for lack of people cannot be rented and are falling into ruin—as soon as the King is informed of these circumstances, the municipal officers of cities where a too numerous population is becoming difficult to govern, receive the order to pick out so many hundreds or so many thousands of inhabitants of both sexes and every condition of life [Reade's people were varied], and to send them to live in the thinly peopled city. I don't deny that it is hard, when a man wants to live and die in the place of his birth, to have to go to live and die far away in some other; that it is hard, when one is attached to his house and property, to have to sell them. [This is Reade's view.] But also what royal benevolence and affection for the man who has to change his residence! [This is the view of the officer and soldiers in Reade.] A free gift of a house, a granting of a pension for the first years, a moratorium on debts."[7]

In another Burgundian inn Gerard, finding a comrade of Denys's who was going to the Low Countries and was ready to carry messages, wrote a long letter to Margaret and "a short, cold letter to his parents; and in it he drew hastily with his pen two hands grasping each other, to signify farewell."[8] This, of course, is in harmony with the statement of the *Compendium:* "While on his journey, he sent to his parents and brothers a letter

[6] Oxf., pp. 203–5; Ev., pp. 211–12.

[7] *Histoire des français des divers états*, II, 95.   [8] Oxf., p. 209; Ev., p. 216.

with hand clasping hand and one sentence added, 'Farewell; I shall never see you again.' "

And now occurred what, to my way of thinking, is the most exciting episode in the novel: the two friends' terrible adventure in the hostelry where they were nearly murdered.[9] The source is a short excerpt given in French translation in Michel and Fournier, but coming from the *Table Talk* of Martin Luther:

Conrad de Ross, Maximilian's secretary, a man of heroic courage, while travelling stopped at an inn where the landlord was a thief. Conrad was well received, and he saw a girl who was weeping. He questioned her in secret, and she told him that she was compelled to live here among robbers, and that the landlord, in the course of the night, would make a signal to bring in some of the neighboring peasants, who had been instructed that in such a case there were travellers in the inn to butcher and plunder. Conrad remained on the watch and passed the night completely armed. When the peasants arrived, he attacked them with the aid of his followers; he killed several and took away with him the landlord well bound.[10]

Reade, once more, has developed this brief and commonplace account into a masterpiece of thrilling narrative. Being requested to pay in advance, Denys foolishly threw down a gold coin on the table, thereby showing he had money. During supper, the serving-maid Manon looked at Denys repeatedly and finally said that she would meet him after the meal. On going to the rendezvous he found her weeping, and at first she would say nothing save that her sweetheart was dead. However, she soon declared that she would speak out clearly, though she were killed for doing so—the reason for this disclosure being that Denys resembled the dead sweetheart. She then informed him that the landlord, impelled by the sight of the gold, had gone for a band of assassins, who would kill both him and Gerard in their beds. Denys now started to go to Gerard's room in order to warn him to flee, but just then the assassins arrived, and, though Denys joined his friend upstairs, the two men were trapped. In the treatment of the theme thus far Reade has been careful to add proper motivation in the gold piece, Denys's resemblance to Manon's dead

[9] Oxf., pp. 210–22; Ev., pp. 217–29.

[10] I, 344–45. The original of this, in Latin and German, may be found in *Luthers Tischreden* (6 vols.; Weimar, 1912–21), I, 379.

lover, and the arrival of the assassins before the friends had a chance to flee. During the rest of the incident he uses suspense in masterly wise. Manon had gone for help. Meanwhile, the friends conversed in terrified whispers, while the ruffians downstairs waited for them to go to sleep. Reade provided additional suspense by having one of the rascals a stentorian-voiced giant who was known as the Abbot and wielded an immense battle-ax in combat. The most noteworthy and original feature in the whole episode, in spite of its melodramatic quality, is that, when the friends killed the first varlet who was sent upstairs by his fellows to murder them, they tied his corpse in a chair, and Gerard, using phosphorus, brightened the features and wrote on the forehead "*La Mort.*" Reade was evidently proud of this unusual touch—probably his own invention—for he characterizes Gerard's act as "one unparalleled perhaps in the history of mankind."[11] The performance, moreover, occasions a dramatic situation when the other robbers, on coming upstairs, see the ghastly figure; it adds a medieval note in their belief that the corpse is possessed by the devil; and it later motivates the interesting accusation of Gerard as a sorcerer. After killing several of the cutthroats, including the Abbot, the two men were saved by the soldiers brought by Manon, and the landlord, was taken prisoner as an accomplice.

The thieves were executed, and funeral ceremonies were performed over the bones, just now discovered, of their former victims. In attending the obsequies, Gerard became friendly with the curé who conducted the ceremony. As a consequence, he beheld various parishioners on the porch of the church paying the vows which they had made during sickness. Among them was the lord of the manor "in gorgeous attire, his cap adorned by a feather with a topaz at its root, his jerkin richly furred, satin doublet, red hose, shoes like skates, diamond-hilted sword in velvet scabbard, and hawk on his wrist."[12] Though it is usually difficult to spot exact sources for descriptions of costume, some details in

[11] Oxf., p. 218; Ev., p. 225. Professor Sutcliffe has called my attention to this expression and two other similar ones in the novel.

[12] Oxf., p. 238; Ev., p. 245.

this passage seem to come from Moryson's statement, "In France as well men as women, use richly to bee adorned with Jewels. The men weare rings of Diamonds, and abroad Jewels in their hats, placed upon the roote of their feathers."[13] The use of the word "root" by both authors seems to prove borrowing. A picture of a "Provençal Noble of the Fifteenth Century," facing the Lacroix and Seré passage which is next to be discussed, may have fused with the Moryson; it presents a lord with furred mantle, feathers in hat, sword, hawk on wrist, and what might be considered, though they are not clearly visible, shoes "like skates."

The lord, having vowed during illness to give his weight in bread and cheese to the poor, was now duly weighed. He attempted, unsuccessfully, to cheat a little, but, nevertheless, refused to diminish his weight by giving his hawk to anyone else to hold. "Shall I for one sorry pound grudge my poor fowl the benefit of holy Church?" he declared. "I'd as lieve the devil should have me and all my house as her, any day i' the year."[14]

Thereafter, Gerard was greatly surprised by seeing the image of a hawk upon the altar. The talkative curé, carrying on the subject, pleasantly related that the hawk there portrayed belonged to the Bishop of Avignon. During service nobles had the custom of putting their hawks on the altar. For two years the lord who had been weighed and a neighboring abbot had had a feud as to who should have the place of honor—the right side of the altar—for his hawk.

Why, the abbot he yielded, as the Church yields to laymen. He searched ancient books, and found that the left hand was the more honourable, being in truth the right hand, since the altar is east, but looks westward. So he gave my lord the soi-disant right hand, and contented himself with the real right hand, and even so may the Church still outwit the lay nobles and their arrogance.[15]

The source of this picturesque little narrative, and perhaps, too, of the previous stressing of the lord's devotion to his bird, is Lacroix and Seré:

Falconry was formerly so highly honored that a gentleman, or even a propertied lady, never appeared in public without hawk on wrist. Many bishops

[13] IV, 230. (Not noted by Wheeler.)

[14] Oxf., p. 238; Ev., p. 245.   [15] Oxf., p. 241; Ev., p. 248.

and abbots imitated them; they all came into churches with their birds, which they put down, during the service, on the steps of the altar, and often on the altar itself! Prelates put them on the side of the Gospel, thus ascribing to themselves the place of honor [*s'attribuant ainsi la place d'honneur*]; the lay lords placed their birds on the right, on the side of the Epistle. During public ceremonies, during solemn receptions, noblemen carried a falcon on the right wrist, just as they carried a sword by the left thigh.[16]

In particular, the expression about the prelates' "ascribing to themselves the place of honor" gave birth, in Reade's fancy, to the amusing dispute between the spiritual and the lay lord, and the former's saving his face by adroit misinterpretation.

Gerard, after this friendly chat, left the curé, but almost immediately found himself under arrest. The charge was sorcery, on the ground of his having made the face of a dead man burn with diabolical flame. Poor Gerard persuaded the magistrate to allow him to be taken to the curé, and, once in the presence of this churchman, so well disposed to him as the result of their talk, related just how the assumed enchantment had been effected. The curé took Gerard's part at once and returned with him to the magistrate. They found there the white sorcerer, Mangis, who was the accuser of Gerard. The details concerning him indubitably are from Monteil, as we shall see. They are colorful and very medieval—just such as would attract the eye of a historical novelist. Moreover, since the borrowing of particulars shows that Reade studied the passage, it is very likely that Monteil's account was what induced Reade to place in his book an incident containing magic.[17]

In Monteil is an account of the sorcerer, Malchus—a name, by the way, very like Mangis. And of Malchus we hear:

People say to him, with impunity, when he is wearing his red shoes, "Malchus, you have your feet in hell," and when he is wearing his stockings of the same color, "Malchus, you are in hell up to your middle." Today he had on

[16] *Le Moyen Age et la Renaissance*, I, "Chasse," xiii. Le Grand d'Aussy (*Histoire de la vie privée des françois*, II, 3–4) tells of noblemen putting hawks on the altar, but says nothing about ecclesiastics doing so or about a dispute between the two sorts of dignitaries.

[17] Reade's account of Mangis covers Oxf., pp. 245–46; Ev., pp. 252–54.

his red shoes and stockings, his pointed hat, and his black coat with blue bands; he was in sorcerer's full dress.[18]

Similarly, Reade's magician was "a singular figure in red hose and red shoes, a black gown with blue bands, and a cocked hat."

Monteil's sorcerer declared, "Under the protection of the venerable ecclesiastics and magistrates of the city, I am a magician of white magic."[19] Reade's enchanter, in like manner, remarked, "A sorcerer I am, but a white one, not a black one." Moreover, at the end, when the curé, with threats, made him retract his accusation, he declared, "I respect holy Church and her will."

Again, the magician of the French author had a bitter grievance. It was against Italian competitors whom the French honored more than their own home products: "Finally, Italian male sorcerers, far more damnable than French ones, include in their art the profanation of the sacraments, and the abominable female sorcerers of that country, changing themselves into cats, go and suck the blood of little children."[20] In the same fashion Reade's necromancer protested, "I ne'er profane the sacraments, as do the black sorcerers, nor turn myself into a cat and go sucking infants' blood, nor e'en their breath." On the contrary, Monteil's enchanter told how people had brought to him animals that ate or drank too much or too little and so perhaps might be under a spell, and how one woman even brought him a hen, fearing that it was a sorceress come to coquet maliciously with the young men of the house.[21] Similarly, Reade's magician was able, among other things, to "tell the peasants when their cattle and their hens are possessed."

Finally, both white sorcerers made it their special business to detect practitioners of the black variety and to report them to the authorities. Monteil's man had adopted his profession with this aim in mind and related how he had helped a police official arrest such a person.[22] Reade's sorcerer made it his business "to detect the black magicians, as I did that whole tribe of them who were burnt at Dol last year" and whose "ashes were cast to the

[18] II, 166.

[19] II, 166.

[20] II, 172.

[21] II, 168–69.

[22] II, 166–67, 173–74.

wind." The curé, at once taking up the gauntlet, replied, "The parliament of Dijon has since sifted the matter, and found they were no sorcerers, but good and peaceful citizens; and but last week did order masses to be said for their souls, and expiatory farces and mysteries to be played for them in seven towns of Burgundy; all which will not of those cinders make men and women again." A like calamity was recounted by the necromancer in Monteil as a lamentable example of some people's tendency to suspect black magic everywhere. The citizens of Arras were thus suspected, and many suffered punishment. He said:

Nevertheless, they were all good Christians and good peaceable citizens. . . . . It was only after long years that the Sire of Beaufort strove for and obtained their rehabilitation, at parliament, which passed a decree to have masses sung every year, to have games held and comedies and expiatory farces represented; all of which did not prevent the ashes of innocent men . . . . being on the wind.[23]

The result of the whole affair was that the curé made Mangis retract his charge, and hence Gerard went a free man again.

In the meantime, while Gerard had been in the peril of death for sorcery, Denys, unsuspecting of his comrade's danger, had been associating with two girls. On first seeing them he accosted them in easy wise, and they received his advances no less readily. As a result he took them to a repast at an inn. Gambling followed eating. They soon won a good sum from him by cheating, and then, on an excuse, slipped away, first one and then the other. On examining his purse he found the girls had helped themselves to the rest of its contents. He vociferated furiously, "Who are they? Where do they bide? They have ta'en my purse and fifteen golden pieces: raise the hue and cry! Ah! traitresses! vipers!" But the money was gone and remained gone.[24] The tale is a reworking, with more naturalness and spirit, of an experience of a certain Courtois d'Arras, narrated by Michel and Fournier. The traveler encounters two girls at a hostelry:

The two women redouble their allurements; all three fall to drinking together; they eat plentifully and in order that there may be more complete sympathy and true amorous sharing, they all drink out of the same cup and eat out

[23] II, 174.

[24] Different stages of this episode are narrated at three points by Reade: Oxf., pp. 243, 247–48, 251; Ev., pp. 250, 254–55, 258–59.

of the same bowl, as is the custom at such betrothals. The hussies, apprised by mine host beforehand, have scented money; but it is too slow about coming out of its purse. Thus they propose gaming; Courtois accepts, and they play *merelle.* But gambling, even with the help of cheating, doesn't satisfy them quickly enough. To settle this purse which is too slow in emptying itself, they purloin it and make off.[25]

Now Gerard ordered a bottle of wine at the inn. On examining it, however, he found that the glass was inordinately thick at the bottom, so that the contents were but scanty. He remonstrated with the landlord, and the latter, in defense, lamented his many troubles. The passage is filled with information about the difficulties of running a medieval inn and provides much local color of the time.[26] The facts are borrowed mostly from the complaint of a hotel-keeper in Monteil, with a few added from Michel and Fournier.

And now to take up the points in the order in which they occur in the complaint. The fashioning of wine bottles so they may contain less than they appear to is drawn from Michel and Fournier.[27] Next, the landlord, touching on his various guests, bewailed the fact that soldiers receiving but two sous a day ate that amount and drank in addition. This is recorded both in Monteil and in Michel and Fournier.[28] Again, the hotel-keeper in Monteil said he had to accommodate friars much more often than he wished. He had a particularly bad time with one young Augustinian who refused to pay, and, when asked for prayers instead, declared that he had them promised a long time ahead; only after lively argument would he promise the landlord a few.[29] This in Reade becomes: "The black and grey friars have made vow of poverty, but not of famine; eat like wolves and give the poor host nought but their prayers; and mayhap not them: how can he tell?" Moreover, the weddings of artisans nowadays, the innkeeper continued, were attended by more people than hostelries could accommodate, and hence were held in the man-

[25] I, 207–8.

[26] Reade's passage occurs, Oxf., pp. 248–50; Ev., pp. 255–58.

[27] II, 69–70.

[28] Monteil, II, 249; Michel and Fournier, I, 245.   [29] II, 250–51.

sions of the gentry, rented for the occasion—a practice which is recounted in Michel and Fournier.[30]

Thereafter Reade's landlord declared it was hard to provide enough food for the coroner's quests which were held in hotels; moreover, laws restricted the amount innkeepers could buy or the times at which they could frequent markets. Butchers, too, they had to bribe. All these details come from Monteil.[31]

Once more, whereas landlords might be jailed for failing to pay their debts, the same rule did not apply to guests at a hostelry, as we learn in both Monteil and Reade. Apropos of a patron who fails to pay, the French author remarks: "You have, indeed, the right to retain his horse. . . . . In truth you may also retain its owner; but, after you have fed him as long as he wishes, one fine morning he breaks his arrest and is free with a small fine."[32] In *The Cloister and the Hearth*, this becomes in vivid phrasing:

> A traveller's horse we may keep for his debt; but where in Heaven's name? In our own stable, eating his head off at our cost. Nay, we may keep the traveller himself: but where? In gaol? Nay, in our own good house, and there must we lodge and feed him gratis. And so fling good silver after bad? Merci; no: let him go with a wanion.

Next returning to sorts of guests, the innkeeper in Reade approved of thieves, who paid well, but abominated various officers of government who made an official visit to a hotel an excuse for eating and drinking free of charge—"a swarm of them, and all with a wolf in their stomachs and a sponge in their gullets." The same facts occur, in less vivid language, in Monteil.[33]

And now for prices. In Monteil, the hotel-keeper, angry at the Augustinians who would not pay, gave a list of the prices of various foods and then of the wages of his cook, valet, and serving maid.[34] The prices catalogued by Reade's host, though not in the same order, are identical in amounts. The novelist, however, avoids monotony skilfully. Thus after "a pair of partridges five sous," he adds, "What think you of that? Heard one ever the like? five sous for two little beasts all bone and feather?" After

[30] I, 340–41.   [32] II, 253.

[31] II, 251–52.   [33] II, 253.   [34] II, 251.

a few other comments put in by Reade to provide variety, mine host returned to some more prices and then ended a paragraph forcefully, "Why what think you I pay my cook? But you shall never guess. A hundred sous a year as I am a living sinner." (This last sentence is in the sensational capital letters dear to Reade's heart.)

Finally, Monteil's landlord told how he went to church and heard the preacher censure all professions, but especially inn-keepers. He added, however, that the statutes of the diocese authorized a hostelry to serve strangers even during the time of church service.[35] Reade builds out the idea more forcefully:

> Last Sunday I went to church. It is a place I trouble not often. Didn't the curé lash the hotel-keepers? I grant you he hit all the trades. . . . . But, mind you, he stripeit the other lay estates with a feather, but us hotel-keepers with a neat's pizzle: godless for this, godless for that, and most godless of all for opening our doors during mass.

Yet the laws, continued the landlord, decreed that strangers should be taken in, "and, say a townsman should creep in with the true travellers, are we to blame? They all vow they are tired wayfarers."

The quotation *Levius quid foemina*, occurring somewhat later in Reade, may be a translation of the expression "Is any thing lighter then a woman?" found in Moryson apropos of a coachful of women conversing.[36] Again, Reade's *Bene quae latuit, bene vixit* is present in Moryson, though with *qui*, as originally written by Ovid.[37] Furthermore, having the corpse of the former criminal landlord, with its bones all broken, displayed on the wheel may perhaps come from the discussion of such practices in Lacroix and Seré.[38] Finally, the account of wolves attacking Paris in 1420 and 1438 and eating fourteen persons in one month between Montmartre and the Porte Saint-Antoine is from Michel and Fournier; indeed, the French passage may have suggested to

[35] II, 255. Michel and Fournier (II, 74) also say inns must take in travelers even during church service.

[36] Oxf., p. 253; Ev., p. 260; Moryson, I, 26. (Noted by Wheeler.)

[37] Oxf., p. 257; Ev., p. 264; Moryson, III, 355. (Noted by Wheeler.)

[38] III, "Pénalité," vi–vii; Oxf., p. 258; Ev., p. 265.

Reade the idea of having wolves appear in a Burgundian town which Gerard and Denys traversed.[39]

The next inn where the two companions put up was kept by a coquettish young woman excessively proud of her pretty hands. In consequence, she seized every possible opportunity to display them. She carved the goose; she handled her hairpins; she clasped her hands devoutly during grace at table; she pointed out the sights of the town, thrusting her hand close to her interlocutor's face; she was so interested in displaying her hands when she gambled with Denys that she actually lost money. The sight of a mouse made her shriek with affected terror. And though attracted by Gerard, she was so desirous of displaying her hands that, while he was telling a story, she feigned yawning time and again in order to raise the ever present hands to her mouth. Gerard was so much offended that he broke off his story and went promptly to bed. Everybody was weary of the girl—this *mijaurée*, as she is called by Reade again and again—and the inn's business was fast declining.[40]

This episode is drawn from a passage in Michel and Fournier, a passage which they quote, in French translation, from Quevedo's picaresque novel, *La Vida del Buscon, llamado Don Pablos*. The mistress of a certain inn is described by Quevedo as

lively, given to winking, fond of laughter, rather coquettish. She lisped a little, she was afraid of mice and was proud of having pretty hands; thus, to display them, she snuffed the candles frequently and carved at table. In church, she always kept her hands clasped; on the street, she was eternally pointing out something; in the house, she was forever having to adjust a pin in her hair; her favorite game was checkers; she was ceaselessly pretending to yawn in order to show her teeth and to hold up her hand before her mouth [*se faire croix sur la bouche*]. In a word, the whole house was full just of her hands, and everybody, even her family, was bored.[41]

Michel and Fournier then add, speaking for themselves, "An inn kept by so affected a girl [*une pareille mijaurée*] must have been little frequented." The recurring French word *mijaurée* of Reade's account, then, is taken over from Michel and Fournier, and the

---

[39] Oxf., pp. 258–59; Ev., pp. 265–66; Michel and Fournier, II, 4.

[40] Oxf., pp. 260–66; Ev., pp. 267–73.   [41] II, 139.

novelist likewise borrows from the same book the French expression *croix sur la bouche*.[42]

Two small borrowings from other passages occur in this episode. The desire of inn hostesses to be great ladies, their consequent insistence on wearing the patrician *chaperon* of velvet on their heads, and their habit of staring vacantly at the courteous bows of guests come from another part of Michel and Fournier.[43] Again, the remark in the novel, "In Germany men sat bareheaded round the stove, and took off their upper clothes, but in Burgundy they kept on their hats, and put on their warmest furs to sit around the great open chimney-places," comes from the passage in Montaigne's *Journey* in which he praises the stoves of Germany and says, "While we [the French] put on our warm furred morning-gowns when we enter the house, they [the Germans] on the contrary strip themselves to their doublets and go bareheaded in the warm room, and clothe themselves warmly to go back into the open air."[44]

Having no fondness for the *mijaurée*, Gerard persuaded Denys to leave the inn the next morning before its mistress had arisen. They did so, but when they had progressed a fair distance, they saw a country fellow pursuing them on a mule. He presented Gerard a package, which, he declared, had been left by the young Dutchman at the inn. On the departure of the messenger Gerard found that the package contained a ring with a handsome amethyst from the *mijaurée*. The episode seems prompted by that in Shakespeare's *Twelfth Night*, where Olivia, after Viola's first visit, sent Malvolio after her with a ring; Malvolio told Viola she had left it at the house, but it was really a present from Olivia.[45] Reade has taken the suggestion from Shakespeare, but he has worked it out differently. His clown's eagerness for a *pourboire* is wholly unlike Malvolio's sour dignity; the *mijaurée* had wrapped the ring up in countless papers so that the messenger would get

[42] *Mijaurée:* Oxf., p. 260; Ev., p. 267; *croix sur la bouche:* Oxf., p. 263; Ev., p. 270.

[43] Oxf., p. 260; Ev., p. 267; Michel and Fournier, II, 75–76.

[44] Oxf., p. 262; Ev., p. 269; *The Diary of Montaigne's Journey to Italy in 1580 and 1581*, trans. E. J. Trechmann (London, 1929), p. 31.

[45] I, v, 283–95; II, ii, 1–39; Oxf., pp. 267–69; Ev., pp. 274–76.

away before Gerard found the jewelry; and, whereas Denys, doting on women, murmured of the hostess "The little dove!" Gerard responded tartly "The great owl!"

Gerard and Denys continued their journey in good fellowship. So satisfied was the former with his companion that he quoted the Ancients: "Better is a bright comrade on the weary road than a horse litter," a saying found in the original Latin and in another English rendering in Moryson.[46] But the happiness was not to continue long. They soon encountered a company of fifty soldiers bound on an expedition under the command of the Bastard of Burgundy. The stern Bastard ordered Denys to join the troop and, when he demurred, threatened to shoot him. Thus Denys submitted, much against his will, and tearfully parted from his friend.[47] Anthony, Bastard of Burgundy, the son of Duke Philip the Good, is mentioned more than once in both Monstrelet and Commines, and Reade may have derived from one of these books the idea of introducing him.

Losing Denys as a companion was a great misfortune to Gerard, but a second trouble now came to him in the theft of his purse. The event is taken from an account by Moryson of his experience with disbanded soldiers in France:

When I had passed halfe this dayes journey, I met with some dozen horsemen, whose Captaine demaunded of me my name and Countrey. . . . . . He (as it seemed to me) thinking it dishonourable to him, if he should himselfe assault a poore fellow, and a stranger, did let me passe, but before I came to the bottome of the hill, I might see him send two horsemen after me, who wheeling about the mountaines, that I might not know they were of his company, suddenly rushed upon me, and with fierce countenance threatening death, presented their Carbines to my brest. I having no abilities to defend mee, thought good not to make any the least shew of resistance, so they tooke my sword from my guide, and were content onely to rob me of my mony.[48]

Reade, in his treatment of this borrowing,[49] again shows himself the humanitarian novelist, for he is careful to emphasize the pitiableness of Gerard's condition. In the first place, the experi-

[46] Oxf., p. 270; Ev., p. 277; Moryson, III, 385. (Noted by Wheeler.)

[47] Oxf., pp. 271–73; Ev., pp. 278–80.

[48] I, 398–99. (Noted by Wheeler.)

[49] Oxf., pp. 273–74; Ev., pp. 281–82.

ence came to him when he was overcome with grief over parting with Denys. Again, the oppressors were not disbanded soldiers who might command some sympathy from the reader because of their own need, but "a gay cavalcade. A gentleman of rank and his favourites in velvet and furs and feathers; and four or five armed retainers in buff jerkins." The company passed Gerard, and then three servants came back to rob him. Since he made show of resistance, one of them leveled a petronel at him. Gerard looked for assistance, but "scarce a hundred yards off the noble-man and his friends had halted, and sat on their horses, looking at the lawless act, too proud to do their own dirty work, but not too proud to reap the fruit." Having the leaders look on instead of just pass by, as in Moryson, sharpens the situation. Another re-tainer, instead of threatening to shoot, tried persuasion with Ger-ard "and assured him it cost a mint to be a gentleman; his mas-ter had lost money at play overnight, and was going to visit his leman, and so must take money where he saw it." Compelled, then, by a social superior who was unworthy of his position, poor Gerard delivered his purse and cursed the nobleman.

Here the narrative leaves the hero to wander onward alone and returns once more to Holland.

Chapter Five

HOLLAND AGAIN AND
GERARD'S LETTER

MARGARET, grieving for her absent lover, excited the sympathy of all the people who were acquainted with her. Dame van Eyck visited the girl and declared that Gerard ought to return home quickly. To bring him back from Italy a letter was written, and the famous painter, Hans Memling, who was going to that country, was picked by Dame van Eyck to carry it. Unfortunately, Memling, according to the novel, loved the flowing bowl too well. Two of his cronies regaled him at a tavern in Tergou, and there, as his potations increased, he gradually became more and more talkative. "He confided to the convivial crew that he was going to show the Italians how to paint: next he sang his exploits in battle, for he had handled a pike; and his amorous successes with females, not present to oppose their version of the incidents."[1] Thereafter, he went on to declare that he was taking a letter to Gerard. One of Gerard's evil brothers, present at the tavern as usual, heard the news. He took counsel with his brother, and the two, anxious to keep Gerard away from home so that they might share his patrimony, persuaded the willing burgomaster to write a substitute letter to Gerard saying that Margaret was dead. Then, encountering Memling on the road after he had finished his long revelry at the tavern, they held him up and exchanged, in his bag, the false for the real letter. The relation of cause and effect, then, is very well brought out by Reade.

The sending of the spurious letter saying that Margaret was dead is, of course, in accordance with the statement in the *Compendium*. Instead of having the parents perform the miserable

[1] Oxf., p. 285; Ev., p. 292.

84

act, however, Reade, as has been already remarked, clears them and makes them more sympathetic figures by having the two evil brothers do it. He likewise involves the other villain of the novel, the burgomaster, who, unlike the brothers, knew how to write and who wanted to keep Gerard away from Tergou because the latter, in possession of an important document, presumably was aware of the burgomaster's fraudulent treatment of Margaret's father.

Memling's great fondness for liquor is likewise important, since a man without this weakness would not have been garrulous enough to announce that he was carrying the letter, and, again would not have given the brothers time to procure a forgery. Mr. Wheeler, in his note to Reade's passage, remarks of Memling, "For his insobriety I can find no authority." One of the books in the *Century* list, Michael Bryan's *Dictionary of Painters*, however, touches on a point of a similar nature. To be sure, the article,[2] of considerable length, gives "John Hemmelinck" as the painter's name, but it also gives Hemling and Memling as other possible spellings and declares his first name is sometimes given as Hans. I gather that Reade employed the form most usual in his day. The larger part of the article is devoted to Memling as a painter, but the following sentence is significant for our purpose: "Van Mander reports, that being of a very dissolute character, he was reduced to the necessity of engaging as a private soldier." Such mention of dissoluteness would easily suggest that the man was likewise overfond of liquor. Moreover, Reade's touching upon Memling's having had amours and having been a soldier makes us feel that this sentence was probably at the bottom of his conception of Memling's character.

The narrative now turns to Denys's experiences with the body of troops after leaving Gerard. He marched over the same Burgundian territory traversed by his friend and himself before. Finally, the commander, Anthony of Burgundy, led his men into Flanders, combined forces with those of his brother Baldwyn, and settled down to the siege of a rebellious city.

[2] *Biographical and Critical Dictionary of Painters and Engravers* (London, 1849), pp. 318–22.

This siege has but little connection with the rest of the novel.[3] Neither hero nor heroine is present, and the only means of tying it to the plot is that Denys is there. In other words, Reade put the siege into his book for its own sake. Now he seems to have had some natural interest in this sort of military operation; at any rate, in his earlier novel, *White Lies*, a siege during the Napoleonic wars occupies an important position and is described in detail.[4] Moreover, his reading of the chronicles of Froissart and, to a less extent, of Monstrelet, both of which are full of sieges, may have brought the matter to his attention once more and have particularly shown what an admirable opportunity for local color a medieval siege offered. At any rate, Reade's account makes full use of this opportunity; in fact, narrative, for once, is less important than straight fact-giving.

I have discovered no siege in Froissart or Monstrelet that corresponds in all its details to that in *The Cloister and the Hearth*. Of course many of the devices found in Reade likewise occur in sieges in these chronicles,[5] but I do not believe one can say that Reade had any one particular siege in mind as a model. The influence is rather one of general atmosphere.[6] A great difference, too, is that the medieval authors were writing for contemporary audiences and thus, even though they went into some detail about the fighting, did not need to inform their readers just how each military engine looked and worked. Reade, on the other hand, did have to and thus was compelled to consult some antiquarian work for this purpose. Three fairly detailed accounts of this type are found in the books of the *Century* list: one in Strutt's *Manners*

[3] The siege occupies pp. 301–8 in Oxf., pp. 307–15 in Ev.

[4] (Boston, 1869), pp. 241–63. (Professor Sutcliffe has called my attention to this other siege.) Naturally a Napoleonic siege is conducted differently from one in the fifteenth century.

[5] Somewhat similar passages in Sir John Froissart (*Chronicles of England, France Spain, and the Adjoining Countries*, trans. Johnes [2 vols.; London, 1855]) are: I, 135–36 (filling the ditch of a castle); I, 137–38, with a picture (another siege, including towers); I, 453 (mines and countermines).

[6] Reade may also have derived some inspiration from a large plate in du Sommerard (*Les Arts au Moyen Age*, Album I, Pl. XIV) representing the siege of a town by Malatesta, Duke of Rimini.

and Customs af the English,[7] a second in a number of the *Gentle-man's Magazine*[8] published a little before *The Cloister and the Hearth*, and a third in Lacroix and Seré. It is very possible, of course, that Reade studied all of these, and he may have taken some suggestions from any or all. The one that is closest to his passage is undoubtedly the account in Lacroix and Seré, a work from which we have already seen him borrowing more than once. Let us now examine specific points taken by Reade from this work—to be exact, from the portion of it on "Military Archi-tecture."

The first act of the besiegers was "to advance their carpenters behind rolling mantelets. . . . . A strong force of cross-bowmen, including Denys, rolled their mantelets up and shot over the workmen's heads at every besieged who showed his nose."[9] This is drawn from Lacroix and Seré:

Archers rarely exposed themselves freely to the shots of the besieged. Espe-cially cross-bowmen, who bent their bows by means of a complicated apparatus and needed time to get their weapons ready to fire, needed to be well *paveschiés* [covered with big shields], as Froissart puts it. Portable wooden parapets, called mantelets were used for the same purpose.[10]

Reade speaks several times of the "curtains" of the city wall. These, according to Lacroix and Seré, were "the parts of the ram-part enclosed between two towers."[11] Again, Reade tells us that the besieged

ran out at night their hoards, or wooden penthouses on the top of the curtains. The curtains were built with square holes near the top to receive the beams, that supported these structures, the true defence of medieval forts, from which the besieged delivered their missiles with far more freedom and variety of range.[12]

This, similarly, is drawn from the French work, which states:

In the case of siege, to increase the height of towers or to add to their insuffi-cient tops, wooden scaffoldings were constructed, on which stood men at arms.

[7] (3 vols.; London, 1775–76), II, 29–31.

[8] CCVI (1859), 342–46.

[9] Oxf., p. 301; Ev., pp. 307–8.

[10] *Le Moyen Age et la Renaissance*, V, "Architecture militaire," xix.

[11] *Ibid.*, leaf ix.   [12] Oxf., p. 302; Ev., p. 308.

In many old fortresses, holes or corbels placed at equal distances in the masonry seem to have served to hold these scaffoldings, which were also placed, as it seems, on the outside of walls which had no machicolations.[13]

Reade gets his word "hoards" for these wooden structures from another passage in Lacroix and Seré, which says that one of the purposes of slinging machines was "to break the hoards [Fr. *hourds*] constructed on the ramparts."[14] Thus we are not surprised when the novelist tells us later that the penthouses after a while were "somewhat shattered" by the "slinging engines of the besiegers."[15]

There are several mentions of machines to discharge stones in Reade. His remarking on the besiegers' "mangonels" seems to be occasioned by their occurrence in Lacroix and Seré (M. Fr. *mangonneaux*) in a list of various slinging engines.[16] The French authors say they will not attempt to distinguish between the different sorts of machines, but that they all corresponded to the "catapult of the Ancients and served to throw bullets or stones and sometimes incendiary material."

Reade, similarly, does not try to separate all the different varieties of engines. He gives, however, a very careful and detailed account of a "great catapult," and, even without a diagram, he makes its operation perfectly clear.[17] This explanation is drawn, I feel sure, from the English edition of Wilars de Honecort's *Sketch-Book*. This medieval French architect made a sketch of the base of a slinging machine with a brief explanation Then the English editor of the work wrote a much fuller and clearer account of the engine with three little medieval pictures and one diagram of his own, which is reproduced in the present book. The whole account of Wilars and the editor fills nine pages[18] and is too long to quote here. It is, however, one that is convincing and lucid and agrees in detail perfectly with Reade's account. Reade cannot have drawn from the French edition of this medie-

[13] V, "Architecture militaire," viii.

[14] *Ibid.*, leaf xii.   [16] V, "Architecture militaire," xxii.

[15] Oxf., p. 303; Ev., p. 309.   [17] Oxf., pp. 304–5; Ev., p. 311.

[18] *The Sketch-Book of Wilars de Honecort*, trans. and ed. Robert Willis (London, 1859), pp. 195–203.

Figure 26.

Robert Willis (ed.), "The Sketch-Book of Wilars de Honecort"

CATAPULT

val work, an edition called the *Album de Villard de Honnecourt*,[19] because the French editor thinks Wilars's machine shot an arrow, not a stone, and worked differently from the way the English editor and Reade interpret it. Conceivably, Reade might have got his idea of this catapult from the description (with a diagram) of such an engine in Lacroix and Seré.[20] It is less likely, however, since the missile there rests on a fork at the end of the beam, not (as in Wilars and Reade) "in a sling attached" to the end of the beam. Again the comparative length of the two ends of the beam in Reade is more in accordance with the diagram of Wilars than with that in Lacroix and Seré. We should also notice that Reade may have got the word *trébuchet* for slinging instruments, from the English edition of Wilars, where it is used often.

A most efficient engine during the siege was "an enormous Turkish catapult" operated by the citizens of the town.[21] Indeed, it was similar in its success to Long Tom, an especially dreadful cannon suddenly produced within the city besieged in *White Lies*. One may remark, since it is interesting to observe such parallels, that just as one of Long Tom's shots "had fallen on a powder wagon and blown it to pieces, and killed two poor fellows and a horse,"[22] so one of the Turkish engine's stones "struck a horse that was bringing up a sheaf of arrows in a cart, bowled the horse over dead like a rabbit, and spilt the cart." The idea of having a Turkish catapult in *The Cloister and the Hearth* would seem very likely to be suggested by the statement of Lacroix and Seré about sieges: "Spanish engineers were mostly Mussulmans and up to the Sixteenth Century, Turks and Arabs were considered superior to Occidentals in the art of sieges."[23]

The filling-up by the besiegers of the town's moat is paralleled by the statement in the French work that the "first operation"

[19] (Paris, 1858).

[20] V, "Architecture militaire," xxiii.   [21] Oxf., p. 305; Ev., p. 311.

[22] P. 247. Another parallel between Reade's two sieges is that a sergeant in *White Lies* displayed a plate to the enemy, as a sign agreed on that both sides should take time off for dinner (p. 244), and that in *The Cloister and the Hearth*, Denys exhibited a piece of bread for the same purpose (p. 304). But such parallels between the two sieges are few.

[23] V, "Architecture militaire," xviii.

of the besieger "was to fill up the ditch and to level the ground to the base of the rampart."[24] Moreover, several of the events of Reade's siege come from the following passage of Lacroix and Seré:

If the siege was prolonged, the besieger protected his approach by fortifications of wood, earth, or even stone, high enough to allow his archers to reach the platforms of the town and to fire advantageously from above on its defenders. Wooden towers of several stories were built piece by piece on the bank of the moat or, rather were constructed out of range of the enemy's engines and then moved up on rollers to the base of the walls. . . . . The Romance name *gata*, cat, given to this machine, is an allusion to the slyness and cleverness of a cat in seizing its prey. . . . . When the arrows discharged from the upper stories of these towers had driven the besieged from their platforms, a bridge was lowered on to the rampart and a hand to hand combat took place. [See the plate of such a tower from Lacroix and Seré reproduced for comparison at this point.] The besieged, to prevent or retard the approach of these terrible machines, fired at them huge stones or flaming arrows; sometimes they mined or flooded the ground on which the tower must roll, so that it became overturned with its own weight. . . . . Sometimes towers were covered with newly flayed hides and coated with clay to protect them from fire.[25]

Now in *The Cloister and the Hearth* the besiegers "built a triangular wooden tower as high as the curtain, and kept it ready for use, and just out of shot." The besieged countered by beginning "to mine underneath that part of the moat the tower stood frowning at." Thereafter,

a strong penthouse, which they called "a cat," might be seen stealing towards the curtain, and gradually filling up the moat with fascines and rubbish, which the workmen flung out at its mouth. [Reade makes the "cat" less high than do Lacroix and Seré.] . . . . [The besieged] burnt the first cat by flinging blazing tar-barrels on it. So the besiegers made the roof of this one very steep, and covered it with raw hides, and the tar-barrels could not harm it.

At a later time

the moat was filled, and the wooden tower began to move on its wheels. . . . . There was something awful and magical in its approach without visible agency, for it was driven by internal rollers worked by leverage. On the top was a platform, where stood the first assailing party protected in front by the drawbridge of the turret, which stood vertical till lowered on to the wall. . . . . The be-

24 *Ibid.*, leaf iii; Oxf., p. 304; Ev., p. 310.
25 V, "Architecture militaire," xix–xx.

ET LA RENAISSANCE.

Fig. 81. Tour roulante avec un pont pour donner l'assaut. Ms. du XVe siècle. Bibl. Nat. de Paris.

Lacroix and Seré

TOWER FOR USE IN A SIEGE

sieged slung at the tower, and struck it often, but in vain. It was well defended with mattresses and hides. . . . . The Knight [a leader of the besieged] bade fire the mine beneath it.

Then the drawbridge of the tower was lowered on to the wall, and the attackers swarmed over; but after a few moments of intense combat, the mine beneath took effect and the tower collapsed.[26]

The besieged undermined the tower, as we have seen, and the besiegers undermined part of the city wall. In this operation, Reade says, the soldiers "undermined the place and underpinned it with beams, and covered the beams thickly with grease and tar."[27] This account is likewise from Lacroix and Seré, who remark of mining:

A subterranean gallery was dug, some distance from the besieged place, and was continued under the foundations of its ramparts and especially of its towers. As the gallery progressed, the earth was supported by planking. When the soldiers arrived under the foundation, they propped it up with joists, so that it rested wholly on these beams. Then they arranged around the props, brushwood and inflammable material, which they later set on fire. When the props were burned, the walls collapsed.[28]

The siege in *The Cloister and the Hearth* finally ended by common agreement after an important leader on each side had been captured and some money had been paid by the citizens of the town. Anthony of Burgundy, moreover, was to go to England to bring back the sister of Edward IV to marry the Duke of Burgundy's son, the Earl of Charolois. Mr. Wheeler points out a slight anachronism in that the Earl of Charolois married this lady (his third wife) only after his father had died and he himself had become duke. Reade may perhaps have based his statement on the following passage of Commines:

And it was purely on this suspicion that Messire William of Cluny, the prothonotary . . . . was despatched into England to the court of King Edward IV.,

[26] These events are scattered through Oxf., pp. 302–7; Ev., pp. 308–13.

[27] Oxf., p. 306; Ev., p. 312. One might add that the use of a mine dug by the assailants ends the narrative of the siege in *White Lies*, as the mine dug by the besieged figures in the closing episode of the siege in *The Cloister and the Hearth*. Obviously the mines work very differently.

[28] V, "Architecture militaire," xx.

who then reigned; and who had been always the mortal enemy of the Count of Charolois. . . . . In his private instruction, he had orders to propose a marriage with Margaret, the King of England's sister; but to treat only and negotiate, without coming to any conclusion. . . . . However, though he had no real intention at first to consummate the marriage, upon account of his inveterate hatred to the house of York, yet affairs were so managed, that several years after, the match was concluded.[29]

Though the passage says that only negotiations were engaged in at this time, Reade may either have misread the account or have chosen to alter the facts and have the marriage actually take place before the Count of Charolois succeeded to his father's title. Reade also has slipped Anthony of Burgundy into the role of Burgundian ambassador. Monstrelet, and likewise Barante in his *Histoire des Ducs de Bourgogne*, declare, in passages which Reade may possibly have noted, that Anthony went to England to engage in a tournament, but they say nothing about his bringing back Edward IV's sister.[30]

The novel now turns to Gerard's family and Margaret. She and Gerard's mother became fast friends. Giles, moreover, was summoned to court to become the duke's dwarf. Finally, Denys arrived at the Tergou household looking for Margaret, to bring her news of her lover, for she was no longer to be found at Sevenbergen. Shrinking from the tumult of slander that the birth of her child would occasion, she, in company with her aged father, had gone to Rotterdam. This fleeing from slander, though of course it would naturally occur to any novelist who had to move Margaret to Rotterdam (the city of Erasmus' birth), may have been prompted by the remark of John Jortin in his *Life of Erasmus:* "His [Erasmus'] mother, a person of ordinary rank, had repaired to Roterdam [*sic*], on purpose to conceal her lying-in."[31]

In Rotterdam, Margaret's father had a paralytic stroke. To earn the family livelihood, therefore, she put up the crocodile (a

---

[29] *The Memoirs of Philip de Commines*, ed. Andrew R. Scoble, (2 vols.; London, 1896), I, 37–38. A note throws some doubt on Commines' accuracy in this passage.

[30] *The Chronicles of Enguerrand de Monstrelet*, trans. Thomas Johnes (2 vols.; London, 1840), II, 345; A. G. P. B. de Barante (12 vols.; Paris, 1839), VIII, 290; IX, 195.

[31] (3 vols.; London, 1808), II, 86.

borrowing already spoken of) and practiced medicine. For a time numerous patients flocked to her, believing her a learned physician, for *populus vult decipi,* as Reade says, making use of a quotation which he might have found in Nathaniel Wanley.[32] The authorities, however, soon forbade her acting as a doctor, and she was compelled to earn money by doing laundry work.

And now comes one of the prettiest episodes in the novel— Margaret's cure of the mayor's daughter. The source, I believe, is surely one of the anecdotes in Wanley:

Antiochus, the Son of Seleucus, daily languished and wasted away under a Disease, whereof the cause was uncertain, to the great trouble and affliction of his Father; who therefore sent for Erasistratus, a famous Physician to attend the care of his beloved Son. Who addressing himself with his utmost dexterity to find out the root of his infirmity; he perceived it was rather from the trouble of his mind, then any effect of his constitution. But when the Prince could not be prevail'd with to make any such acknowledgment; by frequent feeling of his pulse, he observed it to beat with more vigour and strength at the naming or presence of Stratonica, that was the beloved Concubine of his Father; having made this discovery, and knowing the Prince would rather die than confess so dangerous a love, he took this course. He told Seleucus, that his Son was a dead Man; for, saith he, he languishes for the love of my Wife; and what, said Seleucus, have I merited so little at thy hands, that thou wilt have no respect to the love of the young Man? Would you, said Erasistratus, be content to serve the love of another in that manner. I would the gods, said Seleucus, would turn his love towards my dearest Stratonica. Well, said Erasistratus, you are his Father, and may be his Physician. Seleucus gave Stratonica to Antiochus, and sixty thousand Crowns as a reward to the prudent Physician.[33]

It is natural that Margaret, herself grieving for love, should be able to detect a similar trait in another woman, and she would, of course, be able to handle the situation with much tact and sympathy. When she first persuaded the mayor to let her see his daughter, she found the girl languid and melancholy. After a few preliminary questions she told the patient a disguised version of the story of her own love for Gerard. The maiden at once became interested and, when she learned that the story was about Margaret, kissed her. Next Margaret caused the mayor to pay all his employees in the presence of his daughter and herself, keeping her finger lightly on the girl's pulse. She at once dis-

[32] *Wonders of the Little World*, p. 362.   [33] P. 186.

covered that a young clerk was the object of her patient's affection. Then finding the mayor would rather permit the marriage
than lose his child, she procured a lock of the girl's hair and went
into the shop. Soon she returned:

So Doctor Margaret said cheerfully, "Mistress, your lock is gone, I have sold
it."

"And who was so mad as to buy such a thing?" inquired the young lady,
scornfully.

"Oh, a black haired laddie wi' white teeth. They call him Ulrich."

The pale face reddened directly—brow and all.

"Says he, 'Oh, sweet mistress, give it me.' I had told them all whose 'twas.
'Nay,' said I, 'selling is my livelihood, not giving.' So he offered me this, he
offered me that, but nought less would I take than his next quarter's wages."

"Cruel," murmured the girl, scarce audibly.[34]

And thus the marriage took place.

The whole episode is related with Reade's narrative skill and
with much feeling and sympathy too. A note of satire, likewise, is
added in the pompous and undiscerning mayor, satisfying his
conscience with the idea that, though of course he could not permit Margaret to practice regularly as a physician, he might allow her to cure his daughter provided he did not pay her for doing so.

Thereafter there is a short account of the splendid progress of
the English princess, now the wife of the Count Charolois,
through Holland. The details are too general for us to pick a
definite source, but Reade might have studied a six-page account
of the festivities in Barante or the letter of an eyewitness of the
events in the *Paston Letters*.[35] On the other hand, it should be observed, both accounts say that she became Duchess of Burgundy,
not Countess Charolois.

Eventually Denys found Margaret and brought her greetings
from Gerard. Soon afterward, moreover, she received a huge
letter from her lover. She derived therefrom no end of satisfac-

[34] The whole episode is found Oxf., pp. 353–58; Ev., pp. 357–61. It should be
remarked that Mr. Wheeler narrates the Erasistratus story as a similar incident; he
does not declare it is a source, and of course he says nothing about its occurrence in
Wanley.

[35] Oxf., p. 362; Ev., p. 366; Barante, VIII, 4'.2–18; *Paston Letters*, ed. John Fenn
(5 vols.; London, 1787–1823), II, 3–7.

tion and was later persuaded by Denys to go to Gerard's family and read them the letter. The document is given at length in *The Cloister and the Hearth* and serves to inform the reader of Gerard's adventures after the time when he parted from Denys.

The first experience of Gerard's after he had been robbed by the gay gallant comes from the following passage in Monteil, related by an impoverished man:

Suddenly, in the depths of a house draped with black, I perceived a bier covered richly with a cloth of silver; I went to sprinkle holy water upon it, hoping that the man was more fortunate than I in heaven now and that he had been more fortunate than I on earth. I immediately had proved to me that my wishes were in part granted, for there came out of the house a kindly serving maid, who, presenting me a basket full of bread and meat, said to me, "Take this, poor fellow; it's the daily portion of my late master." It was the dead man's daily portion; well and good, my masters,—I had enough to last me four days, eating all I could. Was he fortunate, that dead gentleman? What say you?[36]

The account in *The Cloister and the Hearth* is similar. While Gerard was lying asleep on the snow, a possible prey to wolves, a servant girl awaked him and, finding he was now a poor man, conducted him to "a noble dining-hall hung with black." In the room was a table set "with many dishes," for here in Burgundy it was the custom, from the time that a gentleman died until he was buried, to serve his dinner every day to some poor fellow. Thus Gerard sat and feasted upon an immense meal, although it was only the "daily dinner" of the deceased man. Reade emphasizes the contrast in the episode first by having Gerard asleep on the snow and thereafter by having him sit down to the table instead of merely receiving a basket of food, and by having him given "a right good bed" for the night.[37]

Gerard told one of the servants how he had been robbed and asked whether redress were possible. The man informed him, however, that the heartless gallant was cousin to the lady of the manor, and that since the case would have to be judged before her, she would be more likely to hang Gerard than punish her cousin. This touch seems to depend upon a statement elsewhere in Monteil supposed to be spoken about a noble lady by a lord:

[36] *Histoire des français des divers états*, II, 8.

[37] Oxf., pp. 370–71; Ev., pp. 374–75.

"This lady has, as I do, the absolute right to dispense justice, neither more nor less; her judge, like mine, may banish, deport, hang, and burn; she has, as I do, complete police power."[38]

Next Gerard fell in with a beggar and traveled with him for a considerable time. The beggar acted as his master, providing him with employment and food, and Gerard, in return, gave him half of the money he made by painting or singing. The great difference between these two strangely assorted companions was that while Gerard was guilelessly honest, the beggar was absolute master of all the fraudulent practices of his trade.

Altogether, these adventures with the beggar occupy some twenty pages. One may wonder how Reade first became interested in medieval beggars and how he decided to put them into his novel. Possibly his natural sympathy led him in this direction; but, in view of the great number of suggestions that he adopted from books and then developed, it seems more likely that he read some passage which first gave him the idea. Apart from works especially on beggary which he would have read only after becoming concerned with the subject, there are several bits in the books in the *Century* list that might have prompted his interest. Erasmus has a *Colloquy* between a beggar and a former beggar, now an alchemist, each praising his calling.[39] Then, too, John Heywood's *The Foure PP*—which Reade seems to have liked greatly, to judge from the "especially" prefixed to it in the *Century* list—may have attracted him to low life. Furthermore, various touches in Monteil or in Michel and Fournier (including illustrations in the latter book) may have directed his attention to beggars. The book which, in my opinion, however, is most likely to have started him is Hugo's *Notre-Dame*.[40] We have already seen that this novel influenced *The Cloister and the Hearth* once —in the conception of Giles. Now, in the same manner, the beggar scenes of this French tale are most striking and are likely to remain in the memory. The poet Gringoire managed to stray by night into the Court of Miracles, the spot in Paris where the beggars congregated and where their professional infirmities were all laid aside. Poor Gringoire, captured by these lawless fellows, was

[38] II, 180–81.   [39] I, 300–304.   [40] I, 124 ff.

about to be hanged by them, when Esmeralda saved his life by taking him as her husband and he himself thus embraced the life of a vagrant. So picturesque are these scenes, and so full of local color, that Reade would easily be struck, in perusing them, by the possibilities of beggar life in fiction and be tempted to follow suit. Finally, there is one similarity in wording between Hugo and Reade—a similarity to be touched on later—that seems to show at least some influence in respect to scenes about mendicants.

The details of Reade's beggar interlude come especially from Monteil and the *Liber vagatorum*, the latter a work dealing wholly with this class of paupers. In the first place, the account of Gerard and the beggar's meeting is from Monteil, where a poor man is talking:

> Hardly had I started on my journey when I met a man who was cheerful, animated, and witty in his talk, a fellow who to the gift of playing the blind man added the still more precious gift of playing the legless cripple [*faire le cul-de-jatte*]. We soon struck up a great friendship; we shared a common purse—that is to say, my purse became our common purse. . . . . Since I couldn't yet bring myself to bow down to beg for public charity, my comrade nailed on the front of his cart [where he rode] a tin cup.[41]

In *The Cloister and the Hearth*, Gerard, sunk in melancholy, all of a sudden heard someone come "carolling like a bird." The singer turned out to be "a humpbacked cripple, with a bloody bandage o'er his eye, and both legs gone at the knee." The beggar solicited alms of Gerard, but, finding the latter had no money, he let down "a stout pair of legs out of his back" and turned into a normal man. They became companions, and the mendicant volunteered to feed Gerard if the latter would give him half his earnings. Gerard was too proud to beg, but his companion did so on all occasions.[42] Reade's change of the beggar's sharing all the purse of the other man into his getting only half of Gerard's earnings may perhaps be occasioned by a later remark of the same poor man in Monteil. He declares apropos of being in prison: "I was furnished with leather; I made new shoes; I worked half for my own account, half for the jailer's."[43]

Gerard later constantly referred to his companion by the name

[41] II, 2.   [42] Oxf., pp. 372–74; Ev., pp. 376–78.   [43] II, 5.

of Cul de Jatte, an expression occurring in the former of the two Monteil passages just quoted. In return, the beggar gave him the name of Bon Bec,[44] a name probably coming from two plates in Michel and Fournier.[45]

The beggar put out his foot and boasted that it had been "washed by the greatest king alive, Louis of France, the last holy Thursday that was."[46] Similarly the poor man in Monteil recounted, "The Kings of France, who would not wash the feet of emperors, wash the feet of beggars."[47] Again, the mendicant, hearing Gerard speak of dogs licking the sores of Lazarus, replied, "Dogs lick not a beggar's sores, being made with spearwort, or ratsbane, or biting acids." This is probably taken from Thomas Harman's *Caveat*, a Renaissance book on beggars, though the work is not mentioned in the *Century* list. The passage runs:

> All for the most parte of these wil either lay to their legs an herb called Sperewort, eyther Arsnicke, which is called Ratesbane. The nature of this Spereworte wyll rayse a great blister in a night upon the soundest part of his body; and if the same be taken away, it wyl dry up againe and no harme.[48]

On another occasion Cul de Jatte played a trick on Gerard by pretending to have a fit:

> By and by he gave a groan, and rolled on the ground like a ball, and writhed sore. I was scared, and wist not what to do, but went to lift him; but his trouble rose higher and higher, he gnashed his teeth fearfully, and the foam did fly from his lips; and presently his body bended itself like a bow, and jerked and bounded many times into the air.[49]

Thereafter the beggar revealed that the fit was but simulated; soap in the mouth produced the foam and pricking the nose with a straw, the bloody nostril.

This happening comes from the part of the *Liber vagatorum* which describes the grantners who pretend to be "afflicted with

---

[44] Oxf., p. 376; Ev., p. 380 (for both Cul de Jatte and Bon Bec).

[45] *Le Livre d'or des métiers*, I, plate opposite 312; II, plate opposite 368.

[46] Oxf., p. 374; Ev., p. 378.   [47] II, 5.

[48] Ed. Viles and Furnivall (London, 1869), p. 44. Mr. Wheeler quotes, apropos of Reade's sentence, a passage from Dekker, *Belman of London*, about spearwort and arsenic, but the word "ratsbane" does not occur.

[49] Oxf., p. 378; Ev., pp. 381–82.

the falling sickness": "Some fall down before the churches, or in other places with a piece of soap in their mouths, whereby the foam rises as big as a fist, and they prick their nostrils with a straw, causing them to bleed."[50]

Upon seeing a wheelbarrow outside a village, Gerard's beggar-master proposed, "I'll tie myself in a knot, and shalt wheel me through; and what with my crippledom and thy piety, a-wheeling of thy poor old dad, we'll bleed the bumpkins of a dacha-saltee."[51] This little trick seems to have occurred to Reade's mind when he gazed on a plate in Michel and Fournier of a young man conveying a decrepit beggar in a wheelbarrow.[52] Cul de Jatte likewise bought Gerard a psaltery with which to earn money. The young man writes, "I tuned it and coursed up and down the wires nimbly with my two wooden strikers."[53] The mention of the instrument may have been occasioned by the account of it in Lacroix and Seré, who declare, among other things, "The musician placed the instrument against his breast, and embraced it in order to touch the strings with his fingers or two quills or plectra."[54]

On two occasions Gerard's master obtained bones to sell as relics: the first time, as St. Anthony's thumb and St. Martin's little finger; the second time, as the head of St. Barnabas.[55] Though of course the idea of having false relics introduced may come from many sources, a likely one is *The Foure PP*, since Reade seems to have been especially interested in the play. In this the pardoner displays, for the other three *P*'s to kiss, his spurious relics, including such items as "the great-toe of the Trinite." The whole action is accompanied by lively dialogue.[56]

[50] *The Book of Vagabonds and Beggars*, trans. J. C. Hotten (London, 1860), pp. 21–22. (Noted by Wheeler.) (The *Liber vagatorum* is the title of the original Latin version.)

[51] Oxf., p. 378; Ev., p. 382.   [52] II, plate opposite 84.

[53] Oxf., pp. 376, 379; Ev., pp. 380, 383.

[54] IV, "Instruments de musique," xi.

[55] Oxf., pp. 380, 384; Ev., pp. 384, 387.

[56] Ll. 422 ff. The play may be found in J. M. Manly, *Specimens of the Pre-Shaksperean Drama* (Boston, 1897), I, 483–522.

An experience that made a great impression on the sensitive Gerard was witnessing the execution of a woman:

> They did fling her off the bridge, and fell in the water not far from us. And oh! Margaret, the deadly splash! It ringeth in mine ears even now. But worse was coming; for, though tied, she came up, and cried, "Help! help!" and I, forgetting all, and hearing a woman's voice cry "Help!" was for leaping in to save her; and had surely done it, but the boatman and Cul de Jatte clung round me, and in a moment the bourreau's man, that waited in a boat, came and entangled his hooked pole in her long hair, and so thrust her down and ended her.[57]

The emotion and sympathy displayed are but another reminder that the author of this passage was a writer of humanitarian novels.

The source of this is a passage in *Archaeologia, or Miscellaneous Tracts Relating to Antiquity*, a publication of the Society of Antiquaries of London. This series, to be sure, does not occur in the *Century* list, but a jotting in one of the Reade notebooks owned by Mr. Parrish refers to a near-by page in the same volume, showing that the novelist had consulted the work.

> A memorable instance of drowning occurred in Bavaria in the fifteenth century. On the 14th of October, 1436, Agnes Bernauerinn, wife of Duke Albert the Pious, was thrown off the bridge of the city of Straubing into the Danube by order of her father, Ernest Duke of Bavaria. She appears not to have been put into a sack, and her limbs not to have been securely bound, for she rose to the surface of the water and swam to the shore crying "Help! help!" but the executioner put a long pole into her hair and kept her down.[58]

In order to reinforce the effect of this spectacle and make the beggar repent of his unprincipled ways, Gerard repeated the couplet:

> The Lord is débonair
> Let Sinners nought despair.[59]

In the English translation of an epistle of St. Bernard given by Thomas Coryate occurs the following prose sentence: "Doe not distrust o ye sinners, the Lord is debonaire."[60] Reade may well have obtained his distich by versifying this. Again, poor Cul de

[57] Oxf., p. 381; Ev., pp. 384–85.

[58] XXXVIII, Part I, 61. (This is the first volume for 1860.)

[59] Oxf., p. 381; Ev., p. 385.   [60] *Crudities*, II, 241. (Not noted by Wheeler.)

TROOP OF BOHEMIANS ON THE ROAD

Michel and Fournier

Jatte had a bad experience with a fierce dog who tore off his false leg. So irritated was the man that for a long time he would say nothing but "Curse the *quiens*." The glossary in Hotten's edition of the *Liber vagatorum* gives *quien* as "dog," obviously the source of Reade's use of the expression.[61]

Next Gerard and his companion entered Germany. Then, one day, there "came by a reverend palmer with hat stuck round with cockle shells from Holy Land, and great rosary of beads like eggs of teal, and sandals for shoes. And he leaned aweary on his long staff, and offered us a shell apiece." Gerard gave him some money, but Cul de Jatte later informed his companion that the man was a fraud: "In France we call them 'Coquillarts,' but here 'Calmierers.' "[62] This episode seems to be a composite formed from three sources. The *Liber vagatorum* tells about Christianers or Calmierers:

> These are beggars who wear signs in their hats, especially Roman veronicas, shells, and other tokens, which they sell to each other, in order that it shall be thought they have been in distant cities and foreign parts. For this reason they wear these signs, although they have never come thence, and they deceive people thereby.[63]

Another touch, I think, comes from *Notre-Dame*. In the Court of Miracles are various sorts of false beggars; one of them is a sham pilgrim—called *un coquillart*.[64] Probably, in the third place, we may catch in Reade's wording an echo of Ophelia's song in *Hamlet:*

> By his cockle hat and staff
> And his sandal shoon.[65]

Next Gerard encountered what Cul de Jatte later told him was a "Vopper." The happening is based on a section of the *Liber vagatorum:*

> The XIIIth chapter is about the Voppers. These beggars are for the most part women, who allow themselves to be led in chains as if they were raving

---

[61] *Liber vagatorum*, p. 60 (noted by Wheeler); Oxf., p. 382; Ev., p. 386.

[62] Oxf., pp. 384, 386; Ev., pp. 388, 389.   [63] P. 40. (Noted by Wheeler.)

[64] French text (2 vols.; Paris: Marpon and Flammarion, n.d.), I, 116. Lacroix and Seré (I, "Bohémiens," xi) speak of this sort of pilgrims, but call them *coquillards*, not *coquillarts*.

[65] IV, v, 25–26.

mad; they tear their shifts from their bodies, in order that they may deceive people. . . . . This is vopping, viz. when one begs for his wife's or any other person's sake and says she has been possessed of a devil (tho' there is no truth in it), and he has vowed to some Saint (whom he names), and must have XII pounds of wax or other things whereby the person will be delivered from the power of the devil.[66]

Reade has followed the details of this closely, but he has made it into a lively episode. "We heard savage cries, and came a sorry sight, one leading a wild woman in a chain, all rags, and howling like a wolf." She tore her rags and flew at Gerard with her long nails. The man, who occasionally lashed her, said that she was his wife and that he was seeking alms to buy six (not twelve, as in the *Liber vagatorum*) pounds of wax for St. Anthony.[67]

Thereafter Gerard met a troop of Bohemians. The idea of introducing such a band in his novel may have been suggested to Reade by Monteil's poor man remarking that he joined a company of these people for a time.[68] The account which Reade put into *The Cloister and the Hearth*, however, is an exact description of a plate in Michel and Fournier.[69] The plate, entitled "Troupe de Bohémiens en Voyage," is after a print by the celebrated French artist Callot. Reade's description, which may be compared with a reproduction of the plate in this volume, runs as follows:

With that came along so motley a crew as never your eyes beheld, dear Margaret. Marched at their head one with a banner on a steel-pointed lance, and girded with a great long sword, and in velvet doublet and leathern jerkin, the which stuffs ne'er saw I wedded afore on mortal flesh, and a gay feather in his lordly cap, and a couple of dead fowls at his back, the which, an the spark had come by honestly, I am much mistook. Him followed wives and babes on two lean horses, whose flanks still rattled like parchment drum, being beaten by kettles and caldrons. Next an armed man a-riding of a horse, which drew a cart full of females and children: and in it, sitting backwards, a lusty lazy knave, lance in hand, with his luxurious feet raised on a holy-water pail, that lay along, and therein a cat, new kittened, sat glowing o'er her brood, and sparks for eyes. And the cart-horse cavalier had on his shoulders a round bundle, and thereon did perch a cock and crowed with zeal, poor ruffler, proud of his brave feathers as the rest, and haply with more reason, being his own. And on an ass another wife and new-born child; and one poor quean a-foot scarce dragged

---

[66] P. 31. (Noted by Wheeler.)

[67] Oxf., pp. 384–86; Ev., pp. 388–89.

[68] II, 11.

[69] II, plate opposite 144.

THE CAMP OF THE BOHEMIANS

herself along, so near her time was she, yet held two little ones by the hand, and helplessly helped them on the road. And the little folk were just a farce; some rode sticks, with horses' heads, between their legs, which pranced and caracoled, and soon wearied the riders so sore, they stood stock still and wept, which cavaliers were presently taken into cart and cuffed. And one, more grave, lost in a man's hat and feather, walked in Egyptian darkness, handed by a girl; another had the great saucepan on his back, and a tremendous three-footed clay pot sat on his head and shoulders, swallowing him so as he too went darkling led by his sweetheart three foot high.[70]

Gerard sympathized with the pregnant woman, but Cul de Jatte declared she was a *biltreger* who used a pillow to counterfeit this condition. This type of beggar is spoken of in the *Liber vagatorum*.[71]

Then the two friends encountered the same group of Bohemians again, this time encamped. Reade's account[72] is but a description of a second plate after a print by Callot contained in Michel and Fournier.[73] The picture, for purposes of comparison with the following passage, is reproduced in this volume:

And rising after meat and meditation, and travelling forward, we found them camped between two great trees on a common by the wayside; and they had lighted a great fire, and on it was their caldron; and, one of the trees slanting o'er the fire, a kid hung down by a chain from the tree-fork to the fire, and in the fork was wedged an urchin turning still the chain to keep the meat from burning, and a gay spark with a feather in his cap cut up a sheep; and another had spitted a leg of it on a wooden stake; and a woman ended chanticleer's pride with wringing of his neck. And under the other tree four rufflers played at cards and quarrelled, and no word sans oath; and of these lewd gamblers one had cockles in his hat, and was my reverend pilgrim. And a female, young and comely, and dressed like a butterfly, sat and mended a heap of dirty rags. And Cul de Jatte said, "Yon is the 'vopper,'" and I looked incredulous and looked again, and it was so, and at her feet sat he that had so late lashed her; but I ween he had wist where to strike, or woe betide him; and she did now oppress him sore, and made him thread her very needle [a happy interweaving by Reade of the previous "vopper" episode]. . . . . Natheless we soon espied a wife set with her back against the tree, and her hair down, and her face white, and by her side a wench held up to her eye a new-born babe, with words of cheer, and the rough fellow, her husband, did bring her hot wine in a cup, and

[70] Oxf., pp. 386–87; Ev., pp. 389–90.

[71] Pp. 36–37. (Noted by Wheeler.)   [72] Oxf., pp. 387–88; Ev., pp. 390–91.

[73] II, plate opposite 162; it is entitled "Le Camp des Bohémiens."

bade her take courage. And, just o'er the place she sat, they had pinned from bough to bough of those neighboring trees two shawls, and blankets two, together, to keep the drizzle off her. And so had another poor little rogue come into the world.

Gerard and Cul de Jatte then mixed with the Bohemians, and the latter "talked with the men in some strange Hebrew cant where of no word knew I."[74] Hotten, the editor of the *Liber vagatorum*, says of the beggars' cant, "As Luther states, in his preface, the Hebrew appears to be the principal element."[75] This remark obviously occasioned the previous circumstance in Reade.

On leaving this company Cul de Jatte observed that if Gerard would but come with him to the "rotboss" (beggars' lodging-house),[76] he would show Gerard a vast variety of different sorts of beggars. And thereupon Reade shows his thoroughness by making Cul de Jatte rattle off a long list of cant names. With one or two exceptions, the names at the beginning are German; those in the middle, French; those at the end, English. The German words for various types of mendicants come from the *Liber vagatorum*, and I put in parentheses the pages of Hotten's edition where they occur: *lossners* (11), *dutzers* (24), *schleppers* (26), *gickisses* (28), "*schwanfelders*, whom in English we call 'shivering Jemmies' " (30 and xxxiii), *süntvegers* (35), *schwiegers* (41), *joners* (47), *sessel-degers* (45, *Sefel Diggers*), *gennscherers* (45, *Gensscherers*), and (next skipping a pair of French names)*veranerins* (39), *stabulers* (9, *stabülers*).[77]

The last part of the list—which is English—comes from Thomas Harman's *Caveat*.[78] I give it, inclosing the page references to Harman in parentheses: rufflers (29; Reade used this in his account of the camp of the Bohemians), whipjalks (48, whipiacke in Harman), dommerars (57), glymmerars (61, a demander for

---

[74] Oxf., p. 388; Ev., p. 392.

[75] P. xxxvi. Luther's remark, to the same effect, is on p. 3. (Neither is noted by Wheeler.)

[76] From the *Liber vagatorum*, p. 60. (Noted by Wheeler.)

[77] Oxf., p. 389; Ev., 392. (Mr. Wheeler spots all these German words except *veranerins*.)

[78] Noted by Wheeler.

glymmar), jarkmen (60, jarke man), patricos (60), swadders (60), autem morts (67), walking morts (67).

In the middle come the French terms: "*marcandiers* or *rifodés* (the German *veranerins* and *stabulers* follow)—*piètres, francmitoux, polissons, malingreux, traters.*" I have not found the last term; it may belong to the English list following. The other terms, I believe, all come from Hugo's *Notre-Dame*, where the following list of beggars in a procession in the Court of Miracles is given (the italics are mine): "les courtauds de boutanche, les coquillarts, les hubins, les sabouleux, les calots, les *francs-mitoux,* les *polissons,* les *piètres,* les capons, les *malingreux,* les *rifodés,* les *marcandiers,* etc."[79] I should add that the fourth volume of Monteil has a list of various sorts of beggars[80] including all of Reade's French terms except *marcandiers.* Moreover, Monteil's spellings of *riffodés* and *francs-mitous* make us prefer *Notre-Dame* as a source, and, again, there are no other possible borrowings by Reade from this fourth volume of Monteil, which treats of the seventeenth century. Hence Hugo's passage seems preferable as the origin of Reade's French words.

Thereafter follows a most entertaining adventure of Cul de Jatte told by Reade in lively fashion. The beggar "had put on sores made of pig's blood, rye meal, and glue" and was sitting, in the hope of alms, beside a monastery door. Out came the monks and their dogs. "The great idiots, being as I think, puppies, or little better, fell on me where I sat, downed me, and fell a-licking my sores." The sores promptly came off. "So up I jumped, and shouted 'a miracle! a miracle! The very dogs of this holy convent be holy, and have cured me.' 'Good fathers,' cried I, 'whose day is this?' 'St. Isidore's,' said one. 'St. Isidore,' cried I in a sort of rapture, 'why St. Isidore is my patron saint: so that accounts.' " The populace swallowed the miracle. The monks on the contrary, though they were content to have their monastery enjoy the credit of working wonders, took Cul de Jatte inside the building. "Finally they bade the lay brethren give me a hiding, and take me out a back way and put me on the

[79] *Notre-Dame* (French ed.), I, 91–92. (Not, of course, noted by Wheeler.)
[80] IV, 278–79.

road, and threatened me did I come back to the town to hand me
to the magistrate and have me drowned for a plain imposter.
. . . . Wow but the brethren laid on."[81]

This passage is developed from several bits concerning a mendicant and occurring close together in Monteil. This man taught
a friend "to make ulcers out of glue, meal, and blood."[82] Cul de
Jatte, in Reade, fashioned his of "pig's blood, rye meal, and
glue," the procedure becoming somewhat more specific in the
hands of the novelist. The idea of a sore made of blood, aided
perhaps by the remembrance of Lazarus, suggested to Reade's
fertile mind the episode of the sores coming off, much to the bystanders' astonishment. Then Reade borrowed from another
passage in Monteil about this beggar. Though posing as a cripple:

> One fine afternoon, my comrade while singing, jumping, and playing on a
> tennis court, found himself suddenly encircled by constables. He wasn't dis-
> concerted, nor did he hesitate even for a moment. Sir, he said, going right up to
> the vice-bailiff, isn't today St. Isidore's? Well, he's my patron. Every year I
> fast for the three evenings before his fête; every year he grants me for this one
> day, the cure of all my maladies.[83]

But the fellow's ready invention helped him not, and he had to
go to prison.

Cul de Jatte's similar remark about St. Isidore imposed on the
populace, but the monks knew better and inflicted punishment.
The form it took is drawn from another experience of Monteil's
beggar when he attempted to win money by a bogus fit:

> An old curé, after my first tremblings and contortions, at the moment when
> my cries and convulsions were beginning, remarked to the spectators: Brothers,
> this is a devil we must drive out, not with the cross, but with the handle of the
> cross. Forthwith . . . . the sacristans and clerics began exorcizing my ribs so hard
> and so long that my body advises me even now not to try to win alms again like
> that.[84]

And now occurred the adventure that was to separate Cul de
Jatte and Gerard.[85] One day the former "took the yellow jaun-
dice and went begging through the town." The device is adopted

---

[81] Oxf., 389–90; Ev., 392–93.

[82] II, 2.

[83] Monteil, II, 3–4.

[84] *Ibid.*, pp. 2–3.

[85] Oxf., 390–92; Ev., pp. 394–95.

from the *Schweigers*, in the *Liber vagatorum*, who "take horses' dung and mix it with water, and besmear their legs, hands, and arms with it; thereby appearing as if they had the yellow sickness, or other dreadful disease."[86] Cul de Jatte at first prospered that day in his begging, but, in time, he ran into difficulties with "blind Hans." This fellow, who was "an old favourite with the townsfolk, had his station at St. Martin's porch, the greatest church." Hans is an example of the type of beggars called, in the *Liber vagatorum, platschierers*. "These are the blind men who sit before the churches on chairs" and tell lies.[87] The name Hans is from a near-by page of the same book, where we are warned to beware of blind doctors and are told of one named Hans of Strassburg.[88]

Now the supposedly blind Hans, beholding Cul de Jatte's success, denounced him to the authorities. They arrested the newcomer promptly. At the trial Cul de Jatte demonstrated that his accuser was a fraud; yet the burgomaster sided with Hans on the ground that he was an established civic institution. At this point the hangman, there present, volunteered, "An't please you, first let us see why he weareth his hair so thick and low." He examined, "and lo the upper gristle of both ears was gone." At first Cul de Jatte said he had forgotten how this came about. Thereafter, "when he found this would not serve his turn, he named two famous battles, in each of which he had lost half an ear, afighting like a true man against traitors and rebels." The lie would not serve; the cuts had evidently been made by a hangman, and poor Cul de Jatte was condemned "to prison for one month, and to give a florin towards the new hall of the guilds now abuilding, and to be whipt out of the town, and pay the hangman's fee for the same."

The experience is borrowed from a passage about the beggar in Monteil—a passage from which we have already seen Reade taking one detail:

In a little city of Saintonge where he was playing the blind man, another blind man noticed him and recognized him. Immediately, excited by jealousy

---

[86] Chap. xxvi. (Not noted by Wheeler.) *Schweiger* in Hotten; *schwieger* in Reade.
[87] P. 42. (Not noted by Wheeler.)   [88] P. 47. (Not noted by Wheeler.)

and without any warning, threat, or other preliminary, he denounced him to the vice-bailiff. . . . . [Here comes the incident of his being caught and pretending to be cured on St. Isidore's day—a touch already borrowed by Reade for another passage.] But it was no use; we had to go to prison. . . . . My comrade was condemned to the galleys, and I was to receive ten lashes with a whip, after which I should be obliged to leave the country in three days. [Among Cul de Jatte's punishments was being whipped out of town, with the picturesque addition, by Reade, of having to pay the hangman's fee.] . . . . [As for the comrade], they examined his head and found that under the thick tufts of his hair, he lacked the left ear. I don't know where he had left it or where he had had it cut off; for he had told me everything except this experience. You know how strict the laws are with second offenses.[89]

This final adventure of Cul de Jatte's, then, is a good example of Reade's habit of weaving together bits from different sources and improving the whole with interesting fancies of his own.

Gerard, after interviewing Cul de Jatte once through the prison bars, left him in confinement and pursued his journey. He was not destined, nevertheless, to go far alone:

The next day, passing a grand house, out came on prancing steeds a gentleman in brave attire and two servants; they overtook me. The gentleman bade me halt. I laughed in my sleeve; for a few batzen were all my store. He bade me doff my doublet and jerkin. Then I chuckled no more. "Bethink you, my lord," said I, " 'tis winter. How may a poor fellow go bare and live?" So he told me I shot mine arrow wide of his thought; and off with his own gay jerkin, richly furred, and doublet to match, and held them forth to me. Then a servant let me know it was a penance. "His lordship had had the ill luck to slay his cousin in their cups." Down to my shoes he changed with me; and set me on his horse like a popinjay, and fared by my side in my worn weeds, with my psaltery on his back. And said he, "Now, good youth, thou art Count Detstein; and I, late count, thy Servant. Play thy part well, and help me save my blood-stained soul! Be haughty and choleric, as any noble; and I will be as humble as I may."[90]

Gerard played the count for some time, finding the innkeepers fairly licked his boots, but he could not be so barbarous as were most noblemen of the time. He behaved with kindness to the count and also to the retainers. "He tried to make them all happier than he was; held them ravished with stories, and songs, and set Herr Penitent and Co. dancing, with his whistle and psaltery." Eventually, the count and Gerard parted. "I gave my lord, late Servant, back, his brave clothes for mine, but his horse he made me keep, and five gold pieces, and said he was still my debtor, his penance it had been slight along of me, but profitable. But his best word was this: 'I see 'tis more noble to be loved than feared.' "[91] Reade's narrative about the count lasted for six pages. But in order to avoid monotony, he introduced skilfully two short digressions about the listeners to Gerard's letter. First, Giles arrived in court costume and, when Sybrandt contemptuously pointed to a little chair, tore Sybrandt out of a big one and assumed it himself. Second, a reference in the letter to Denys's fondness for women occasioned an interchange of remarks between him and Margaret.

The main theme of this experience with the German count is drawn from a similar one with a French noble related by the poor man in Monteil:

> Hardly had I sat down [in a cheap inn] when the landlord, accompanied by a valet in livery, came to speak to me: A gentleman is looking everywhere for a poor man to go to Paris on a horse which he himself will lead, on foot, by the bridle. "Good," said I, "I know what it is; he has made a vow; I'm his man." "In that case," said the landlord pointing to the valet in livery, "go with this fine fellow." [Reade, more specific, tells the cause of the vow; in addition he provides more suspense by having the nobleman begin to strip Gerard.] I followed the man. He led me to the inn of his master. "Into the saddle with you quick!" cried the gentleman to me as soon as he noticed me: "we've a long journey to go today." We set off. We were four, and we marched in this order: first, the squire, on horseback; the gentleman on foot leading by the bridle the horse on which I was seated; the liveried valet, who had come after me and who was also on horseback closed the procession. When we came to a hostelry, the gentleman stayed in the kitchen and ate the coarsest victuals out of a wooden bowl; I was conducted into the hall, put at the table which the gentleman would have occupied and respectfully served by the liveried valet. While we were on the road, the gentleman sometimes turned to me saying: "Come on! Courage, brother! Courage! Pray God for me; you see how well we are treating you."[92]

When they finally arrived in Paris they went to mass in a church, and the gentleman, having completed his vow, dismissed the poor man; he absolutely refused, however, the latter's entreaties for a little money.

[91] Oxf., p. 398; Ev., p. 401.   [92] II, 8–9.

One great difference between the two accounts is the way Gerard behaves: he treats both count and retainers with great kindness. Accordingly, at the end, he and the nobleman part in a spirit quite unlike the French book, for the count has finally learned it is better to be loved than feared. This addition, of course, is quite in harmony with the ethical note characteristic of Victorian literature, and with Reade's humanitarianism. Another difference between the French and the English accounts is the addition in the English of a change of clothes between Gerard and the count. This comes from another passage in Monteil, two or three pages before the one which we have just been considering. In this:

> I was at a street corner with three other poor men when there passed a certain cavalier very richly dressed. We accosted him, holding out our hands and sounding our prayer. "Ah!" said he, turning toward me and looking at me, "you're my size; let's change clothes." At the same time, he took off mine, threw me his, and went off.[93]

Later the poor man learned that the cavalier had to sell his lands because of extravagance and, in order to do this, had first to demonstrate to the magistrates his poverty; hence his desire for shabby clothes.

Several other borrowings are included in the narrative of Gerard's sojourn with the count. At one inn he was requested to present the establishment with his coat-of-arms, and painted it himself. We have already discussed Reade's source for this custom of medieval inns.

A second incident is from Montaigne's *Journey*. Gerard writes in his letter: "I observed a young man of the country to meet a strange maiden, and kissed his hand, and then held it out to her. She took it with a smile, and lo! acquaintance made; and babbled like old friends. Greeting so pretty and delicate I ne'er did see." Thus Gerard told his noble servant to greet the next girl in the same manner, and the result was similar. Nevertheless, "presently came up a band of her companions. So this time I bade him doff his bonnet to them, as though they were empresses; and he did so. And lo! the lasses drew up as stiff as hedge-stakes,

[93] II, 6.

and moved not nor spake." All this is takingly worked up from a statement in Montaigne, who, speaking of German girls, says: "You salute by kissing the hand, and offering to touch theirs. Otherwise, if in passing you make them a bow and doff your hat, most of them will be stuck there without any movement; and that is their time-honoured custom."[94]

Another borrowing concerns the wearing of rose garlands in Germany and comes from Moryson. Though the quotation of both passages in full would occupy too much space, I shall try to show how well Reade handles what he takes. Moryson says:

> All other [women except gentlewomen] from the highest to the lowest, commonly weare garlands of roses, (which they call Crantzes). For they keepe Roses all Winter in little pots of earth, whereof they open one each saturday at night, and distribute the Roses among the women of the house, to the very kitchin maide; others keepe them all in one pot, and weekely take as many Roses as they neede, and cover the rest, keeping them fresh till the next Summer. And the common sort mingle guilded nutmegs with these Roses, and made garlands thereof: Only women weare these Garlands in Winter, but in Summer time men of the better sort weare them within doores.[95]

Then follows a lengthy account, first, of how the buds are preserved in pots and, second, how they are treated when taken out of the pots to be worn.

Reade follows Moryson closely as to the facts but he handles them more skilfully. He begins by an appreciation of the custom of wearing garlands:

> For know, dear Margaret, that throughout Germany, the baser sort of lasses wear for head-dress nought but a "crantz," or wreath of roses, encircling their bare hair, as laurel Caesar's; and though of the worshipful scorned, yet is braver, I wist, to your eye and mine which painters be, though sorry ones, than the gorgeous, uncouth, mechanical head-gear of the time.[96]

Next Reade turns to the method of preserving the buds and in his account condenses Moryson's lengthy remarks. Then, following the time order, he discusses opening the pots for the dis-

[94] Oxf., pp. 394–95; Ev., p. 398. Montaigne, p. 29. (Reade borrowed from the second part of this passage in describing Denys's bowing to German girls.)

[95] *An Itinerary Containing His Ten Yeeres Travell through the Twelve Dominions*, IV, 209–10. (Noted by Wheeler.)

[96] Oxf., p. 395; Ev., p. 398.

tribution of roses—a point discussed early in Moryson—and, thereafter, the means of treating them before wearing—a point coming late in his source. After this, Reade turns to the modification of the usual fashion by means of combining gilded nutmegs —which comes rather early in Moryson; the aesthetic Gerard quite properly disapproves of the nutmegs. And finally the novelist closes with another bit of appreciation of his own, which he puts into Gerard's mouth: "And it does the eye's heart good to see these fair heads of hair come, blooming with roses, over snowy roads, and by snow capt hedges, setting winter's beauty by the side of summer's glory. For what so fair as winter's lilies, snow yclept, and what so brave as roses?" The fact that men sometimes wore roses is omitted by Reade as unsuitable. The novelist, then, has improved Moryson's discussion of the matter by making the order more logical, by condensing necessary explanation, and by adding an aesthetic note at the beginning and at the end in order to provide something of an idyllic atmosphere.

While Gerard was still in the company of the German count, he visited some remarkable stables which he described in his letter in detail.[97] In fact, the careful Gerard had much of Baedeker in his system. The account is taken from Moryson's picture of the extensive stables of the Elector of Saxony.[98] Reade's sketch follows Moryson's but condenses it, as previously. Moreover, he postpones the great number of horses—"not less than two hundred horses"—to the end, to serve as a climax. When Gerard had viewed the stables where the horses lived in luxury, he visited the cottage of one of the grooms—a cottage of one room—where the man's "wife and children of all ages, from five to eighteen" lived in squalor. Replying to a question of Gerard's, the count admitted he knew the princely owner of the stable and had often drunk with him "in a marble chamber above the stable," a chamber furnished with strange and curious objects. Then said Gerard, " 'Tis well . . . . : now for thy penance, whisper thou

---

[97] Oxf., pp. 397–98; Ev., pp. 400–401.

[98] I, 19–21. (The borrowing about the stables is noted by Wheeler.) One should observe that Moryson's account of these stables is also in Southey's *Common-Place Book* (2d ser.), p. 348. This work of Southey's occurs in the *Century* list.

in yon prince's ear, that God hath given him his people freely, and not sought a price for them as for horses. And pray him look inside the huts at his horse-palace door, and bethink himself is it well to house his horses, and stable his folk."

The feeling of the passage is strongly humanitarian and thus eminently characteristic of Reade. The groom's cottage is the novelist's own invention, and after a brief description of the "marble chamber"—much condensed from Moryson—there occurs the plea for the unfortunate just quoted, a plea, it need hardly be said, that has no original in the Elizabethan volume. In his more detailed sketch of the chamber above the stable Moryson is especially interested in a round table "with many inscriptions perswading temperance." He gives two of them, both in Latin and in translation, one against drunkenness and one against gluttony. "Yet I dare say," continues Moryson, "that notwithstanding all these good precepts, few or none ever rose (or rather were not carried as unable to goe) from that table." In other words, Moryson, as well as Reade, has introduced a moral into his description, and each of the two morals is eminently characteristic of the epoch when its writer lived.

Next Gerard saw a wedding feast where "the guests were plying the business of drinking sad and silent, but ever and anon cried loud and dolefully, 'Seyt frölich! Be merry.' "[99] This is from Moryson's observation that the Germans in drinking "sadly ply the buisinesse, sometimes crying one to the other, Seyte frolich, Be merry."[100]

On parting company with the count Gerard betook himself to Augsburg. He was most favorably impressed with the city and celebrated its virtues and those of its citizens rapturously. A most important influence, I believe, was *Norica*, the modern work purporting to be an account of Renaissance Nuremberg, written by a contemporary. Though not great, it is a most interesting little book, full of enthusiasm over the city, its arts, and its people. The supposed author of the diary interviewed, at great length, Vischer, Krafft, Stoss, Sachs, and especially Dürer, and described their works rapturously. As he continued his visit, "Nürn-

[99] Oxf., p. 98; Ev., p. 401.   [100] IV, 37.

berg became dearer to me every day," he said, "and the thought of parting ever more bitter."[101] In addition, "more and more did I admire the bronze structure [of Vischer's shrine of St. Sebaldus], with its larger and smaller figures, its shafts and arches, its gables and turrets."[102] The people of the city—particularly the artists— were noble souls, cordial to strangers, and free from jealousy of each other. Thus when the diarist first went to see Peter Vischer, he found him and two acquaintances drawing. Though interrupted, they received him cordially, and, after a time, made him judge of which had produced the best drawing. When he decided in favor of Vischer, the others were not in the least annoyed. "Yes," declared one, "Master Vischer has succeeded best to-day." Then all three courteously presented the visitor with their drawings.[103]

The tone of Gerard's description of Augsburg is similar, for he becomes most enthusiastic in his comments. The streets are full of beautiful buildings. The burgomaster is wise and courteous: "God bless the city where the very burgomaster is cut of Solomon's cloth!" "Dear Margaret, it is a noble city, and a kind mother to arts." "In arts mechanical no citizens may compare with these." And when Gerard and these other men painted a pack of cards and his queen was the best done of all, "my fellow-craftsmen saw her, and put their arms round my neck and hailed me master. Oh, noble Germans! No jealousy of a brother workman: no sour looks at a stranger."[104] The last example, indeed, seems directly inspired by the scene in *Norica* where Vischer made the best drawing.

In view of these similarities, I believe that in creating the atmosphere of his Augsburg, Reade was surely influenced by the corresponding tone of Nuremberg in *Norica*.[105] Moreover, since the visit to Augsburg has nothing to do with the plot of the novel

[101] *Norica or Tales of Nürnberg*, trans. from the German of August Hagen (London, 1851), p. 170.

[102] P. 227.   [103] P. 68.

[104] All these occur in Oxf., pp. 399–400; Ev., pp. 402–4.

[105] Moryson has an account of Augsburg (I, 40–43), but is he far less enthusiastic than Gerard.

and is a long passage of description pure and simple, it is very likely that, but for the interest that *Norica* stirred up in him, there would have been no sketch of Augsburg in *The Cloister and the Hearth* at all.

One may perhaps wonder why Reade selected Augsburg for Gerard to visit instead of Nuremberg or some other German city which was not too far distant from Italy. Though inspired by *Norica*, he was unwilling, very likely, to be too close to another modern book, as he would have been if he had chosen Nuremberg. Moreover, Augsburg was a great medieval city. Moryson visited the place and, in comparing it and Nuremberg, is in doubt which to rank first.[106] Labarte, in his *Handbook of the Arts of the Middle Ages and Renaissance*, a work in the *Century* list, frequently puts the two on an equality.[107] Montaigne, finally, describes his visit to Augsburg and says it is "considered the finest town in Germany."[108] In a word, then, with the possible exception of Nuremberg, Augsburg would be the most likely German city to be visited and warmly praised by Gerard.

When Gerard arrived at Augsburg the gates were closed, but he was enabled to gain ingress by means of "a famous postern called der Einlass." The detailed account of this he derived from Montaigne's *Journey*. The two accounts agree in mentioning the following steps for entering the city by this gate: two preliminary guards, an iron gate opened by machinery, a covered bridge, speaking to the porter the first time, his ringing of a bell, the consequent opening of other barriers, a dark hall, another gate, a lighted hall, a vessel into which to put the entry fee (two batzen for a horseman), and another door letting one out into the city.[109] Moryson, too, gives an account of this gate, but he is far less specific. There is no mention of the first two guards; no distinction of the various gates (only "divers gates" are spoken of); no mention of the bell-ringing, of the two halls, or of the two batzen. There is only one detail, indeed, which Reade appropriated from Moryson, the name of the gate, *der Einlass*.[110] When

---

[106] I, 36.   [107] (London, 1855), pp. 27, 38, 44.   [108] *Journey*, p. 52.

[109] Oxf., p. 398; Ev., pp. 401–2; Montaigne, pp. 60–61.

[110] I, 41. (Wheeler wrongly thinks Reade's whole description is from Moryson.)

once within the city Gerard stayed at an inn called The Three
Moors, a name coming, probably, from Les Trois Maures mentioned by Michel and Fournier.[111]

The next morning the wanderer started sight-seeing:

> According to my way of viewing towns to learn their compass and shape, I
> mounted the highest tower I could find, and setting my dial at my foot sur-
> veyed the beautiful city . . . . and I, now first seeing a great citie, did crow with
> delight, and like cock on his ladder, and at the tower foot was taken into custody
> for a spy; for whilst I watched the city the watchman had watched me. The
> burgomaster received me courteously, and heard my story; then rebuked he
> the officers.[112]

This episode is based on a hint taken by Reade from some general advice to any traveler given by Moryson.

> When he wil observe the scituation of any City, let him (if he may without
> jelousie of the Inhabitants,) first climbe one of the highest steeples, where having
> taken the generall scituation of the City, he shall better remember in order the
> particular things to be seene in the City. To which end, let him carry about him
> a Dyall, which may shew him the North, South, East, and West, which knowne,
> he shall lesse erre in the description of the City, and this he may observe pub-
> likely onely with his eyes, for avoiding of jelousie, and after, being retired into
> his Inne, may draw it in paper, if he thinke good.[113]

Gerard's method of getting a general idea of the city is exactly
that recommended by Moryson. Moreover, Reade has made en-
sue that very arousing of suspicion of which Moryson warns the
traveler to beware. Gerard's dial, or compass, also comes from
Moryson. It was mentioned once previously in the novel.[114]

From the tower Gerard beheld "churches tiled with copper
burnished like gold." This is probably from Montaigne's mention at Augsburg of a church "roofed with copper—and that is
not very uncommon here." Gerard was likewise impressed with
the windows "so clean and burnished as 'tis most resplendent and
rare." This, too, may come from Montaigne's saying German
windows shone brightly from being often polished.[115]

Gerard likewise praised Augsburg as "a kind mother to arts.

[111] I, 338.   [112] Oxf., p. 399; Ev., p. 402.

[113] III, 384. (Wheeler notes the occurrence of the dial but not the borrowing of
the rest of the episode.)

[114] Oxf., p. 118; Ev., p. 125.   [115] Pp. 62, 53.

Here they cut in wood and ivory, that 'tis like spider's work, and paint on glass."[116] This, I believe, is drawn from Labarte, who mentions the city often in his discussion of the fine arts. To be specific, he expatiates on sculpture in wood on page 27, referring to Augsburg; then, on pages 29–30 he takes up ivory-carving, touching on the same city; still later—on pages 64–77—he discusses the painting of glass windows, but with scarcely any mention of individual German cities.

In his account of Augsburg, Gerard inserts the following remark:

> Each mechanic wears a sword. The very weavers at the loom sit girded with their weapons, and all Germans on too slight occasion draw them [weapons] and fight; but no treachery; challenge first, then draw, and with the edge only, mostly the face, not with Sir Point; for if in these combats one thrust at his adversary and hurt him, 'tis called ein schelmstück, a heinous act, both men and women turn their backs on him; and even the judges punish thrusts bitterly, but pass over cuts. Hence in Germany be good store of scarred faces.[117]

The first part of this is from Montaigne, who says, "In Germany I noticed that everybody wears a sword at his side, even workmen." The latter part is from Moryson:

> The Germans are apt to quarrell, and sometimes they fight after their fashion, which is a slash or two with the edge of a sword . . . . but to stab or make a thrust is vulgarly called ein schelemstücke, that is, the act of a villaine, and the very judges esteeme it a most abominable act.[118]

Reade's touch about the many scarred faces may, conceivably, come from his having heard about this state of affairs in Germany as the result of modern student duels.

Gerard again says of Augsburg: "Fountains in every street that play to heaven, and in the gardens seeming trees, which being approached, one standing afar touches a spring, and every twig shoots water, and souses the guests to their host's much delectation." The source of this is Montaigne, who says the town is "quite peopled with fountains" and who describes two contriv-

---

[116] Oxf., p. 399; Ev., p. 402.

[117] Oxf., p. 399; Ev., p. 403.

[118] Montaigne, p. 94; Moryson, III, 403. (The Moryson passage is noted by Wheeler.)

ances in gardens which may be turned on to drench unsuspecting guests.[119]

Another interesting mechanism is adroitly described by Gerard:

These cunning Germans do set in the chimney a little windmill, and the smoke struggling to wend past, turns it, and from the mill a wire runs through the wall and turns the spit on wheels; beholding which I doffed my bonnet to the men of Augsburg, for who but these had ere devised to bind ye so dark and subtle a knave as Sir Smoke, and set him to roast Dame Pullet?

This is occasioned by Montaigne's mention that in Germany spits are often "turned by a sort of sail of pinewood, broad and light, which they place in the funnel of their chimneys, and which revolve very rapidly in the draught of the smoke and the steam of the fire."[120]

Now Gerard related how he went to the house of a senator. One of the other guests was "one Veit Stoss, a wood-carver," who may have been introduced by Reade because of a long account of him in *Norica*.[121] At the senator's house the party centered about

his stupendous wine-vessel. It is ribbed like a ship, and hath been eighteen months in hand, and finished but now, and holds a hundred and fifty hogsheads, and standeth not, but lieth; yet even so ye get not on his back withouten ladders two, of thirty steps. And we sat about the miraculous mass, and drank Rhenish from it, drawn by a little artificial pump, and the lasses pinned their crantzes to it, and we danced round it, and the senator danced on its back, but with drinking of so many garausses, lost his footing and fell off, glass in hand, and broke an arm and a leg in the midst of us. So scurvily ended our drinking bout for this time.[122]

There are several borrowings in this picturesque episode. The crantzes of the girls, prettily introduced here, come, as we have already seen, from Moryson. From another passage in the same author are taken the numerous *garausses*.[123] Furthermore, the custom of having huge wine vessels is likewise from Moryson: "The very Princes strive . . . . who shall have the hugest and

[119] Oxf., p. 400; Ev., p. 403; Montaigne, pp. 55–56, 58.

[120] Oxf., p. 400; Ev., p. 403; Montaigne, p. 23.

[121] Pp. 227–46.

[122] Oxf., p. 401; Ev., p. 404.   [123] IV, 36. (Noted by Wheeler.)

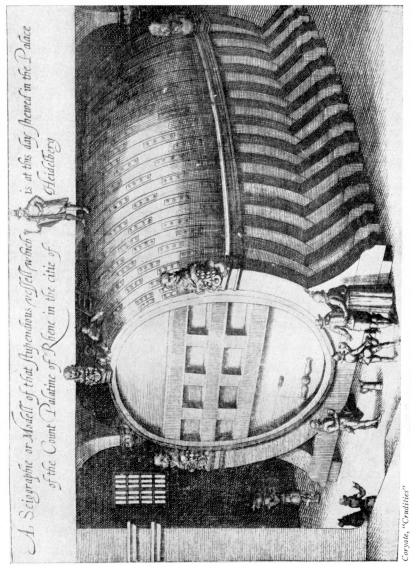

A Scigraphe or Modell of that stupendous vessell which is at this day shewed in the Palace of the Count Palatine of Rhene in the citie of Heidelberg

THE GREAT TUN AT HEIDELBERG

most capable vessels in his Cellar. Some of these vessels containe more then a thousand measures, each of seventy Cans or Pots, and are ascended by twenty or thirty staires."[124] It will be noted that the immense cask in *The Cloister and the Hearth* was climbed by means of "thirty steps"—the very same number. Finally, the most important borrowing is from Coryate, for the whole description of Reade's wine vessel and the episode connected with it are all taken from Coryate's description of the Great Tun at Heidelberg and his illustration thereof. The illustration is reproduced in this volume. Coryate's description runs as follows, the italicizing being mine:

For it is the most remarkable and famous thing of that kinde that I saw in my whole journey, yea so memorable a matter, that I thinke there was never the like fabrick . . . . in all the world, and I doubt whether posterity will ever frame so monstrously strange a thing. . . . . For thy better satisfaction I have inserted a true figure thereof in this place (though but in a small forme). . . . . Also I have added an *imaginary kinde of representation of my selfe upon the toppe of the same, in that manner as I stood there with a cup of Rhenish wine in my hand.* . . . . It was begunne in the year 1589, and ended 1591 [Reade's cask took eighteen months to make]. . . . . Moreover thou must consider that this vessel is not compacted of boords as other barrels are, but of solid great beames [cf. Reade's "ribbed like a ship"]. . . . . When the Cellerer draweth wine out of the vessel, he ascendeth *two severall degrees* of wooden staires [Reade's "ladders two"] . . . . and *so goeth up to the toppe.* About the middle whereof there is a bung-hole or a venting orifice into the which he conveigheth a *pretty instrument of some foote and halfe long, made in the forme of a spout,* wherewith he draweth up the wine. . . . . A Gentleman of the Court accompanied me to the toppe together with one of the Cellerers, and exhilarated me with two sound *draughts of Rhenish wine.* For that is the wine it containeth . . . . I advise thee (I say) if thou dost happen to ascend to the toppe thereof to the end to tast of the wine, that in any case thou dost drinke moderately, and not so much as the sociable Germans will persuade thee unto. For if thou shouldest chance to over-swill thy selfe with wine, peradventure such a giddinesse will benumme thy braine, that *thou wilt scarce finde the direct way downe from the steepe ladder without a very dangerous precipitation.*[125]

Reade has condensed his description from Coryate's account and picture and has imagined the senator's performance from hints in the earlier writer. However, the novelist has reduced the capacity from Coryate's 528 hogsheads to only 150.

[124] IV, 35. (Not noted by Wheeler.)

[125] II, 218–21, and plate opposite 224. (Neither is noted by Wheeler.)

Apropos of the printing of Augsburg, Gerard quotes, "Imprimit una dies quantum non scribitur anno." Coryate quotes this "old verse," but with the reading *vix* instead of *non*.[126] Perhaps Reade, mindful of the increasing speed of modern, compared with Renaissance, presses, changed the wording to make it more up to date.

Then Gerard, leaving his beloved Augsburg,[127] journeyed into Italy.

[126] II, 278. (Noted by Wheeler.)

[127] I have tried, in vain, to find specific borrowings about Augsburg from Münster's *Cosmographia*. Münster discusses the city, especially its political and ecclesiastical history, for twelve pages (600–612 in the Latin edition of 1554 printed in Basel).

Chapter Six

THE ITALIAN JOURNEY

THE long letter of Gerard to Margaret, which she read to his family, continued with his experiences in Italy. After leaving Augsburg he became separated from the merchants with whom he was traveling and had a thrilling adventure in a windmill. As far as mere excitement is concerned, this has always seemed to me superior to any other scene in the novel, except the attempted murder of Gerard and Denys in the Burgundian inn.

Reade drew the idea of this experience from a quotation in Michel and Fournier, which in turn came from an account of the life of the bandit Fetzer, written by himself. The robber narrates that he was imprisoned in an old mill situated on the ramparts of a town. He and his companion, wishing to escape, made their way to the very top of the structure:

The idea came to me that the old sails of the mill would be useful to us if we could lay hold of them without being perceived; we actually pulled two of them to us. With the first, I said to myself, we shall be able to slip down to the gallery that surrounds the tower at the height of the mill-stone and, with the second, get down to earth. No sooner said than done: the sail was attached, after a fashion, to the balcony where we were, and seizing the canvas firmly in my arms, I began to descend. Unfortunately, the wind blew like the devil, and a gust which burst forth dashed me so violently against that cursed wall that all my bones cracked. Blinded by the folds of the sail, stunned by the bruises, I no longer knew where I was or what I was doing. Had I reached the gallery? had I passed it? My strength failed; my fingers grew weak and let go; I fell.[1]

Thus, having reached the ground, the two men escaped in spite of the alarm given by a sentinel.

The account, though brief, is striking. Indeed, Michel and Fournier, remark of Fetzer: "A splendid novel could be made out of the story of his life." Reade, too, was certainly the man to

[1] *Le Livre d'or des métiers*, II, 175.

121

appreciate any possible thrills that presented themselves. He took the suggestion here, I think unquestionably, and fashioned from it the story of Gerard's escape from the top of the windmill by riding upon the revolving sails. Of course this is not the method of Fetzer. Instead the bandit took two old sails no longer on the arms of the mill, and, after fastening them to the structure, climbed down as if by a rope. The reader, however, may easily misinterpret the passage on the first reading—at least English-speaking people may misinterpret the passage in the original French—and gain the idea that the sails were still on the arms of the mill and that Fetzer made his way downward by riding on them as they revolved. I must confess that I made this error myself and, of four friends to whom I showed the extract—three Americans and one Frenchman—all the Americans, on the first reading, got the same conception. It is not unreasonable, then, to suppose that Reade, on first perusing the excerpt, made the same mistake, or at least had this mode of descent suggested to his imaginative mind. If this is so—and it appears a most natural way of explaining this unusual adventure—we have the central and most original touch in the whole episode.

Reade, as usual, has built out the whole suggestion with the most vivid invention and suspense.[2] Gerard managed to get separated from his associates and thought he was lost. He came to an old mill surrounded, the careful Reade tells us, with barrels of spirits and a haystack. Discovering no one within, he lay down to sleep there. Eventually he awoke and found himself in the midst of evil-looking men. He made his excuses in Italian, to which they replied with ominous grins. Since the mill door was now bolted, he asked to spend the night and was taken to a room far aloft, occupied by one truckle bed clamped to the floor. To obtain as much protection as possible in this menacing situation he left the couch and lay down against the door in order to obstruct entrance. After a time the bed vanished into a yawning well. Knowing the assassins would come up when they found he had not been killed, Gerard began to weave a rope of straw, but, realizing he had but little time, he looked out of the window.

[2] Oxf., pp. 402–7; Ev., pp. 404–10.

There, slowly revolving, were the sails of the mill. He lowered himself by the short straw rope, caught at a sail, and gradually traveled downward until he was catapulted off onto the grass beneath. Now he heard the assassins running upstairs in the mill, and, since an injured leg kept him from fleeing, he heaped straw, drenched in spirits, against the door and set it on fire. The flame soared aloft and, when the villains opened the door to come out, the fire rushed in and destroyed the building. All the miscreants were burned except one, who, after fighting with Gerard, ran away on the approach of the latter's companions.

One element in this happening—the rope of straw—seems to be taken from the escape of another bandit from prison by this means. The account is in Michel and Fournier, only two pages away from the Fetzer anecdote.[3] It is possible, too, that the falling-away of the bed is suggested by Lacroix and Seré's speaking of the "*oubliette*, a sort of well where were placed prisoners condemned to die of starvation or where they were killed by being precipitated from an elevated place, the floor of which fell away under their feet."[4]

When Gerard reached Lombardy, he was delighted with its loveliness and described its beauty for half a page.[5] These details Reade derives from several passages in Thomas Coryate that are near together. Coryate, too, was extremely enthusiastic, dubbing the land "the very Paradise, and Canaan of Christendome," whereof the equivalent in Reade is "a land flowing with milk and honey." Coryate continues (the italicizing is mine): "It is wholly *plaine*, and beautified with such abundance of *goodly rivers*, pleasant *meadowes*, fruitfull vineyardes, fat pastures, *delectable gardens, orchards*, woodes, and what not, that the first view thereof did even refocillate my spirits, and tickle my senses with inward joy."[6] In Reade this becomes "all sloping *plains, goodly rivers*, jocund *meadows, delectable orchards*, and blooming *gardens*."

[3] II, 177.

[4] *Le Moyen Age et la Renaissance*, V, "Architecture militaire," xvi. Reade borrowed extensively from this division of Lacroix and Seré.

[5] Oxf., p. 409; Ev., pp. 412–13.

[6] *Crudities*, I, 238. (Wheeler says the description of Lombardy is "taken largely from Coryate.")

The "draught oxen" with "white linen on their necks," in the English novel, come from Coryate (the purpose of the linen being to keep off flies),[7] and "the folk, especially women, wear delicate strawen hats with flowers and leaves fairly imitated in silk, with silver mixed" is boiled down from a longer passage in Coryate:

I observed most delicate strawen hats, which both men and women use in most places of that Province [Piedmont], but especially the women. For those that the women weare are very prety, some of them having at the least an hundred seames made with silke, and some pretily woven in the seames with silver, and many flowers, borders, and branches very curiously wrought in them.[8]

Again a passage in the novel running "This day we crossed a river prettily in a chained ferry-boat. On either bank was a windlass, and a single man by turning of it drew one whole company to his shore" is condensed from Coryate's corresponding description:

This Italian transporting was done after a pretty manner. For whereas there is a great long rope that reacheth over the river, tied by certaine instruments on both sides thereof, assoone as the horses and passengers are put into the boat, one of the boatmen that tarryeth on land turned a certaine wheele about by meanes of that rope, by the motion of which wheele the boat is driven on to the other banke.[9]

Finally, Reade's "young wench" "dreading the evil eye," when looked at by an old woman, may come from Lacroix and Seré's saying that this fear was widespread in medieval Italy.[10]

Gerard reached Venice safely. In his account he spoke of "this sea-enthroned and peerless citie, in shape a bow"; the last expression comes from Coryate's words applied to the bar or bank protecting Venice from the sea—"crooked in forme of a bow."[11] Moreover, Gerard wrote of "that market-place of nations, orbis, non urbis, forum, St. Mark his place." Coryate, who was much struck with this famous square and the possibility of hearing there "all the languages of Christendome," says "a man may very properly call it rather Orbis then Urbis forum."[12]

---

[7] *Ibid.*, p. 240.   [9] *Ibid.*, p. 233.

[8] *Ibid.*, p. 228.   [10] IV, "Sciences occultes," xxii–xxiii.

[11] Oxf., p. 409; Ev., p. 413; Coryate, I, 304. (Not noted by Wheeler.)

[12] Oxf., p. 409; Ev., p. 413; Coryate, I, 314. (Not noted by Wheeler.)

Instead of being able to visit the sights of Venice immediately, Gerard was confined to his chamber by his injured leg. He amused himself during this period by listing the national traits of the three foreign nations he had encountered: the Germans, the French, and the Italians. He came to the conclusion that "each nation hath its proper wisdom, and its proper folly; and, methinks, could a great king, or duke, tramp like me, and see with his own eyes, he might pick the flowers, and eschew the weeds of nations, and go home and set his own folk on Wisdom's hill."[13] This view is Charles Reade's own. In fact, in one of his notebooks we find this suggestion for a new science:

Each nation has its wisdom and its folly, and is wiser than other nations in some points, sillier in others. Clings to them equally. Could one man by the industry of a single life compile the strong and weak points of the several nations in one view he would be "the Father of all Statesmen." Yankee phrase.[14]

The four or five meaty pages written by Gerard on the three aforementioned nationalities constitute such a study on a small scale.

First for the Germans. Gerard considered their too free use of liquor their chief failing, and Reade, in his remarks on the subject,[15] draws from Moryson. Let us examine the borrowings in detail. Moryson says: "And to say truth, the Germans are in high excesse subject to this vice of drinking, scarce noted with any other nationall vice."[16] Reade condenses this to "Their general blot is drunkenness." The Germans, continues Moryson, compel a stranger to drink, crying, "Kanstunight sauffen und fressen, so kanstu keinem hern wol dienen,"[17] an expression taken over by the novelist. Reade's next remark about the melancholy drinking and *Seyt frölich* are from Moryson,[18] as has been noted previously. Moryson now observes:

When they are extraordinarily merry, they use a kind of garaussing, called kurlemurlebuff, wherein they use certaine touches of the glasse, the beard,

13 Oxf., pp. 409–10; Ev., p. 413.
14 E. G. Sutcliffe, "Charles Reade's Notebooks," *Studies in Philology*, XXVII, 77.
15 The varied remarks on German drinking are Oxf., p. 410; Ev., pp. 413–14.
16 *An Itinerary Containing His Ten Yeeres Travell through the Twelve Dominions*, IV, 34. (Not noted by Wheeler.)
17 *Ibid.*, p. 35. (Noted by Wheeler.)   18 *Ibid.*, p. 37. (Noted by Wheeler.)

some parts of the body, and of the Table, together with certaine whistlings, and phillippings of the fingers, with like rules, so curiously disposed in order, as it is a labour of Hercules to observe them.[19]

Reade borrows this with but slight changes:

The best of their drunken sport is "Kurlemurlehuff," a way of drinking with touching deftly of the glass, the beard, the table, in due turn, intermixed with whistlings and snappings of the finger so curiously ordered as 'tis a labour of Hercules, but to the beholder right pleasant and mirthful.

Next Reade goes on:

Their topers, by advice of German leeches, sleep with pebbles in their mouths. For, as of a boiling pot the lid must be set ajar, so with these fleshly wine-pots, to vent the heat of their inward parts: spite of which many die suddenly from drink; but 'tis a matter of religion to slur it, and gloze it, and charge some innocent disease therewith.

The first part of this is much boiled down from Moryson; a comparison of the two, in fact, exemplifies how much more efficient is modern than Elizabethan prose style:

Many of the Germans going to sleepe, doe by the advice of the Physitian, put little stones into their mouthes, to keepe them open: for as a boyling pot better seethes the meat if the fier be covered, so the fier be moderate: but if it be extraordinarilie great and hot, the potlid must be taken off, lest it boyle over; so it is good to helpe a mans concoction if he sleepe with his mouth shut, so his diet be sparing or moderate: but in such excesse as the Germans use, not onely the mouth, but (if it might be) the very brest is to bee opened, that the heate of the inward parts may have vent.[20]

The second part of Reade's sentence is drawn from an earlier remark of Moryson's: "A Physician, a familiar friend of mine, tolde mee that many Germans dying suddenly upon excesse of drinking, were ordinarily (for hiding of the shame) given out to die of the falling sickenesse."[21]

Reade proceeds: "Their women come among the tipplers, and do but stand a moment, and, as it were, kiss the wine-cup; and are indeed most temperate in eating and drinking, and, of all women, modest and virtuous." This is from two adjacent sen-

---

[19] *Ibid.*, p. 38. (Noted by Wheeler.)

[20] *Ibid.*, p. 39. (Not noted by Wheeler.)

[21] *Ibid.*, p. 37. (Not noted by Wheeler.)

tences of Moryson, except that Reade puts first the subject matter of Moryson's second sentence:

Onely the Weomen of Germany are most temperate in eating and drinking,
and of all I did ever see, most modest in all kinds of vertue . . . . [except the
women of Bohemia, a point borrowed by Reade for a much later passage in his
novel]. The Weomen of Germany have a custome to helpe their Husbands or
Friends, by sipping of the cup. . . . .[22]

This leads to Gerard's remarking that Dutch women were much
inferior, proposing to the men and bullying them when married;
he cited an example of a Dutchman's having to get his wife's
permission to go out—the result, Catherine remarked, "of a
woman wedding a boy." This comes from Moryson's saying
that, in Holland, women outnumbered men and were likely thus
to marry husbands younger than they and bully them.[23] He cites
the same example of the husband asking to go out, but Reade invents, from the preponderance of women, their habit of proposing.

Gerard continued, "In the south where wine is, the gentry
drink themselves bare; but not in the north: for with beer a noble
shall sooner burst his body than melt his lands." This is taken
from Moryson's two remarks on the same page, that in Upper
Germany (i.e., the south) wine is usually drunk; in Lower Germany, beer.[24] Gerard now continued: "They are quarrelsome,
but 'tis the liquor, not the mind; for they are none revengeful.
And when they have made a bad bargain drunk, they stand to it
sober." Moryson again, in two passages, is the source: (1) "For
many quarrelling in drink are killed," and (2) their habit of
drinking during business but confirming the decisions when
sober.[25]

Next for the French, though I have not found the source of
so many points as for the Germans. Gerard pronounces them
"moderate in drinking, and mix water with their wine, and sing
and dance over their cups, and are then enchanting company."

[22] *Ibid.*, p. 41. (Not noted by Wheeler.)
[23] *Ibid.*, pp. 468–69. (Noted by Wheeler.)
[24] *Ibid.*, p. 36. (Not noted by Wheeler.)
[25] *Ibid.*, pp. 37, 39. (Neither is noted by Wheeler.)

The source is Moryson: "Drunkennesse is reprochfull among the French, and the greater part drinke water mingled with wine. .... [Yet some drink too much.] When these kinds of men sit at drinking, they use much mirth and singing .... as the French in generall are by nature chearefull and lively."[26]

"They often hang their female malefactors," Gerard continues, "instead of drowning them decently, as other nations use."[27] The source of this is the very article in *Archaeologia* from which Reade took the drowning of a woman witnessed by Gerard and Cul de Jatte. The article observes:

Modern refinement, which regards with disgust the coarseness and brutality of past ages, will scarcely allow that our ancestors were actuated by feelings of delicacy in condemning women to be drowned instead of being hung as men; but such appears to have been the fact. It is probably to be ascribed to that reverence for the female sex which was a characteristic of the Teutonic race.

On the same page, and continuing on the next page, the article goes on to record the hanging of one woman at Limoges in 1414 and of another in Paris in the reign of Charles VII.[28] The two instances provide the fact that the French often hanged women, and the quotation produces Gerard's repugnance.

Again, Gerard's statement, "The furniture in their [French] inns is walnut, in Germany only deal," is from Montaigne's remark in speaking of furniture, that "our [French] walnut is much superior to their [German] pine." Moreover, Reade says, "French windows are ill. The lower half is of wood, and opens; the upper half is of glass, but fixed; so that the servant cannot come at it to clean it. The German windows are all glass, and movable, and shine far and near like diamonds." This, too—at least in part—is from Montaigne: "What makes their [German] window-panes shine so brightly is that they have no fixed windows in our fashion, and that their frames can be taken out when they please, and they furbish the glasswork very often."[29]

Gerard makes the observation about France: "At many inns they show the traveller his sheets to give him assurance they are

---

[26] Oxf., p. 411; Ev., pp. 414–15; Moryson, IV, 142. (Not noted by Wheeler.)
[27] Oxf., p. 411; Ev., p. 415.   [28] XXXVIII, Part I, 54–55.
[29] *The Diary of Montaigne's Journey*, p. 53 (for both furniture and windows).

clean, and warm them at the fire before him." Moryson makes this remark thrice. Gerard again says that "in France worshipful men wear their hats and their furs indoors, and go abroad lighter clad," whereas the exact opposite occurs in Germany. This comparison, taken from Montaigne's *Journey*, was used once before in our novel in the description of the hostelry of the *mijaurée*.[30]

Discussing both French and Germans for a few paragraphs, Gerard remarks, "In Germany the snails be red," an appropriation from Coryate.[31] Another saying in the next paragraph, "In Germany the petty laws are wondrous wise and just. Those against criminals, bloody," may come from Moryson's "Yet I must needs confess, that the Germans are generally most severe in Justice. . . . . In criminall offences they never have any pardons from Court."[32]

Finally, Gerard takes up the Italians. "They judge a man, not by his habits, but his speech and gesture. Here Sir Chough may by no means pass for falcon gentle, as did I in Germany, pranked in my noble servant's feathers."[33] This point is drawn from Moryson's remark that the Italians "respect nothing lesse then [i.e., than] the apparrell and outward habit," and from his saying elsewhere that "The Germans in great part measure a strangers dignity by the richnesse of his apparrell."[34] Reade combines the two in felicitous wise. Next Gerard proceeds concerning the Italians: "Wisest of all nations in their singular temperance of food and drink. Most foolish of all to search strangers coming into their borders, and stay them from bringing much money in."[35] The first sentence of this is Moryson's "in truth the Italians dyet is so sparing," and the second Coryate's report of this nation's searching travelers to be sure they do not carry too much money.[36]

---

[30] Oxf., p. 411; Ev., p. 415; sheets: Moryson, III, 478; IV, 140, 141 (the first is noted by Wheeler); hats and furs: Montaigne, p. 31.

[31] Oxf., p. 412; Ev., p. 415; Coryate, II, 204. (Noted by Wheeler.)

[32] IV, 287–88. (Not noted by Wheeler.)   [33] Oxf., p. 412; Ev., p. 416.

[34] III, 398; IV, 209. (Neither is noted by Wheeler.)

[35] Oxf., pp. 412–13; Ev., p. 416.

[36] Moryson, IV, 96; Coryate, I, 227. (Wheeler notes the second but not the first.)

Reade's saying that the Venetian women turn their hair yellow "by the sun and art" is from Moryson.[37] The novelist's statement, "Ye enter no Italian town without a bill of health, though now is no plague in Europe," may be from Moryson, Coryate, or Montaigne, all of whom speak of this custom, Coryate, in fact, uses the words "bill of health" just as Reade does.[38] *The Cloister and the Hearth* continues about Italy: "The innkeepers cringe and fawn, and cheat, and, in country places, murder you. Yet will they give you clean sheets by paying therefor." This is from Moryson: "The Italian Hosts are notable in fawning [Reade's word] and crouching for gaine." Details follow about their extortion and the means of avoiding it. Moreover, Moryson recommends the traveler "to goe to the best Inne and of most fame, that he may be more safe from the losse of his money or hazard of his life"—Reade's "murder you." The voyager must not expect feather beds, continues the Elizabethan, "onely he shal have cleane sheetes, at least if he curiously demand them."[39] Gerard's disapproving mention of "a little bifurcal dagger to hold the meat, while his knife cutteth it" may be from either Coryate or Moryson.[40]

The ointment for the itch—with the Italian expression *unguento per la rogna*—is from Moryson, but Reade dexterously invents the "urchin," who sold it "to three several dames in silken trains, and to two velvet knights."[41] Gerard goes on: "Their bread is lovely white. Their meats they spoil with sprinkling cheese over them." The first of these facts is from Moryson's "the very Porters feede on most pure white bread";[42] the second from Coryate's "a custome . . . . which did not a little dis-

[37] All the points in this paragraph from Reade's novel occur Oxf., p. 413; Ev., p. 416; Moryson, IV, 220. (Noted by Wheeler.)

[38] Moryson, I, 145, 158; II, 75; Coryate, I, 214 (the Coryate passage is noted by Wheeler); Montaigne (trans.), p. 86, 100, 173.

[39] Moryson, clean sheets: IV, 100–102; III, 474. (None of these noted by Wheeler.)

[40] Coryate, I, 236; Moryson, I, 448; IV, 98, 99. (Noted by Wheeler.) Southey (*Common-Place Book* [1st ser.], p. 144) quotes the Coryate passage.

[41] Moryson, IV, 101–2. (Noted by Wheeler.)

[42] IV, 96. (Not noted by Wheeler.)

please me, that most of their best meats which come to the table are sprinkled with cheese, which I love not so well as the Welchmen doe."[43] Thereafter, Gerard praises the Italians for making "roses and gilliflowers" blossom out of season and describes the method. All this, including the roses and gillyflowers and the cows from whom the practice was derived, is borrowed from Moryson, but Reade, as usual, greatly condenses the passage.[44]

Gerard next declares, "Women have sat in the doctors' chairs at their colleges." This fact is drawn from a volume entitled *Italy*, by Antonio Gallenga, writing under the pseudonym L. Mariotti. The book does not occur in the *Century* list, but there is a reference to this part of it in one of the Reade notebooks owned by Mr. Parrish. Gallenga writes, apropos of a law professor at Bologna (the italics are mine):

> His daughter, Novella, who, in the prime of her age, was so far proficient in such arid studies as to fill the professor's *chair* during her father's absence, and deliver her lectures; taking, however, good care to screen her lovely face behind a curtain, 'lest her beauty should turn those young heads she was appointed to edify and enlighten.' It is, however, but justice to remark, that the story is equally applied to one of Accursius' daughters [a medieval Italian authority on law], and that the names of other ladies occur among the list of *doctors* at Bologna.[45]

Gerard next bursts out, "Italy too, for artful fountains and figures that move by water and enact life." This statement is taken from one of two possible sources, or perhaps from both. Much the more probable of the two is Montaigne. This writer had a real passion for fountains, as we have already seen in his account of Augsburg (in fact, in the present passage Gerard declares that this German city is second, in this respect, only to Italy). Thus in a half-dozen passages he describes the fountains of Italy in detail, and some three of these are fountains where animals move by water or squirt.[46] Reade's second possible

[43] I, 236. (Noted by Wheeler.)

[44] Oxf., pp. 413–14; Ev., p. 417; Moryson, IV, 87. (Noted by Wheeler.)

[45] Oxf,. p. 414; Ev., p. 417; Antonio Gallenga, *Italy* (2 vols.; London, 1841), I, 225–26.

[46] Montaigne, *Journey*, animal fountains: pp. 106, 112–13, 164–66 (this is the fountain spoken of in Wanley); others: pp. 107, 111, 270.

source, though less likely, is the following paragraph in Wanley's *Wonders of the Little World:*

> At Tibur or Tivoli near Rome, in the Gardens of Hippolitus d'Este, Cardinal of Ferrara, there are the Representations of sundry Birds, sitting on the tops of Trees, which by Hydraulick Art, and secret conveyances of water through the trunks and branches of the trees, are made to sing and clap their wings; but at the sudden appearance of an Owl out of a Bush of the same Artifice, they immediately become all mute and silent.[47]

Being on the subject of fountains, Gerard, with his usual love of information, goes on, after another reference to the smoke-turned spits of Augsburg, to give some more facts (the italics are mine):

> Two towns there be in Europe, which, scorning giddy fountains, bring water tame in *pipes* to every burgher's door, and he filleth his *vessels* with but turning of a *cock*. One is London, so watered this many a year by pipes of a league from Paddington, a neighboring city; and the other is the fair town of Lubeck. Also the fierce English are reported to me wise in that they will not share their land and flocks with wolves; but have fairly driven those marauders into their mountains.[48]

Moryson declares of Lübeck: "Water is brought to every Citizens house by *pipes*, and all the Brewers dwelling in one street have each of them his iron *Cock*, which being turned, the water fals into their *vessels*." And once more about Lübeck: "Without Millen Port there is a Conduit of water, which serves all the Towne, the more notable because it was the first of that kinde, *which since hath beene dispersed to London* and other places."[49] Moryson's remark about London made Reade, proud of the city where he lived, bring it in. He may have added "the pipes of a league from Paddington, a neighboring city" from John Stow's *Survey of London* (a book mentioned in one of Mr. Parrish's Reade notebooks). Stow tells of introducing a water supply into London in the reign of Henry III "by pipes of lead": "The water-course from Padington to Iameshed hath 510.rods; from Iameshed on

---

[47] P. 228. The same paragraph occurs also in William Turner, *A Compleat History of the Most Remarkable Providences* (London, 1697; a volume mentioned in Mr. Parrish's Reade notebooks), Part III, chap. xv.

[48] Oxf., p. 414; Ev., pp. 417–18.

[49] I, 7, 8. (Wheeler notes the first passage but not the second.)

the hill, to the Mewsgate, 102.rods; from the Mewsgate to the Crosse in Cheape, 484.rods."[50] These three figures added together make a little over three miles, Reade's "league." The last part of the excerpt quoted from Reade is based on Moryson again: "I formerly said, that the Wolves were altogether destroied in England and Wales, so as the Sheepe feede freely in the fields and Mountaines."[51]

Gerard now observes of the Italians: "Their name for a cowardly assassin is 'a brave man,' and for an harlot, 'a courteous person,' which is as much as to say that a woman's worst vice, and a man's worst vice, are virtues. But I pray God for little Holland that there an assassin may be yclept an assassin, and an harlot an harlot, till domesday." This is taken from Coryate, "There are certaine desperate and resolute villaines in Venice, called Braves,"[52] and "The woman that professeth this trade is called in the Italian tongue Cortezana, which word is derived from the Italian word cortesia that signifieth courtesie."[53] The moralizing comment added by Reade is particularly suited to Gerard's character.

Gerard was soon able to visit the sights of Venice in a litter. With his usual zeal for travel, he inspected everything eagerly and then passed on two or three pages crammed with facts, to Margaret. The sources from which Reade drew are Moryson and Coryate, intermingled. Gerard begins with a few remarks about the exterior of St. Mark's Church (the italics are mine):

Outside it, towards the *market-place*, is a noble *gallery*, and *above* it *four* famous *horses*, cut in *brass* by the ancient Romans, and seem all moving, and *at the very next step must needs leap down* on the beholder. About the church are *six hundred pillars of marble*, porphyry, and *ophites*.[54]

These facts are taken from Moryson:

And in all places about the Church, there be some *six hundred pillars of marble*. . . . . Above these pillars on the outside of the Church is an open *gallery*, borne up with like pillars. . . . . And *above* this *gallery*, and over the great doore of the

---

[50] (London, 1633), p. 11.

[51] IV, 169. (Not noted by Wheeler.)

[52] I, 413. (Not noted by Wheeler.)

[53] I, 402. (Noted by Wheeler.)

[54] Oxf., pp. 414–15; Ev., p. 418.

Church, be *foure horses of brasse*, guilded over, very notable for antiquity and beauty; and they are so set, *as if at the first step they would leape into the market-place.*[55]

Moryson then tells how the *Romans* made these statues. A little later, too, he says of the porch, "And there be erected foure great pillars of *Ophites.*"[56]

The next thing described in *The Cloister and the Hearth* is the treasure of St. Marks'.[57] The first part of this is from Coryate; the middle part from Moryson; and a touch at the end from Coryate again. Gerard begins, "Inside is a treasure greater than either at St. Denys, or Loretto, or Toledo." Coryate runs, at much greater length: "For this treasure is of that inestimable value, that it is thought no treasure whatsoever in any one place of Christendome may compare with it, neyther that of St. Denis in France, which I have before described, nor St. Peters in Rome, nor that of Madona de Loretto in Italy, nor that of Toledo in Spaine. . . . ."[58] Reade now continues: "here a jewelled pitcher given the seigniory by a Persian king." Coryate: "a certaine Pitcher adorned with great variety of pretious stones, which Usumcassanes King of Persia bestowed upon the Signiory." Reade once more: "also the ducal cap blazing with jewels, and on its crown a diamond and a chrysolite, each as big as an almond: two golden crowns and twelve golden stomachers studded with jewels, from Constantinople; item, a monstrous sapphire; item, a great diamond given by the French king." These now are drawn from Moryson:

I saw the Ducall Cap . . . . being of inestimable value, for the multitude and price of the Jewels, especially of a diamond upon the crowne of the Cap, and a chrysolite set in the midst. [Reade adds "each as big as an almond" for vividness.] I saw two crownes of Kings with twelve stomachers of pure gold set with rich jewels (which the Noblewomen wore at Constantinople before the Turkes

[55] I, 166. (Not noted by Wheeler.) Coryate has some description of the horses of St. Mark (I, 348–49), but Moryson is much closer to Reade.

[56] I, 168. (Not noted by Wheeler.)

[57] Oxf., p. 415; Ev., p. 418.

[58] All the Coryate borrowings about the treasury are in I, 356. (None are noted by Wheeler.)

tooke it) and twelve other Crownes all of pure massy gold [omitted by Reade to avoid monotony] . . . . I saw a saphyre of extraordinary bignes, and a Diamond which the French King Henry the third gave to this state.[59]

Reade concludes by mentioning "item, a prodigious carbuncle; item, three unicorns' horns." Of these, the former is from Coryate's mention of "an exceeding great Carbuncle"; on the other hand, the three unicorns' horns, which one might perhaps call the most attractive exhibit, were spoken of by both the Elizabethan travelers.

Gerard now turns to a description of the sacred objects in the church, the chief being St. Mark's body.[60] Again the passage is a mosaic of borrowings from Moryson and Coryate, who together, as in the case of the treasury, account for all the circumstances in Reade.

"I stood and saw the brazen chest that holds the body of St. Mark the Evangelist," says Gerard. "I saw with these eyes, and handled, his ring and his gospel written with his own hand, and all my travels seemed light." These points come from Moryson: "When you enter the body of the Church, there is the great Altar, under which lies Saint Marke, in a chest of brasse,"[61] and, in a later place, "the ring of Saint Marke, and his Gospell written with his owne hand,"[62] These last two objects occur in Moryson's long list of relics from which Reade borrows afterward. The novelist separates them from the rest, it appears, partly to break up the lengthy enumeration but more because, being related to St. Mark, they should be mentioned, he feels, next the saint's body. Gerard now proceeds:

Dear Margaret, his sacred body was first brought from Alexandria by merchants in 810, and then not prized as now; for between 829, when this church was builded, and 1094, the very place where it lay was forgotten. Then holy priests fasted and prayed many days seeking for light, and lo the Evangelist's body brake at midnight through the marble and stood before them.

[59] The Moryson borrowings about the Treasury are from I, 171–72. (Noted by Wheeler.)

[60] The description of the sacred objects is Oxf., p. 415; Ev., pp. 418–19.

[61] I, 168. (Not noted by Wheeler.)

[62] I, 172. (These borrowings from Moryson are not noted by Wheeler.)

Gerard enlarges upon the episode to secure vividness and adds that he saw the "crevice" through which the body had burst. The first part of this passage is from Coryate's reference to "the body of S. Marke the Evangelist and Patron of Venice, which was brought hither by certaine Merchants from Alexandria in Egypt . . . . in the year 810. To whose honor they built this Church about nineteen yeares after."[63] The latter part, in turn, is from Moryson:

> On the left hand by the Altar of Saint James is a place, where (if a man may believe it) the body of Saint Marke, by a crevice suddenly breaking through the marble stone, appeared in the yeere 1094. to certaine Priests who had fasted and praied to find the same, the memory of the place where it was laied at the building of the Church about 829. being utterly lost.[64]

Next Gerard, having finished St. Mark and his relics, turns to other sacred objects:

> After that they showed me the Virgin's chair, it is of stone; also her picture, painted by St. Luke, very dark, and the features now scarce visible. This picture, in time of drought, they carry in procession, and brings the rain. I wish I had not seen it. Item, two pieces of marble spotted with John the Baptist's blood; item, a piece of the true cross and of the pillar to which Christ was tied; item, the rock struck by Moses, and wet to this hour; also a stone Christ sat on, preaching at Tyre; but some say it is the one the patriarch Jacob laid his head on, and I hold with them, by reason our Lord never preached at Tyre.[65]

The section about the picture of the Virgin is from Coryate: a "picture of the Virgin Mary, which they say was made by S. Luke the Evangelist . . . . the hue of it doth witnesse that it is very auncient." To be sure, Moryson mentions the picture, but, since he has no fact from which Reade would infer its indistinctness, we prefer Coryate. From Coryate, too, comes the account of parading the picture to secure rain, a habit at which he looks askance.[66] All the other relics are taken from Moryson,[67] though Reade

---

[63] I, 354. (Wheeler notes the borrowing of the date from Coryate.) Moryson says (I, 165): "The body of which Saint being brought hither by Merchants from Alexandria: this Church was built in the yeere 829." (Moryson does not mention the date 810.)

[64] I, 169. (Not noted by Wheeler.)   [65] Oxf., p. 415; Ev., p. 419.

[66] I, 355. (The picture is noted by Wheeler.)

[67] I, 172. (None are noted by Wheeler.)

changes the order. The noteworthy objects other than relics occurring in Moryson's list are omitted by the pious Gerard. Again Gerard's using his reason in the matter of the stone at the end of the passage is not found in Moryson and is characteristic of the canny Dutchman.

Having described St. Mark's and its treasure, Gerard now turns to the other sights of the city. First we learn about the state nursery for the children of courtesans, and the hole in the outer wall through which the child must be small enough to be squeezed if the state is to take charge of it. This information is condensed from Coryate's account.[68] Gerard goes on, "Coming out of the church we met them carrying in a corpse, with the feet and face bare." The source of this is Coryate's "They carry the Corse to Church with the face, handes and feete all naked."[69]

"On a great porphyry slab in the piazza," the novel proceeds, "were three ghastly heads rotting and tainting the air, and in their hot summers like to take vengeance with breeding of a plague. These were traitors to the state," and Gerard, in characteristic fashion moralizes briefly. This occurrence is drawn from Coryate's description of "a certaine Porphyrie stone" on which were "laide for the space of three dayes and three nights, the heads of all" traitors.[70] Next Gerard was interested "to see over against the duke's palace a fair gallows in alabaster, reared express to hang him, and no other, for the least treason to the state." Coryate, too, has a description of "a marvailous faire paire of gallowes made of alabaster" for the same purpose.[71]

"Hard by, on a wall," continues Gerard, "the workmen were just finishing . . . . the stone effigy of a tragical and enormous act enacted last year." It was of four brothers who desired to inherit more land; hence, at the same banquet, "these twain drugged the wine, and those twain envenomed a marchpane," with the result that all died. Coryate saw this representation (it was already finished, not in the process of construction as in the

[68] Oxf., p. 415; Ev., p. 419; Coryate, I, 407. (Noted by Wheeler.)

[69] Oxf., p. 416; Ev., p. 419; Coryate, I, 393. (Not noted by Wheeler.)

[70] Oxf., p. 416; Ev., p. 419. Coryate, I, 330. (Noted by Wheeler.)

[71] Oxf., p. 416; Ev., pp. 419–20. Coryate, I, 330–31. (Noted by Wheeler.)

novel), and he narrates the story of these "Noble Gentlemen of Albania" who arrived by ship in Venice. Two presented "certaine poysoned drugges at a banquet," and the other two "ministred a certaine poysoned march-pane," with fatal results.[72] Gerard, of course, is much impressed by the moral of this and quotes the saying:

> Quand Italie sera sans poison
> Et France sans trahison
> Et l'Angleterre sans guerre,
> Lors sera le monde sans terre.

These verses Reade found quoted (from Leigh's *Observations*) in Robert Southey's *Common-Place Book*.[73] In Southey the word *et* does not occur at the beginning of the second and third lines. Reade evidently made this slight addition to connect the verses better.

While viewing the ships at the quayside in Venice, Gerard "espied among the masts one garlanded with amaranth flowers." The custom is taken from Moryson, who, on one occasion, "tooke ship, upon the Mast whereof was a garland of Roses, because the master of this ship then wooed his wife, which ceremony the Hollanders use."[74] Reade has made a pretty, though short, incident of this: a homesick Dutchman in a foreign city saw the flowers and knew, from the sign, that the ship came from Holland; he felt a surge of emotion and then it mounted higher, for by the inscription on the stem he found that the vessel belonged to his brother. Reade has changed roses into amaranth, and Moryson's "wooed his wife" into "courting a maid." Gerard learned from the skipper that another boat was sailing for Holland that evening, and on it he sent to Margaret the long letter which she read aloud to his family.

The next scene in Gerard's adventure is presented to us directly instead of being related in a letter. It is the famous ship-

---

[72] Oxf., p. 416; Ev., p. 420; Coryate, I, 331–32. (Noted by Wheeler.)

[73] (3d ser.), p. 415. Perhaps I should add that Mr. Wheeler, very careful about tracing quotations, was unable to find this one.

[74] Oxf., p. 416; Ev., p. 420; Moryson, I, 114. (Noted by Wheeler.)

wreck. As has been long recognized,[75] it is derived from one of Erasmus' *Colloquies* and keeps to its source closely. It is, moreover, the longest passage I have found in *The Cloister and the Hearth* based continuously and closely on any one source. (I am excluding long scenes that are developed from a suggestion freely.) Now it is quite possible that Reade was struck by this colloquy, *The Shipwreck* (*Naufragium* in the original Latin)—it seems, indeed, to me the most vivid and dramatic of all the *Colloquies*—and decided that it offered so admirable an opportunity for a fine scene that he must have a shipwreck in his novel too. But it is also possible that the following little narrative occurring in *Norica* gave him the idea of introducing a disaster at sea.[76] The story is related by the famous sculptor, Adam Krafft, about his youthful experiences:

Adam left his native town of Nürnberg as a young man, to seek his fortune in foreign parts, and to return home as soon as possible with a well-filled purse. Nothing remained as a consolation, to Magdalena [his betrothed] but her lover's oath of inviolable fidelity. Ten years she waited for the return of her friend, but in vain. No tidings of him reached her; and her relations, who beset her with proposals of marriage, said to her over and over again, that Adam would never more return; for that he must either be dead, or long since settled and married in foreign lands . . . . [Adam wandered into Italy]. He found every where plenty of work, and his money increased every week, especially in Naples. Now he thought of returning; and as a ship was going from Naples to Genoa, he seized the opportunity to return to his home as soon as possible. . . . . Suddenly a storm and foul weather arose, the ship was tossed about here and there, and the ship's crew were in despair; the masts were cut down, and the lives of such numbers were given up to chance. After sailing about comfortless for many days, the ship came to land, and the lives of the people were saved. [Unfortunately they landed in Tunis and were made slaves, but eventually Adam got back to Germany and married the girl.]

The parallelism between the general situation here and that in *The Cloister and the Hearth* is obvious: the hero's artistic skill, his leaving home, his going to Italy, his earning much money there, the girl at home waiting for her fiancé, the rival suitor, the constancy of the lovers, are all alike. Reade, unless he skipped the passage, must have noticed the similarity. And if he did notice it, it would be very easy, when he happened upon the storm occurring as another misfortune of the hero's, to decide to have.

[75] *Notes and Queries* (10th ser., 1905), IV, 313.   [76] Pp. 178–80.

a like storm harass Gerard. In this case the Erasmus colloquy occurred to him as a good source of material. Since the account in
Norica is so brief, we can hardly hope for parallelism in details.
It may, however, be worth while to point out that Adam Krafft
had just sailed from Naples when the tempest arose, and that
Gerard's ship was between Naples and Rome,[77] whereas the
Erasmus' shipwreck took place off the Dutch coast. The question cannot, I believe, be decided surely, and each person may
think as he chooses.

Now let us turn our attention to Reade's borrowings from
Erasmus' colloquy and particularly to the way he treats them.[78]
We should note in passing, however, that the colloquy is far
more vivid than most of the works from which the novelist drew
and that it is hence more difficult to improve upon than the average source. The parallel between Erasmus and Reade, as I have
said, is close.

Reade begins his account with the people on the beach who
are watching a ship offshore oppressed with a tempest. Erasmus,
on the other hand, does not bring in these observers until late
in the story. Reade has made this change in order to begin his
narrative calmly and then work up the emotion.

Next Reade transports us to a more tense scene, the deck of the
ship, and shows us everyone stricken with fear. Among the passengers, he tells us, was Gerard. But Gerard is not individualized
from the others; he is mentioned only so that we may know how
this ship scene is connected with the rest of the novel. Through
a general description of the passengers, the reader feels the per-
vading atmosphere of terror. No passengers are yet marked off
from the rest, and, though there was general fear, the danger of
the ship's going to pieces was not yet immediate. The dread of
all present was expressed in vows. "The sailors, indeed," says
Reade, "relied on a single goddess. They varied her titles only,
calling on her as 'Queen of Heaven,' 'Star of the Sea,' 'Mistress

---

[77] Oxf., p. 420; Ev., p. 424.

[78] The shipwreck in Reade covers Oxf., pp. 420–28; Ev., pp. 424–32. The Erasmus colloquy is found in *The Colloquies*, II, 7–18.

of the World,' 'Haven of Safety.' "[79] These details are from a later point in Erasmus:

There you might have seen a wretched Face of Things; the Mariners, they were singing their *Salve Regina*, imploring the Virgin Mother, calling her the Star of the Sea, the Queen of Heaven, the Lady of the World, the Haven of Health, and many other flattering titles, which the sacred Scriptures never attributed to her.[80]

(The correspondence of epithets is perfect between Reade and Erasmus, the difference in English phrasing being accounted for by the fact that Reade rendered the Latin differently from the translator here quoted.) Reade now continues:

An English merchant vowed a heap of gold to our lady of Walsingham. But a Genoese merchant vowed a silver collar of four pounds to our lady of Loretto; and a Tuscan noble promised ten pounds of wax lights to our lady of Ravenna; and with a similar rage for diversity they pledged themselves, not on the true Cross, but on the true Cross in this, that, or the other, modern city.[81]

This is based on an Erasmus passage coming soon, but not immediately, after the one previously quoted:

Some made Vows. There was an Englishman there, that promis'd golden Mountains [*montes aureos*, which Reade renders colloquially "a heap of gold"] to our Lady of Walsingham, so he did but get ashore alive. Others promis'd a great many Things to the Wood of the Cross, which was in such a Place; others again to that which was in such a Place; and the same was done by the Virgin Mary, which reigns in a great many Places, and they think the Vow is of no Effect, unless the Places be mentioned.[82]

Reade, it will be noted, has improved the order by putting all the vows to the Virgin together, and has made the passage more vivid by inserting two other specific Virgins—those of Loretto and Ravenna—instead of Erasmus' general statement.

The process of making vows, in the novel, is momentarily interrupted: "Suddenly a more powerful gust than usual catching the sail at a disadvantage, the rotten shrouds gave way, and the sail was torn out with a loud crack and went down the wind smaller and smaller, blacker and blacker, and fluttered into the sea, half a mile off, like a sheet of paper."[83] This sentence is a far

[79] Oxf., p. 421; Ev., p. 425.

[80] *The Colloquies*, II, 10.

[81] Oxf., p. 421; Ev., p. 425.

[82] *The Colloquies*, II, 10–11.

[83] Oxf., pp. 421–22; Ev., p. 425.

more vivid counterpart of Erasmus' "The Winds were nothing the less boisterous for our Presents [certain things had been thrown overboard], but by and by burst our Cordage, and threw down our sails."[84]

After this interruption the vows proceeded in Reade:

Then one vowed aloud to turn Carthusian monk, if St. Thomas would save him. Another would go pilgrim to Compostella, bareheaded, barefooted, with nothing by a coat of mail on his naked skin, if St. James would save him. Others invoked Thomas, Dominic, Denys, and above all, Catherine of Sienna.[85]

These lines are taken from two passages in Erasmus' colloquy, the first being directly after the vows to the Virgin. "Some made Promises to become Carthusians. There was one who promised he would go a Pilgrimage to St. James at Compostella, bare Foot and bare Head, cloth'd in a Coat of Mail, and begging his Bread all the Way."[86] The last saints in Reade are taken from a much later point in Erasmus' *Shipwreck*, where a Dominican, swimming after leaving the ship, called on "St. Dominick, St. Thomas, St. Vincent, and one of the Peters, but I can't tell which [Reade substitutes Denys for Vincent and omits the Peters]: But his chief Reliance was upon Catherina Senensis."[87]

After this insertion from a later point Reade goes on with the passage in Erasmus about vows and takes over the loud-mouthed vow to St. Christopher and the admission, *sotto voce*, that the poor saint, even though he preserved his suppliant, would never receive the gift promised him.[88] Still other people, Reade declares, lay flat and apostrophized the sea, applying to it four complimentary epithets. The circumstance is from Erasmus, and the four epithets are exact translations, but Reade has shifted the position of the happening.[89] Erasmus had it after the sailors' invocations to the Virgin and before the vow of the English merchant to our lady of Walsingham, whereas Reade, more logically, places it when all the invocations and vows to saints are finished.

---

[84] *The Colloquies*, II, 9.   [86] *The Colloquies*, II, 11.

[85] Oxf., p. 422; Ev., p. 425.   [87] *Ibid.*, p. 16.

[88] Oxf., p. 422; Ev., p. 426; *The Colloquies*, II, 11.

[89] Oxf., p. 422; Ev., p. 426; *The Colloquies*, II, 10.

Now that Reade has established his general atmosphere and shown how all the people felt, he next turns to two exceptions. A Roman woman nursing her child, and a gigantic friar, unlike the other frightened persons on the ship, were wholly calm. Both are drawn from Erasmus, where they occur about halfway through the episode. The novelist, detecting the interest they would excite in his readers, chose wisely to introduce them earlier, but not until the general tone of fear had been established. Erasmus says of the woman: "There was no Body among them all behaved herself more composed than a Woman, who had a Child sucking at her Breast. . . . . She only neither bawl'd, nor wept, nor made Vows, but hugging her little Boy, pray'd softly."[90] The Englishman enlarges most effectively on this short description; in particular he added the fact that "sixteen hundred years had not tainted the old Roman blood in her veins; and the instinct of a race she had perhaps scarce heard of taught her to die with decent dignity."[91] Reade now goes on:

A gigantic friar [he turned out later to be a Dominican] stood on the poop with feet apart, like the Colossus of Rhodes, not so much defying, as ignoring, the peril that surrounded him. He recited verses from the Canticles with loud unwavering voice; and invited the passengers to confess to him. Some did so on their knees.[92]

This, too, depends on Erasmus:

Upon this, up starts an old Priest about three-score Years of Age. . . . . Then standing in the middle of the Ship, he preach'd a Sermon to us, upon the five Truths of the Benefit of Confession, and exhorted every Man to prepare himself, for either Life or Death. There was a Dominican there too, and they confess'd those that had a Mind to it.[93]

Reade's recitation of "verses from the Canticles" appeals to a modern person more than "a Sermon . . . . upon the five Truths of the Benefit of Confession." Moreover, Reade has wisely made Erasmus' two clergyman into one, thereby gaining in emphasis. Again he makes the most of the contrast between the only two calm people on the ship: "Thus, even here, two were found who maintained the dignity of our race: a woman, tender, yet heroic,

[90] *The Colloquies*, II, 12–13.   [92] Oxf., pp. 422–23; Ev., p. 426.
[91] Oxf., p. 422; Ev., p. 426.   [93] *The Colloquies*, II, 13.

and a monk steeled by religion against mortal fears." Both characters, finally, are to appear more than once in the novel; hence
Reade has done well in making their first appearance dramatic.

At this point in Reade, acts showing more acute peril took
place. "The sail being gone, the sailors cut down the useless mast
a foot above the board." Similarly in Erasmus, "he orders to
cut the Shrouds and the Mast down by the Board."[94] Moreover,
in the novel, "the captain left the helm and came amidships pale
as death. 'Lighten her,' he cried. 'Fling all overboard.' " Then,
while the sailors were executing the order, he explained that
"there came a globe of fire close to the ship. When a pair of them
come it is good luck" (they are called Castor and Pollux); but
if only one comes, disaster follows. "Therefore, like good Christians, prepare to die."[95] In Erasmus, "the Pilot, all pale as Death
comes to us"; he exhorted "every one to prepare himself for
Death. . . . . But in the first Place, says he, we must lighten the
Ship."[96] All this occurs at an earlier point in Erasmus than in
Reade, who preferred to keep it until the situation had become
more tense. The appearance of the ball of fire comes from a still
earlier portion of Erasmus, near the beginning of the colloquy:
"A certain Ball of Fire began to stand by him, which is the worst
Sign in the World to Sailors, if it be single; but a very good one,
if double. The Antients believed these to be Castor and Pollux."[97]
In Erasmus, it should be observed, the fire actually appeared;
Reade, on the contrary, must have felt that there would be less
objection, on the part of modern readers, if it were only spoken of
by the captain. When Reade's captain was asked how long the
ship would last, he replied about half an hour.[98] In Erasmus the
captain, who is more talkative than in the novel, twice spoke
about this matter, the first time specifying three hours, the second,
fifteen minutes.[99]

The throwing-overboard of valuables in accordance with the
captain's command, in *The Cloister and the Hearth*, occurs likewise

[94] Oxf., p. 423; Ev., p. 427; *The Colloquies*, II, 9.

[95] Oxf., p. 423; Ev., p. 427.

[96] *The Colloquies*, II, 8.   [98] Oxf., p. 423; Ev., p. 427.

[97] *Ibid.*, p. 7.   [99] *The Colloquies*, II, 9, 13.

in Erasmus, but at an earlier point than in the novel. Since it is a forceful example of extreme peril, Reade has chosen—properly, I think—to put it in later. Erasmus runs:

> There was in the Company, a certain Italian, that had been upon an Embassy to the King of Scotland. He had a whole Cabinet full of Plate, Rings, Cloth, and rich wearing Apparel . . . . he had a Mind either to sink or swim with his beloved Riches. . . . . If you and your Trinkets were to drown by yourselves, says he [the pilot], here's no Body would hinder you; but it is not fit that we should run the Risque of our Lives, for the Sake of your Cabinet: If you won't consent, we'll throw you and your Cabinet into the Sea together. . . . . So the Italian submitted, and threw his Goods over-Board, with many a bitter Curse to Gods both above and below, that he had committed his Life to so barbarous an Element.[100]

Reade uses the episode, but he makes it even more vivid and racy. Instead of an Italian, the owner of the treasure was an old Jew. Several passengers were about to throw his sack overboard:

> "Holy Moses! [he cries] what would you do? 'Tis my all; 'tis the whole fruits of my journey; silver candlesticks, silver plates, brooches, hanaps. . . . ."
>
> "Let go, thou hoary villain," cried the others, "shall all our lives be lost for thy ill-gotten gear?" "Fling him in with it," cried one.[101]

They flung the sack in for him—more natural than persuading him to do so, as in Erasmus—and, if it had floated, he would have jumped in afterward.

In the novel the seafarers now caught sight of a church and prayed to its saint. A similar event took place in Erasmus.

In the colloquy, after the account of the different saints invoked, the narrator is asked whether he prayed to the saints and answers "No":

> Because Heaven is a large Place, and if I should recommend my Safety to any Saint, as suppose, to St. Peter, who perhaps, would hear soonest, because he stands at the Door; before he can come to God Almighty, or before he could tell him my Condition, I may be lost. . . . . I e'en went, the next Way to God the Father, saying, *Our Father which art in Heaven*. There's none of the Saints hears sooner than he does, or more readily gives what is ask'd for.[102]

---

[100] *Ibid.*, pp. 8–9. The frequent breaks are caused by short interested remarks of the listener in the colloquy.

[101] Oxf., pp. 423–24; Ev., p. 427.   [102] *The Colloquies*, II, 12.

Detaching this from the rest of the discussion of the invocation of saints, Reade imagines a short dramatic episode: the other passengers accused Gerard of being a pagan because he had appealed to no saint, and Gerard answered with exactly the same arguments used in the Erasmus excerpt.[103]

Reade's scene has been heightened gradually from the beginning, and he is now ready, since the ship is about to sink, to discuss the attempts to save lives. In both Erasmus and the novel the sailors launched the life-boat, and there was a general rush to get aboard. Reade dubs those who climbed in "egotists," and there were thirty of them. In Erasmus, too, we later find out, the boat had thirty persons get into it.[104] Only a few were still left aboard the ship in Reade. One of them was praying devoutly to a wooden statue of the Virgin which had been taken down; indeed, wherever the waves washed it on deck, he followed on his knees—a nice bit of invention on the novelist's part.

As for the heroic matron and her child in Erasmus:

> We set her upon a broad Plank, and ty'd her on so fast that she could not easily fall off, and we gave her a Board, in her Hand to make Use of instead of an Oar, and wishing her good Success, we set her afloat, thrusting her off from the Ship with Poles, that she might be clear of it, whence was the greatest danger. And she held her Child in her left Hand, and row'd with her right Hand. . . . . Now when there was nothing else left, one pull'd up a wooden Image of the Virgin Mary, rotten, and rat-eaten, and embracing it in his Arms, try'd to swim upon it.[105]

Reade has developed a touching scene from this. Gerard was the man who aided the Roman matron, and he lashed her, not to a plank, but to the statue of the Virgin—a more dramatic situation. In view of her being able, possibly, to reach shore alive, she lost something of her former calm. In fact, she hesitated whether or not she should take the opportunity of being saved and letting Gerard perhaps drown, but the love of her child conquered and she accepted.[106]

---

[103] Oxf., p. 424; Ev., p. 428.

[104] Oxf., p. 424; Ev., p. 428; *The Colloquies*, II, 14, 15.

[105] *Ibid.*, pp. 14–15.   [106] Oxf., p. 425; Ev., p. 429.

Gerard's manner of saving himself likewise comes from Erasmus. The latter says:

I look'd round about me, at Length I bethought myself of the Stump of the Mast, and because I could not get it out alone, I took a Partner; upon this we both plac'd ourselves, and committed ourselves to the Sea. I held the right End, and my Companion the left End. While we lay tumbling and tossing, the old preaching Sea-Priest threw himself upon our Shoulders. He was a huge Fellow. We cry out, who's that third Person? He'll drown us all. But he very calmly bids us be easy, for there was Room enough, God will be with us.[107]

Reade greatly improves this happening. Instead of having a nobody help launch the mast, he has "the gigantic friar," in whom we are already interested, do so. In fact, it is this man in his calm strength who induced Gerard to heave overboard this piece of timber, whereas in the *Colloquies* he rather selfishly made use of the mast which the other men had labored over. Thus in Reade the clergyman keeps our respect far more than in Erasmus, and the third person who jumped on, unasked, is the nobody.[108] While the three were bobbing around on their mast in the *Colloquies*, the thigh of the man who helped launch it was broken by a spike, and he let go his hold and sank. Reade has improved this circumstance also. He has the head of the uninvited passenger "smashed like a cocoa-nut by a sledge-hammer," a greater physical horror and yet one which grieves us less, since we have less esteem for the victim.

The way the friar and Gerard reached shore upon their mast is wholly taken by Reade from Erasmus. The latter runs as follows:

When we had been some Time swimming at this Rate, and had made some Way, the old Priest being a very tall Man, cries out, Be of good Heart, I feel Ground; but I durst not hope for such a blessing. No, no, says I, we are too far from Shoar to hope to feel Ground. Nay, says he, I feel the Ground with my Feet. Said I, perhaps it is some of the Chests that have been roll'd thither by the Sea. Nay, says he, I am sure I feel Ground by the Scratching of my Toes. Having floated thus a little longer, and he had felt the Bottom again, Do you do what you please, says he, I'll leave you the whole Mast, and wade for it. And so he took his Opportunity, at the Ebbing of the Billows, he made what Haste he could on his Feet, and when the Billows came again, he took Hold of his Knees with his Hands, and bore up against the Billows hiding himself, under

[107] *The Colloquies*, II, 15.   [108] Oxf., p. 426; Ev., pp. 429–30.

them as Sea Gulls and Ducks do, and at the Ebbing of the Wave, he would start up and run for it. I seeing that this succeeded so well to him, followed his Example. There stood upon the Shoar Men, who had long Pikes handed from one to another, which kept them firm against the Force of the Waves, and he that was last of them held out a Pike to the Person swimming towards him. All that came to Shoar, and laying hold of that, were drawn safely to dry Land.[109]

This vivid narrative is copied closely as to events by Reade, with some added good touches.[110] Thus the friar remarked, "There, I felt it with my toes again; see the benefit of wearing sandals, and not shoon." Furthermore, when the natives hauled the ecclesiastic ashore, he at once started to Rome on the church's business, not even looking back at the sea—an action most characteristic of the sort of man this Jerome is in the novel.

All the survivors were kindly treated by the natives in both Erasmus and Reade. Erasmus says that, of all persons on the ship, only seven were saved.[111] Reade, likewise, though he does not mention the number, has just seven preserved: Gerard, the friar, the captain, the Jew, the Roman matron, and two more.[112] The fact that he had the last two nameless persons saved indicates that he had his eye on Erasmus' "seven." Moreover, of his own accord Reade adds considerable irony: "The thirty egotists came ashore, but one at a time, and dead." On the other hand, the captain, feeling it was useless to resist Castor and Pollux and making no effort to save himself, was brought to land on part of the wreck, and the Jew, too much concerned with his lost wealth to care about himself, reached the coast on another fragment.

Reade's final touch, which has no parallel in Erasmus, is excellent. Gerard suddenly felt a hand on his shoulder:

He turned. It was the Roman matron, burning with womanly gratitude. She took his hand gently, and raising it slowly to her lips, kissed it; but so nobly, she seemed to be conferring an honour on one deserving hand. Then, with face all beaming and moist eyes, she held her child up and made him kiss his preserver.[113]

[109] *The Colloquies*, II, 16–17.

[110] Oxf., pp. 426–27; Ev., pp. 430–31.   [112] Oxf., p. 427; Ev., p. 431.

[111] *The Colloquies*, II, 17.   [113] Oxf., pp. 427–28; Ev., pp. 431–32.

This turn provides a suitable climax for the scene—much more so than a welter of bodies on the shore—and it likewise is significant, since the preservation of the mother and child has an important influence on the future course of the novel.

Reade then has handled this long and elaborate borrowing very ably. In the first place, he has improved the order of the events. In Erasmus—especially during the earlier part—the happenings are rather scattered in effect and somewhat illogical; Reade has arranged them so that they lead up in harmonious fashion from the less to the more tense. Second, though Erasmus is vivid, Reade at certain times has improved on him. In the third place, the novelist has supplied human interest by developing and emphasizing two personalities, those of the friar and the Roman matron.

Chapter Seven

ROME AT LAST

AFTER being saved from the shipwreck, Gerard proceeded to Rome. There he took a lodging and tried to secure work as a copyist. Being poor, he cut down on his food. "In these 'camere locande' the landlady dressed all the meals, though the lodgers bought the provisions," as we read. Thus she at once detected that he was eating very little and reproved him, asking "whether Adversity was a thing to be overcome on an empty stomach." "Patienza, my lad!" she declared; "times will mend, meantime I will feed you for the love of heaven."[1]

This episode is suggested by a sentence in Fynes Moryson: "it is much more commodious for him that hath some experience and skill in the tongue [Italian], to buy his owne meat, since in Camere locande (i.e., hired chambers) the Hostesse at a reasonable rate of the chamber, is tied to dresse his meate."[2] The taking-over of the words *camere locande* proves the borrowing, but Reade invents the pretty touch of the landlady's taking pity on the young man and feeding him at her own expense.

Feeling friendly with Gerard, the landlady now told him about another lodger whom she called by his Christian name Pietro:

Pietro had come from Florence with money in his purse, and an unfinished picture; had taken her one unfurnished room, opposite Gerard's, and furnished it neatly. When his picture was finished, he received visitors. . . . . [He proved unable, however, to get what he thought was a suitable price for the work, though he tried a long time.] The last month, she had seen one moveable after another go out of his room, and now he wore but one suit, and lay at night on a great chest.[3]

[1] Oxf., p. 430; Ev., p. 434.

[2] *An Itinerary Containing His Ten Yeeres Travell through the Twelve Dominions*, IV, 100. (Wheeler notes the borrowed words *camere locande*, but not the hostess' dressing the meat.)

[3] Oxf., p. 430; Ev., p. 434.

150

This man, it turns out, is the famous painter Pietro Perugino. Reade has taken from Giorgio Vasari, whose work appears in the *Century* list, some details about Perugino's poverty: "This artist, seeking to escape from the extreme of penury in Perugia, departed to Florence, hoping, by means of his abilities, to attain to some distinction. He there remained many months without even a bed to lie on, and miserably took his sleep upon a chest."[4] Reade, then, has drawn from Vasari the information about Perugino's early unsuccessful attempt to succeed as an artist, his consequent poverty, and especially the picturesque detail of his being obliged to sleep on a chest. He has, however, changed the scene of that poverty from Florence to Rome. To be sure, Perugino, according to Vasari, went to Rome later, but it was on the invitation of a pope, and he earned a great deal of money there.

Reade in some respects, moreover, has not pictured Perugino's character in the scenes of *The Cloister and the Hearth* in which he appears, as did Vasari. The Italian biographer depicts him as a very hard worker but extremely materialistic in his aims, being willing to undertake anything for money. Reade, on the other hand, has made him more erratic in his working, but devoted to his art for its own sake. Moreover, he has portrayed the artist as impulsive and excessively proud, inferring the last trait from his being unappreciated as a painter.

At a later point in the novel, when he finally gained prosperity, Perugino engaged in dissipation; in Reade's phrasing, he "was one of those who bear prosperity worse than adversity." Moreover, Reade calls him "not only a libertine, but half a misanthrope, and an open infidel."[5] The quality of dissipation is probably derived from Vasari's remark that Perugino's chief aim in life was "to obtain the power of someday living in ease and quietness." His trait of being "an open infidel," in turn, comes from Vasari's statement, "Pietro possessed but very little religion, and could never be made to believe in the immortality of the soul,

[4] *Lives of the Most Eminent Painters, Sculptors, and Architects*, trans. Mrs. Jonathan Foster (5 vols.; London, 1850–52), II, 306.

[5] Oxf., pp. 481, 482; Ev., p. 489.

nay, most obstinately did he reject all good counsel, with words suited to the stubbornness of his marble-hard brain."[6]

Gerard became acquainted with Perugino on the score of their common interest in art, though he found the Italian haughty. As he sat in the artist's room, the landlady came up with Gerard's dinner; it was a ragout.[7] The nature of the food is surely drawn from Moryson's statement about Italians: "They use no spits to roast flesh, but commonly stew the same in earthen pipkins."[8] After eating a little, Gerard began:

"I am an ill-mannered churl, Signor Pietro. I ne'er eat to my mind, when I eat alone. For our Lady's sake put a spoon into this ragout with me; 'tis not unsavoury, I promise you."

Pietro fixed his glittering eye on him.

"What, good youth, thou a stranger, and offerest me thy dinner?"

"Why, see, there is more than one can eat."

"Well, I accept," said Pietro: and took the dish with some appearance of calmness, and flung the contents out of the window.

Then he turned, trembling with mortification and ire, and said: "Let that teach thee to offer alms to an artist thou knowest not, master writer."[9]

This lively incident is suggested by some remarks of Moryson's on the Italians (the italics are mine):

And at the table, perhaps one man hath a hen, another a piece of flesh, the third a potched egges, and each man severall meat after his diet [i.e., different food according to his taste]: but *it is no courtesie for one to offer another part of his meate, which they rather take to be done in pride*, as if he thought that he that had a sallet of egges could not have a hen or flesh, if hee listed for want of money. To conclude, *they hold it no honour or disgrace to live plentifully or sparingly, so they live of their owne.*[10]

This is the sort of thing that we have seen catching Reade's attention more than once before. In addition, the passage occurs very near to the *camere locande* which Reade borrowed; in fact, the latter part is on the same page. Accordingly, I think there is no doubt that the novelist from this hint imagined the picturesque incident of throwing the dinner out of the window as the result of offended pride.

[6] II, 306–7.

[7] Oxf., p. 432; Ev., p. 436.　　　[8] IV, 98–99. (Not noted by Wheeler.)

[9] Oxf., p. 432; Ev., p. 436.　　　[10] IV, 99–100. (Not noted by Wheeler.)

Gerard smothered his anger and, speaking to Perugino in measured terms, made him consent, by way of reparation for the lost dinner, to show him the painting. Unable to gain recognition of its merits from connoisseurs, the Italian kept it in his room, ready to stab whoever slandered it. He finally consented to show it to Gerard, and the latter, drawing his sword in case Perugino should become violent, delivered a criticism of the work's good and bad points:

First, signor, I would have you know that, in the mixing of certain colours, and in the preparation of your oil, you Italians are far behind us Flemings. But let that flea stick. For as small as I am, I can show you certain secrets of the Van Eycks, that you will put to marvellous profit in your next picture.[11]

The fault as to "the mixing of certain colours" is drawn, I think, from Mrs. Merrifield. She observes:

There is another reason why one layer of colours should be suffered to dry perfectly before another was applied; namely, to prevent their cracking. Some of the early Italian artists, and particularly Pietro Perugino, appear to have bought their experience in this respect. Several of the pictures of Pietro are stated to have suffered from this cause.[12]

Gerard, to be sure, has not gone into particulars as to why the colors were combined improperly as Mrs. Merrifield has done in the passage quoted and in its continuation; if he had, it would have been unsuitable in a dramatic harangue, sword in hand. But at least "mixing of certain colours" might be a brief way of Reade's indicating this fault in some of Pietro's works. Again Mrs. Merrifield later calls Perugino "the first who practised the Flemish method of oil painting in Perugia."[13] From this last statement, I believe, Reade derived the idea of having Pietro at this time faulty "in the preparation of your oil," but later, by Gerard's teaching (as promised here), in possession of "certain secrets of the Van Eycks" that made him, as Mrs. Merrifield says, an early exponent of "the Flemish method of oil painting" in Italy. Moreover, the fact that Reade unquestionably borrowed other points, as we have seen, from this treatise of Mrs. Merrifield makes the probability of influence here almost a certainty. It is

[11] Oxf., p. 435; Ev., p. 438.

[12] *Original Treatises on the Arts of Painting*, I, cccv.   [13] *Ibid.*, p. cccix.

also very likely that when Reade had decided to have Margaret van Eyck a character in his novel and a friend of Gerard's, the mention of Perugino as an early practitioner of Flemish oil painting in Italy made him choose this Italian to appear in the novel and to learn from Gerard some of the secrets of Flemish technique.

Gerard then eulogized the imagination shown in the picture. Thereafter he voiced one objection: "The drapery here is somewhat short and stiff. Why not let it float freely, the figures being in air and motion?" This may, perhaps, be drawn from a criticism of Perugino's paintings in Luigi Lanzi's *The History of Painting in Italy*, a work mentioned in one of the Reade notebooks owned by Mr. Parrish: "He exhibits poverty in the drapery of his figures; his garments and mantles being curtailed and confined."[14] After this, Gerard warmly praised the landscape background, "a spacious plain, each distance marked, and every tree, house, figure, field, and river smaller and less plain, by exquisite gradation, till vision itself melts into distance." This is good criticism of the liquid air effects of Umbrian painting, and Reade may have derived it from his own observation of Italian art or from some book which I have not encountered. In any case, Gerard praised the painting so highly that the artist became his warm friend.

Gerard's landlady introduced him one day to her friend Teresa, and he was astonished to find it was the Roman matron whom he had saved from the wreck. Finding he wanted employment as a scribe, she at once tried to help him. Apropos of the cynicism of Rome, however, she remarked, "La corte Romana non vuol' pecora senza lana," a quotation found in Moryson.[15] One of her friends suggested that Gerard should look up Fra Colonna, an enthusiast over the arts and ancient scholarship, and Gerard followed the advice.

At this point Reade inserts a little account of the scholarship of the Italian Renaissance. This account—as is evident especially after the first—he condenses from Hallam's *Introduction to the Literature of Europe*. A quotation of parallel passages will reveal the indebtedness.

[14] Trans. Thomas Roscoe (3 vols.; London, 1852–54), I, 343.

[15] Oxf., p. 437; Ev., p. 441; Moryson, III, 459. (Noted by Wheeler.)

HALLAM: Petrarch, in 1342 . . . . endeavoured to learn Greek. . . . . Boccaccio, some years afterward, succeeded better with the help of Leontius Pilatus. . . . . The true epoch of the revival of Greek literature in Italy, these attempts of Petrarch and Boccace having produced no immediate effect, though they evidently must have excited a desire for learning, cannot be placed before the year 1395.[16]

READE: The true revivers of ancient learning and philosophy were two writers of fiction—Petrarch and Boccaccio. Their labours were not crowned with great, public, and immediate success, but they sowed the good seed.[17]

Reade's remark, "each learned Greek who landed there [in Italy] was received fraternally," is a condensation of passages in Hallam.[18] Furthermore, Hallam, speaking of "early Hellenists" in Italy, says: "The first, and, perhaps, the most eminent and useful of these, was Guarino Guarini of Verona, born in 1370." On the next two pages Poggio and Valla are mentioned among scholars who knew Greek.[19] From these facts Reade has obtained the statement, "The fourteenth century, ere its close, saw the birth of Poggio, Valla, and the elder Guarino."[20]

HALLAM: Gemistus Pletho, a native of the Morea, and one of those who attended the council of Florence in 1439, being an enthusiastic votary of the Platonic theories in metaphysics and natural theology, communicated to Cosmo de'Medici part of his own zeal; and from that time the citizens of Florence formed a scheme of establishing an academy of learned men, to discuss and propagate the Platonic system. . . . . Meantime, a treatise by Pletho, wherein he not only extolled the Platonic philosophy . . . . but inveighed without measure against Aristotle and his disciples, had aroused the Aristotelians of Greece.[21]

READE [condensing Hallam]: Early in the fifteenth [century] Florence under Cosmo de Medici was a nest of Platonists. These headed by Gemistus Pletho, a born Greek, began about A.D. 1440, [Hallam said Gemistus Pletho attended the Council of Florence in 1439] to write down Aristotle. For few minds are big enough to be just to great A without being unjust to capital B.[22]

[16] Henry Hallam, *Introduction to the Literature of Europe in the Fifteenth, Sixteenth, and Seventeenth Centuries* (2 vols.; New York, 1868), I, 69–70.

[17] Oxf., p. 443; Ev., p. 450.

[18] *Introduction to the Literature of Europe* . . . . , I, 72–73, 93.

[19] *Ibid.*, pp. 70, 71, 72.

[20] Oxf., p. 443; Ev., p. 450.

[21] *Introduction to the Literature of Europe* . . . . , I, 94.

[22] Oxf., p. 443, Ev., p. 450.

HALLAM: [The dispute] soon spread to Italy; Theodore Gaza embracing the cause of Aristotle with temper and moderation, and George of Trebizond, a far inferior man, with invectives against the Platonic philosophy and its founder . . . . Cardinal Bessarion, a man of solid and elegant learning, replied to George of Trebizond in a book entitled Adversus Calumniatorem Platonis.[23]

READE: Theodore Gaza defended that great man [Aristotle] with moderation; George of Trebizond with acerbity, and retorted on Plato. Then Cardinal Bessarion, another born Greek, resisted the said George, and his idol, in a tract "Adversus Calumniatorem Platonis."[24]

After some information about Fra Colonna, Reade turns again to the progress of learning in the Renaissance, continuing to draw from Hallam.

HALLAM: The patronage of Cosmo de' Medici, Alfonso King of Naples, and Nicolas of Este, has already been mentioned. Lionel, successor of the last prince, was by no means inferior to him in love of letters.[25]

READE: Other lettered princes besides Cosmo had sprung up. Alfonso King of Naples, Nicolas d'Este, Lionel d'Este, etc.[26]

HALLAM [continuing]: But they had no patron so important as Nicolas V. (Thomas of Sarzana), who became pope in 1447 . . . . Nicolas founded the Vatican library, and left it, at his death in 1455, enriched with 5000 volumes. . . . . Several Greek authors were translated into Latin by direction of Nicolas V; among which are the history of Diodorus Siculus and Xenophon's Cyropaedia, by Poggio . . . .; Herodotus and Thucydides by Valla, Polybius by Perotti, Appian by Decembrio, Strabo by Gregory of Tiferno and Guarino of Verona, Theophrastus by Gaza, Plato de Legibus, Ptolemy's Almagest, and the Praeparatio Evangelica of Eusebius, by George of Trebizond.[27]

READE [condensing once more]: Above all, his [Fra Colonna's] old friend Thomas of Sarzana had been made pope, and had lent a mighty impulse to letters; had accumulated 5,000 MSS in the library of the Vatican, and had set Poggio to translate Diodorus Siculus and Xenophon's Cyropaedia, Laurentius Valla to translate Herodotus and Thucydides, Theodore Gaza, Theophrastus; George of Trebizond, Eusebius, and certain treatises of Plato, etc. etc. [It is to be noted that Reade leaves out less well-known authors.][28]

[23] Introduction to the Literature of Europe . . . . , I, 94.
[24] Oxf., p. 443; Ev., pp. 450–51.
[25] Introduction to the Literature of Europe . . . . , I, 91.
[26] Oxf., p. 444; Ev., p. 451.
[27] Introduction to the Literature of Europe . . . . , I, 91.
[28] Oxf., p. 444; Ev., p. 451.

Hallam discusses Poggio's works and those of Valla, saying that Valla's most important work was on the Latin language. His character, moreover, was "very irascible and overbearing."[29] From these statements Reade has pleasantly imagined a dispute between the two scholars, though none is mentioned by Hallam: "The monk [Fra Colonna] found Plato and Aristotle under armistice, but Poggio and Valla at loggerheads over verbs and nouns, and on fire with odium philologicum."[30]

Fra Colonna is a striking character in *The Cloister and the Hearth* and one eminently characteristic of his epoch. Though a Dominican, he was little concerned with religion and, in doctrine, was a skeptic. His chief interests were antiquity and the fine arts, and he devoted himself with the greatest ardor to the study of them and to collecting.

Much of the information about Fra Colonna, Reade derived from the account of the real man of this name in Marchese's work. The latter's account runs as follows:

Among the families expelled from Lucca . . . . was that of Colonna, which, like many others of the period, sought and found hospitality in Venice. Our Francesco was born there in the year 1433, and received a splendid education, in every respect worthy of his talents and social position. . . . . Temanza, however, supposes that Francesco, when a very young man, travelled in the East, visiting Greece, Egypt, and Constantinople to store his mind with varied and rarest erudition. [Reade says, "He travelled many years in the East."][31] He states, moreover, that he saw all Italy, and that he made a long sojourn in Rome, where he collected these antiquarian notices with which his book abounds. . . . . Father Federici has discovered documents which prove that in the year 1455 Colonna belonged to the institute of the Preaching Friars [the Dominicans], *i.e.*, when he was but twenty-two years of age. [Reade says, "At twenty he turned Dominican friar."] . . . . All writers agree in saying that he was skilled in Latin, Greek, Hebrew, and Syriac. [Reade says he was "versed in Greek and Latin, Hebrew and Syriac"—an exact borrowing—and, again, that "he knew seven or eight languages."] But the pursuit that constituted his chiefest delight was that of antiquity, and especially of that branch of it which has relation to the Fine Arts. . . . . Chronology, Numismatics, and monumental inscriptions were all familiar to him [Reade calls him "an eager student of lan-

---

[29] *Introduction to the Literature of Europe* . . . . , I, 92–93.

[30] Oxf., p. 444; Ev., p. 451.

[31] All the Reade parallels quoted within brackets are Oxf., p. 444; Ev., p. 451.

guages, pictures, statues, chronology, coins, and monumental inscriptions"—
the last three being an exact parallel], and in each of these departments he acquired much knowledge during his travels. [Reade says that he "returned laden
with spoils"—meaning manuscripts and the knowledge of languages.][32]

Marchese, furthermore, speaks of Fra Colonna as the "author
of the Art-Romance, entitled The Dream of Polifilo,"[33] a point
in which Reade agrees with him. In some respects, to be sure,
Reade departs from Marchese. For instance, Fra Colonna, according to Marchese, is an architect, whereas in the novel he goes
no further than appreciating the art of building; moreover, he
is not apparently connected with the great Colonna family of
Rome, whereas in Reade he is, though called "a young nobleman of Florence" originally. In view of the general correspondence and of very close similarities in two or three cases, however,
it seems unquestionable that this work of Marchese influenced
Reade in his conception of Fra Colonna; indeed, except for
Reade's perusing the Italian's book, there might well have been
no such man in the novel. In Marchese, Fra Colonna, though
characteristic of the age, is not a living figure. The English novelist, in contrast, has made him thoroughly alive and, with his en-
thusiasms and eccentricities, completely interesting.

Fra Colonna, recognizing Gerard's skill as a copier of manuscripts, at once became his friend and introduced him to wealthy
patrons. On one occasion the two attended at the palace of Cardinal Bessarion a banquet which is described by Reade as follows:

They were about a mile from the top of that table; but, never mind, there
they were; and Gerard had the advantage of seeing roast pheasants dished up
with all their feathers as if they had just flown out of a coppice instead of off the
spit: also chickens cooked in bottles, and tender as peaches. But the grand
novelty was the napkins, surpassingly fine, and folded into cocked hats, and
birds' wings, and fans, &c., instead of lying flat. This electrified Gerard:
though my readers have seen the dazzling phenomenon without tumbling backwards chair and all.

After dinner the tables were split in pieces, and carried away, and lo under

---

[32] V. F. Marchese, *Lives of the Most Eminent Painters, Sculptors, and Architects of the
Order of S. Dominic*, trans. C. P. Meehan (2 vols.; Dublin, 1852), I, 284–86.

[33] *Ibid.*, p. 282.

each was another table spread with sweetmeats. The signoras, and signorinas, fell upon them and gormandized; but the signors eyed them with reasonable suspicion.

"But, dear father," objected Gerard, "I see not the bifurcal daggers, with which men say his excellency armeth the left hand of a man. . . . ."

As soon as the ladies had disported themselves among the sugar-plums, the tables were suddenly removed, and the guests sat in a row against the wall. Then came in, ducking and scraping, two ecclesiastics with lutes, and kneeled at the Cardinal's feet and there sang the service of the day; then retired with a deep obeisance: in answer to which the Cardinal fingered his skull cap as our late Iron Duke his hat.[34]

Aside from the neat reference to the "bifurcal daggers" of which we have already spoken, Reade is indebted for this account, so rich in local color, to the description of two different feasts in Montaigne's *Journey*. One of these was served by the governor of the Castle of Sant'Angelo, and at this banquet the ladies were seated, whereas their husbands had to remain standing in order to serve them: "They served up abundance of roast fowls, reclothed with their natural feathers as when alive; capons cooked entire in glass bottles. . . . . The ladies' table, which was of four dishes, could be taken to pieces, and underneath it was another, ready laid and covered with sweetmeats."[35]

The other banquet in Montaigne was given by the Cardinal de Sens. This was a much more sedate affair, beginning with a very long responsive grace by two chaplains and furnishing, in the middle, some reading of Scripture for the guests' entertainment. The napkins in Reade's account are, I suspect, derived from a suggestion in this passage; the religious ceremony at the end certainly is.

Upon this [a large silver square which holds a salt-cellar] there is a napkin folded in four; on this napkin, the bread, knife, fork and spoon. On the top of all this another napkin, which you are to make use of, leaving the rest in the state in which it is. . . . . The table was removed immediately after grace, and the chairs arranged at once along one side of the room, on which the Cardinal made them sit after him. Then came two ecclesiastics, well dressed, with some instruments or other in their hands, who knelt on one knee before him, and gave him notice of some service or other which was being celebrated in some church [*et lui firent entendre je ne sçay quel service qui se faisoit en quelque Eglise;* which Reade

---

[34] Oxf., pp. 445–46; Ev., pp. 452–53.   [35] P. 138.

understands to mean they themselves sang a service actually]. He said not a word to them, but as they rose after having spoken and were going away, he raised his bonnet to them slightly.[36]

Reade's account, though exceedingly colloquial, is much more lively than the plain narrative of Montaigne. It is filled, likewise, with a genial merriment appropriate to a feast. The author increases the vividness of the phraseology and likewise develops hints in the original by drawing upon his imagination. Thus "roast fowls, reclothed with their natural feathers as when alive" (*volaille rôtie, revêtue de sa plume naturelle comme vifve*) becomes "roast pheasants dished up with all their feathers as if they had just flown out of a coppice instead of off the spit." "He raised his bonnet to them slightly" (*il leur tira un peu le bonnet*) is made more vivid and brought up to date for Victorian readers by the rendering "fingered his skull cap as our late Iron Duke his hat." Finally, the mention of delicacies on the undertable before the ladies is built out into Reade's colorful description of how "the ladies disported themselves among the sugar-plums," while the husbands held back suspiciously.

Gerard prospered as a scribe with the help of Fra Colonna. He was even given the task of copying in the Vatican "a glorious grimy old MS" of Plutarch. Montaigne, we may note in this connection, was much struck by a manuscript of Plutarch in the Vatican.[37] Gerard thriftily saved his earnings, and he also brought Perugino to the attention of the great.

Fra Colonna occasionally took Gerard on a walk through Rome and gave him the benefit of his knowledge of the ancient buildings that used to occupy various spots. Marchese says of Fra Colonna:

He has given us the most distinct and exact notion of the five orders, with the interpretation of Vitruvius, and the most correct measurement of the ancient Roman fabrics, together with the dimensions of harbours, palaces, piazzas, bascourts, temples, all most accurately designed, even out of the debris of the ancient edifices which are crumbling in Rome.[38]

[36] Pp. 126–27.

[37] Oxf., p. 446; Ev., p. 453; Montaigne, *Journey*, p. 142.

[38] I, 292.

Though Fra Colonna's skill in such matters comes from Marchese, the particular remarks he makes to Gerard on a walk through Rome[39] are drawn from Montaigne, being usually condensed. An examination of parallel passages will reveal the indebtedness.

MONTAIGNE: It is easy to judge, from the Arch of Severus, that we are more than two pikes' length above the ancient level; and, in point of fact, almost everywhere one walks on the tops of ancient walls which the rain and the coaches lay bare.[40]

READE: He showed Gerard that twenty or thirty feet of the old triumphal arches were underground, and that the modern streets ran over ancient palaces.

MONTAIGNE: It has often happened that, after digging a long way into the ground, they would come upon only the head of a very high column, which was still standing on its feet down below.[41]

READE: [The modern streets ran] over the tops of the columns.

MONTAIGNE: The space encircled by the walls, which is more than two-thirds vacant, comprehending the ancient and modern Rome.[42]

READE: The comparatively narrow limits of the modern city.

MONTAIGNE: The buildings of this bastard Rome which they were at the present time appending to the antique ruins, though they were fine enough to excite the admiration of the present age, reminded him exactly of those nests which the sparrows and crows in France append to the arches and walls of the churches which the Huguenots not long ago demolished.[43]

READE [who produces an English version of Montaigne's statement]: I tell thee this village they call Rome is but as one of those swallows' nests ye shall see built on the eaves of a decayed abbey. [Thus does Fra Colonna, an Italian character, talk a Frenchman's sentiments in an Englishman's phraseology.]

MONTAIGNE: Merely looking at the remains of the Temple of Peace. . . . . It does not seem possible that two such buildings could stand on the whole space of the Capitoline Hill, on which were quite twenty-five or thirty temples.[44]

[39] Fra Colonna's remarks on ancient Rome occur Oxf., pp. 448–49; Ev., pp. 455–56.

[40] P. 120.

[41] P. 133. Pp. 131–33 contain Montaigne's reflections on ancient Rome.

[42] P. 130.   [43] P. 132.   [44] Pp. 132–33.

READE: You see the fragments of the Temple of Peace. How would you look could you see also the Capitol with its five-and-twenty temples?

MONTAIGNE: Monte Savello is nothing but the ruins of part of the Theatre of Marcellus.[45]

READE: Do but note this Monte Savello: what is it, an it please you, but the ruins of the ancient theatre of Marcellus?

MONTAIGNE: When we see that so mean a refuse as that of bits of tiles and broken pots could have risen in ancient times to a heap of such vast size that it is equal in height and breadth to many natural mountains.[46] [The footnote to this passage, in the 1774 French edition of Montaigne used by Reade, runs (translated): "It forms what is called today Monte Testaceo."][47]

READE: And as for Testacio, one of the highest hills in modern Rome, it is but an ancient dust heap; the women of old Rome flung their broken pots and pans there, and lo; a mountain.

Another episode from which Reade drew—concerning an exorcism—runs as follows in Montaigne:

They were holding him [the afflicted man] on his knees before the altar, with some cloth or other round his neck by which they held him fast. The priest read in his presence a number of prayers and exorcisms, commanding the devil to quit this body, and he read them out of his breviary. After that he directed his words to the patient, speaking now to him, now to the devil in his person, and then abusing him, giving him good blows with his fist, spitting in his face. The patient replied to his questions with a few inept replies, now for himself, saying how much he felt the stirrings of his evil, now for the devil, how he feared God, and how much those exorcisms worked upon him. After this, which lasted a long time, the priest, as a last effort, retired to the altar, and took the pyx, in which was the *Corpus Domini*, in his left hand, in the other hand holding a lighted taper, upside down, so that he made it melt and burn away, muttering orisons the while, and at the end fierce and threatening words against the devil, with as loud and authoritative a voice as he could assume. When the first candle was burnt down nearly to his fingers, he took another, and then a second, and then the third. . . . .

He told us that this was a devil of the worst sort, an obstinate devil, who would give much trouble to cast out. He then told ten or a dozen of us gentlemen who were there a number of stories about this art and of his ordinary ex-

[45] P. 133.   [46] P. 132.

[47] *Journal du voyage de Michel de Montaigne en Italie* (2 vols.; Rome and Paris, 1774), II, 117.

periences of it, and in particular that the day before he had freed a woman from a big devil, who, in coming out of her, discharged out of this woman, through her mouth, nails, pins, and a tuft of his hair.[48]

Reade transfers this narrative to *The Cloister and the Hearth* but changes some of the details.

There they found the demoniac forced down on his knees before the altar with a scarf tied round his neck, by which the officiating priest held him like a dog in a chain.

Not many persons were present, for fame had put forth that the last demon cast out in that church went no farther then into one of the company: "as a cony ferreted out of one burrow runs to the next."

When Gerard and the friar came up, the priest seemed to think there were now spectators enough; and began.

He faced the demoniac, breviary in hand, and first set himself to learn the individual's name with whom he had to deal.

"Come out, Ashtaroth. Oho! it is not you then. Come out, Belial. . . . . Come out, Nebul. Aha! what, have I found ye? 'tis thou, thou reptile; at thine old tricks. Let us pray! . . . .

The priest then rose from his knees, and turning to the company said, with quiet geniality, "Gentles, we have here as obstinate a divell as you may see in a summer day." Then, facing the patient, he spoke to him with great rigour, sometimes addressing the man, and sometimes the fiend, and they answered him in turn through the same mouth, now saying that they hated those holy names the priest kept uttering, and now complaining they did feel so bad in their inside.

It was the priest who first confounded the victim and the culprit in idea, by pitching into the former, cuffing him soundly, kicking him, and spitting repeatedly in his face. Then he took a candle and lighted it, and turned it down, and burned it till it burned his fingers; when he dropped it double quick. Then took the custodial; and showed the patient the Corpus Domini within. Then burned another candle as before, but more cautiously. . . . .

"Good father," said Gerard, "how you have their names by heart. Our northern priests have no such exquisite knowledge of the hellish squadrons. . . . ."

He [the priest] then told the company in the most affable way several of his experiences; concluding with his feat of yesterday, when he drove a great hulking fiend out of a woman by her mouth, leaving behind him certain nails, and pins, and a tuft of his own hair, and cried out in a voice of anguish, " 'Tis not thou that conquers me. See that stone on the window sill. Know that the angel Gabriel coming down to earth once lighted on that stone: 'tis that has done my business."

[48] *Journey*, pp. 139–40.

The friar [Colonna] moaned. "And you believed him?"

"Certes! who, but an infidel had discredited a revelation so precise?"

"What, believe the father of lies? . . . ."[49]

Reade's framework in this passage is clearly drawn from Montaigne, but the details are enlivened or elaborated by the novelist's fancy. He first compares the maniac to "a dog in a chain" and thereafter adds, for the sake of humor, the spectator's fear that the devil will take refuge in one of them. Similarly he introduces a new element, namely, the priest's desire to have a good audience. In his elaboration of Montaigne, Reade thereafter renders the action gradually more intense by making the priest pass from rebuking to actually buffeting the patient, whereas in the French diary the two steps are intermingled. In these happenings, too, as indeed in the whole passage, Reade manifests much anticlericalism. Thereafter in both authors the exorcist had recourse to burning candles and presenting the custodial, with the humorous addition in Reade of the priest's hurting his fingers. At the end of each account the priest told the spectators about his previous experiences, particularly with one whom Reade dubs "a great hulking fiend."

Though the basis of the account is from Montaigne, some details are from Moryson. The Elizabethan traveler says:

I say my selfe did see a Priest casting a devill (as they said) out of an old woman with strange inchantments, and hee did so familiarly call that Divell [Reade uses this spelling, in his dialogue, for its archaic flavor] and all his Legion by their names [this suggests to Reade the idea of calling the long list of names], as I much wondred thereat; for wee Northerne men have not such exquisite knowledge of the hellish Squadrons. [Reade's "Our northern priests have no such exquisite knowledge of the hellish squadrons."] And it is ridiculous but true, that while I seemed thus astonished, a young Priest without a beard came to me, and told me a long fable, of a horrible Divel which had been there cast out, yet before his departure, shewed to the Priest a stone on the next window, upon which the Angel Gabriel stood, when he foretold the Virgin Marie of Christs Nativitie, crying that hee was cast out by the holinesse of that stone [all this about the other devil and the stone is borrowed by Reade], not of the Priest. This I heard with great attention, and with shew of astonishment, but

[49] Oxf., pp. 449–51; Ev., pp. 456–58.

with my selfe I thought it strange, that they should in this beleeve the Divell the father of lies. [From this, Reade has taken Fra Colonna's objection at the end of the passage.][50]

Now Gerard began an adventure involving a great Roman lady.[51] He was summoned one day to a palace to write a letter for a princess. The letter never was completed, but Gerard soon found himself, instead, engaged in painting the young lady's portrait in many sittings. The signorina was called Claelia Cesarini. This name Reade got from Montaigne, who tells us that he visited the palace of "Jan George Cesarin" (as the name occurs in the French edition of 1774,[52] though a note on the opposite page gives an Italian form of the surname ending in -*i*). Montaigne goes on, "He has also the portraits of the handsomest living Roman ladies, and of the Signora Clelia-Fascia Farnese [French edition: "Claelia-Fascia Farnèse"], his wife, who is, if not the most agreeable, beyond comparison the most lovable woman who was then in Rome, or, for all I know, anywhere else."[53] Though the name of this Roman aristocrat is borrowed from Montaigne, the character of Reade's lady is wholly different, being haughty, imperious, and passionate.

We next witness a series of ecclesiastical ceremonies on Holy Thursday, which are useful in the novel since they provide much local color. They come from Montaigne's *Journey*. The Pope's progress through the streets is thus described in the novel:

> Presently the Pope came pacing majestically at the head of his cardinals, in a red hat, white cloak, a capuchin of red velvet, and riding a lovely white Neapolitan barb, caparisoned with red velvet fringed and tasselled with gold; a hundred horsemen, armed cap-à-pie, rode behind him with their lances erected, the butt-end resting on the man's thigh. The cardinals went uncovered, all but one, de Medicis, who rode close to the Pope and conversed with him as with an equal. At every fifteen steps the Pope stopped a single moment, and gave the people his blessing, then on again.[54]

[50] Moryson, III, 446. (Some of these Moryson borrowings are noted by Wheeler.) Moryson speaks of this experience again in I, 214.

[51] Oxf., pp. 451 ff.; Ev., pp. 458 ff.

[52] Fr. ed., II, 218.

[53] Eng. trans., p. 169.   [54] Oxf., p. 454; Ev., pp. 461–62.

This is drawn from Montaigne's account of the passing of this dignitary through the streets on another occasion than Holy Thursday.

On the 3rd day of January 1581, the Pope passed before our window. . . . . At his side was the Cardinal de Medicis, who was talking with him covered, and was taking him to dine with him. The Pope had a red hat, his white apparel and red velvet hood, as usual, mounted on a white hackney with harness of red velvet, with gold fringes and lace. He mounts his horse without the assistance of a groom, and yet he is in his eighty-first year. Every fifteen yards he gave his benediction. After him came three Cardinals, and then about a hundred men-at-arms, lance on thigh, and armed at all points except the head.[55]

Another ceremony in Montaigne—this time on Holy Thursday—runs as follows:

On Maundy-Thursday, in the morning, the Pope, in full pontificals, takes his stand on the first portico of St. Peter's, on the second flight, the Cardinals assisting, himself holding a torch in his hand. There, on one side, a canon of St. Peter's reads, in a loud voice, a Latin bull, excommunicating an infinite number of people, among others the Huguenots, by that very name, and all the princes who detain any of the estates of the Church; at which article the Cardinals de Medicis and Caraffa, who stood next to the Pope, laughed very heartily. . . . . After that the Pope threw the lighted torch down among the people, and, in jest or otherwise, Cardinal Gonzaga another; for there were three of them lighted. Those fell on the people; down below the most terrible scramble takes place for bits of the torch, and fists and sticks are used with very good effect. While the commination is being read, there is also a large piece of black taffeta which hangs over the parapet of the said portico before the Pope. The excommunication over, they turn up this black cover and another of a different colour is disclosed; and the Pope then gives his public benedictions.[56]

From this excerpt Reade draws the following incident:

Soon the Pope and cardinals, who had entered the church by another door, issued forth, and stood with torches on the steps, separated by barriers from the people; then a canon read a Latin Bull, excommunicating several persons by name, especially such princes as were keeping the Church out of any of her temporal possessions. [Reade omits mention of the Huguenots, since they would be unsuitable.]

At this awful ceremony Gerard trembled, and so did the people. But two of the cardinals spoiled the effect by laughing unreservedly the whole time.

When this was ended, the black cloth was removed, and revealed a gay panoply; and the Pope blessed the people, and ended by throwing his torch

[55] Pp. 127–28.   [56] P. 156.

among them; so did two cardinals. Instantly there was a scramble for the torches: they were fought for, and torn in pieces by the candidates, so devoutly that small fragments were gained at the price of black eyes, bloody noses, and burnt fingers; in which hurtling his holiness and suite withdrew in peace.[57]

In his treatment of the borrowing Reade stresses the cardinals' frivolity in contrast to the devotion of Gerard and the populace. He likewise enlivens the episode generally, and he alters the order of details so as to close with a rough-and-tumble fight instead of a blessing, thus securing a more spirited climax.

Reade now continues his borrowing from Montaigne's description of ecclesiastical ceremonies. In both the English novel and the French diary the Vera icon, in "a square frame, like that of a mirror" was exhibited to a crowd by a priest with red gloves. The people gazed upon the sight with cries of pity and with tears in their eyes.[58]

In both Montaigne[59] and Reade[60] a procession of flagellants passed, many of them laughing as they whipped themselves. Certain of the bystanders offered them wine, but the flagellants usually accepted it only to wet, and thus separate, the strands of their lashes, which were clotted with blood. In both authors, furthermore, a young woman took pity on a mere boy in the procession. In Montaigne, "he turned round to us and said to her with a laugh: 'Basta, dille che fo questo per li sui peccati, non per li miei.' " ("It's all right; tell her I am doing this for her sins, not for mine.") In Reade, "the fair urchin" acts similarly: " 'Basta,' said he, laughing, ' 'tis for your sins I do it, not for mine.' " Reade then completes the episode suitably from his own imagination and connects it with one of the characters in the novel by making Fra Colonna declare the practice is derived from the ancient Roman festival of the Lupercalia.

Next Gerard and the friar went to hear the pope say mass. The original of this passage in Montaigne runs as follows:

The Pope administered the Sacrament to a number of others, and with him officiated at this service the Cardinals Farnese, Medicis, Caraffa, and Gonzaga.

[57] Oxf., pp. 454–55; Ev., p. 462.

[58] Oxf., p. 455; Ev., pp. 462–63; Montaigne, *Journey*, pp. 156–57.

[59] Pp. 158–59.   [60] Oxf., pp. 455–56; Ev., p. 463.

There is a certain instrument for drinking from the chalice, in order to provide safety against poison. It seemed strange to him that, both at this mass and others, the Popes and Cardinals and other prelates were seated, and, during nearly the whole mass, covered, talking and chatting together. These ceremonies appeared to him altogether to partake more of magnificence than of devotion.[61]

The account in Reade is similar, but more condensed:

Next they got into one of the seven churches, and saw the Pope give the mass. The ceremony was imposing, but again spoiled by the inconsistent conduct of the cardinals, and other prelates, who sat about the altar with their hats on, chattering all through the mass like a flock of geese.[62]

The rendering is more lively and emphasizes more the irreverent conduct of the ecclesiastics.

Then Reade goes on to develop a hint from a note in the 1774 French edition of Montaigne, which he used. In this the French expression for "provide safety against poison" has a footnote running (in translation) "to take precautions against poison. The testing had already been done by the 'Preguste.' "[63] Reade, seeing in this suggestion an opportunity for an additional bit of anticlericalism, has the Eucharist tasted by a special official, or *preguste*, before the pope. Hereupon the naïve and devout Gerard, believing implicitly in transubstantiation, objected that such caution was wholly unnecessary. However, the skeptical Fra Colonna replied curtly, "So says faith; but experience tells another tale," and then declared that until his book, *The Dream of Polifilo*, was finished he lived for it, and no poison was to come near him.

Again, on the same day, Gerard and his friar went to see the so-called heads of Peter and Paul at the Lateran. The passage is drawn from Montaigne's account of the same ceremony. The details coincide perfectly; in both accounts we read of the preliminary ringing of bells, the drawing of a curtain by jerks, the shape and appearance of the heads themselves, and the practice of exhibiting them thrice and each time long enough for the spectators to say an "Ave Maria." To this scene, similarly, Reade attaches a characteristic discourse by the skeptical friar, who de-

[61] *Journey*, pp. 122–23.   [62] Oxf., p. 456; Ev., p. 463.   [63] Fr. ed., II, 91.

rived the ceremony from the ancient practice of showing waxen images of great men at funerals but declared this modern imitation far inferior.[64]

One day Gerard, in his copying-room in the Vatican, was visited by the aged pope, Pius II (Aeneas Sylvius), who came to behold the new copy of Plutarch. Reade gives us a remarkable and charming picture of this famous pope and scholar.[65] His view of the Italian may be summed up in one sentence of the novel: "A high bred, and highly cultivated gentleman, who had done, and said, and seen, and known everything, and whose body was nearly worn out." And so he is depicted in this scene: sophisticated, intellectually subtle, elegant, but lacking in energy.

In his conception of this pope Reade may well have drawn some ideas from Milman's *History of Latin Christianity*, which though not occurring in the *Century* list, he seems to have read, if we may judge from a jotting in one of Mr. Parrish's Reade notebooks.[66] Milman narrates of Aeneas Sylvius while the latter was still young:

> So, then, the Siennese adventurer had visited almost every realm of Northern Europe, France, Germany, Flanders, Scotland, England; he is in the confidence of Cardinals, he is in correspondence with many of the most learned and influential men in Christendom. No sooner was Aeneas fixed at Basle, than his singular aptitude for business, no doubt his fluent and perspicuous Latin, his flexibility of opinion, his rapidly growing knowledge of mankind . . . . opened the way to advancement; offices, honors, rewards crowded upon him.[67]

Moreover, when Aeneas Sylvius became pope, Milman says of him, "Few men of more consummate ability had sat on the throne of St. Peter,"[68] and again, "How strangely, how nobly did Pius II., at the close of his life, redeem the weaknesses, the treachery, the inconsistency, the unblushing effrontery of self-interest of his earlier years."[69] Finally, too, Milman calls him a "refined and accomplished man."[70]   From such remarks as these Reade might

---

[64] Oxf., p. 457; Ev., p. 464; Montaigne, *Journey*, pp. 159–60.

[65] Oxf., pp. 458–63; Ev., pp. 465–70.

[66] It runs: "See Aeneas Sylvius. Cited Milman."

[67] *History of Latin Christianity* (8 vols.; New York, 1860–61), VIII, 74.

[68] *Ibid.*, p. 120.   [69] *Ibid.*, p. 121.   [70] *Ibid.*, p. 122.

well draw his conception of the old pope's wide experience, his skill in handling people shown in the conversation with different persons, the grace of his elocution, the intellectual subtlety of his talk on animals, and the note of considerable high-mindedness which pervades this discourse.

His interlocutors ask the old pope about the novel which he wrote in his earlier years, to which inquiry the pontiff replies, "Well then, the work in question had, as far as I remember, all the vices of Boccaccio, without his choice Italian." This seems to reflect Milman's sentence: "He was forty when he wrote his celebrated Romance, Euryalus and Lucretia, a romance with neither incident nor invention; in its moral tone and in the warmth of its descriptions, as in its prolixity, a novel of Boccaccio, but without his inimitable grace."[71]

Previously, in the novel, the company had discussed Boccaccio, and the pope had given his opinion: "An excellent narrator, Capitano, and writeth exquisite Italian. But in spirit a thought too monotonous. Monks and nuns were never all unchaste: one or two such stories were right pleasant and diverting; but five score paint his time falsely, and sadden the heart of such as love mankind. Moreover, he hath no skill at characters."[72] This dictum, aside from the benevolent spirit toward humanity, shows the easy-going morality ascribed to him by Milman's remark: "Aeneas was an Italian in his passions, and certainly under no austere, monkish self-control. His morals were those of his age and country."[73] The sentence about Boccaccio's lack of skill at character-drawing seems to be Reade's own view, for we find in one of his notebooks the statement: "The figures in Boccaccio's stories have some little distinctive character: but about as much as the peas in a pod."[74]

Fra Colonna requested the pope to pass judgment between Gerard and another young man. Their dispute was over the question whether "the blessing of the beasts of burden" was a foolish institution or not. Reade may have derived his informa-

[71] *Ibid.*, p. 73.   [72] Oxf., p. 458; Ev., p. 466.   [73] VIII, 71.

[74] E. G. Sutcliffe, "Charles Reade's Notebooks," *Studies in Philology*, XXVII, 79.

tion about this ceremony from William Hone's *Every-Day Book*.[75] Hone writes as follows:

On St. Anthony's day, the beasts at Rome are blessed, and sprinkled with holy water. . . . . Lady Morgan says, that the annual benediction of the beasts at Rome, in a church there dedicated to St. Anthony, lasts for some days: "for not only every Roman from the pope to the peasant, who has a horse, a mule, or an ass, sends his cattle to be blessed at St. Anthony's shrine, but all the English go with their job horses and favourite dogs."

The old pope tried to avoid having to judge an argument, but Fra Colonna told him it was his duty to quiet the dispute between two violent youths. Hence the old man submitted with the quotation οὐκ ἔστὶν ὅστις ἐστ' ἀνὴρ ἐλεύθερος. This is an inexact rendering of a line from Euripides: οὐκ ἔστι θνητῶν ὅστις ἐστ' ἐλεύθερος.[76] This is quoted rightly in *Mores Catholici;* hence it seems likely that Reade found it there, but was careless as to the exact wording. The old pope then delivered, on the subject, an informal discourse embodying much good sense and full of charm.

One day, while on his way through the streets of Rome, Gerard saw a printed copy of Lactantius, produced by Sweynheim and Pannartz at Subiaco, Italy.[77] He at once realized that the press would soon drive him out of business as a calligrapher in Rome.

Reade was interested in early printing since he had already been coauthor of a play, *The First Printer*, acted in 1856. The particular information about Sweynheim and Pannartz, the two Germans who first brought printing into Italy, seems to come from Hallam's *Introduction to the Literature of Europe:*

Sweynheim and Pannartz, two workmen of Fust, set up a press, doubtless with encouragement and patronage, at the monastery of Subiaco in the Apennines, a place chosen either on account of the numerous manuscripts it contained, or because the monks were of the German nation; and hence an edition of Lactantius, issued in October, 1465.[78]

Presumably, when he read Hallam, Reade was attracted by this account because of his previous interest in early printing, and

---

[75] *Every-Day Book and Table Book* (3 vols.; London, 1835), Vol. I, col. 117.

[76] Euripides *Hecuba* 864; *Mores Catholici*, III, 601.

[77] Oxf., p. 464; Ev., p. 472.   [78] I, 99.

thus determined to introduce these two Germans, as he does here and at a later point of his novel. Lacroix and Seré, it should be noted, have the same information about the two men,[79] but they give no points used by Reade that are not obtainable also in Hallam. Moreover, Hallam has Reade's spelling of "Sweynheim" (Lacroix and Seré have "Swynheym") and mentions, as the French authors do not, that Subiaco is "in the Apennines." Reade has the bookseller remark to Gerard, "Oh, the *Lactantius;* that was printed on the top of the Apennines."

Meantime, Gerard had continued painting Claelia Cesarini. She fell in love with him and tried to corrupt him, *callida et calida solis filia* that she was. This quotation Reade derived from Coryate's applying it to the courtesans of Venice.[80] Finally, enraged by his not reciprocating her love, Claelia prepared to end him and gathered armed men in her palace to effect his death. Gerard begged passionately for his life, and the princess finally let him go, with the command to leave Rome at once.

Gerard prepared to take a ship to Amsterdam and was happy at the idea of returning. Then suddenly the great calamity happened: The letter forged by his two brothers and the burgomaster was brought to him by Hans Memling. Crushed by the false news of Margaret's death, he became dangerously ill; thereafter, on recovering, he began a life of wild dissipation. One of his companions was Perugino.

After Gerard had lived thus for some time, Perugino one day wished to organize a boat party on the Tiber. He secured a galley and twelve buffaloes to pull it upstream. A group of dissipated young men took part, and each one of them had to bring with him a beautiful girl. Gerard was the last of the group to appear, and he was escorting a lady of surpassing loveliness. The buffaloes pulled the boat slowly, and one of the gay fellows, jumping ashore, pricked a buffalo with his sword. The savage animal at once hooked him with a horn and sent him flying into the Tiber, whence his friends rescued him. The other girls, jealous of the superior beauty of Gerard's lady, began to carp at her, and

[79] V, "Imprimerie," xvii.

[80] Oxf., p. 471; Ev., p. 479; Coryate, *Crudities*, I, 405. (Noted by Wheeler.)

she retorted with satirical jibes. Soon thereafter a galley drifting in the opposite direction passed their boat. In it was seated the Princess Claelia with a group of admirers, and she gazed full upon Gerard and his lady. When the other ship had passed by, two of the girls in the galley of revelers began to suspect Gerard's lady. They threw a handful of nuts into her lap, and by the way she brought her legs together instinctively, instead of separating them as would a woman accustomed to skirts, they found the supposed girl was a boy. He was indeed the boy who ground Perugino's colors.[81]

In this episode there are several borrowings. In the first place, the important element of the boating party is suggested by a single sentence of Montaigne's, "They have their boats on the Tiber towed upstream with ropes by three or four pairs of buffaloes."[82] The twelve buffaloes secured by Perugino thus were an especially luxurious provision. Another bit is drawn from the following remark of Moryson:

> In the Roman territory I have seene many Beasts called Buffoli, like Oxen, but greater and more deformed, having great hornes with foule nostrels cast up into the Ayre: It is a slow and dull Beast, yet being provoked, hath malice enough, and the backe thereof is commonly bare of haire, and ever almost galled.[83]

From this comes the description in a speech by one of the revelers, "We ne'er saw monsters so vilely ill-favoured; with their nasty horns that make one afeard, and their foul nostrils cast up into the air."[84] Moreover, from the latter part of Moryson's remark Reade drew the humorous idea of having one of the gallants try to prick a buffalo and get tossed into the river.

Another most important element in Reade's episode—the disguising of the boy as a girl—comes from Cellini's autobiography. Professor Clyde K. Hyder of the University of Kansas noticed the influence and drew my attention to the similarity. On going

[81] Oxf., pp. 482–87; Ev., pp. 489–94.   [82] *Journey*, p. 160.

[83] IV, 83. (Wheeler notes this passage as a possible source for the first mention of the buffaloes but does not remark the borrowing of the descriptive words or the adventure of the reveler.)

[84] Oxf., p. 483; Ev., pp. 490–91.

over the matter in detail since, I find that an agreement in wording proves the borrowing, but I have not detected any sure influence from other parts of Cellini. Reade used Thomas Roscoe's
translation of the famous book as the resemblance in phraseology
demonstrates. Cellini runs as follows:

> After we had been several times in company together, our worthy president
> [Perugino figures in this part in Reade] thought proper to invite us to sup at his
> house one Sunday, directing that every man should bring his *chère amie* (whom
> he called *cornacchia*) with him [*chère amie*, which is not a close rendering of the
> Italian expression here, is the phrase reappearing later in the incident in
> Reade], and he who brought no lady should be obliged to treat the company
> with a supper. [In Reade, "Each libertine was to bring a lady; and she must be
> handsome, or he be fined."]

Cellini thought of a clever trick and prevailed upon a sixteen-
year-old boy, named Diego, to dress up as a girl and go with him.

> When we came to the place, the whole company were already met, and all
> rose to salute me. [Gerard and his girl arrived last also.] .... As soon as I had
> taken the handkerchief from the head of my beautiful companion, Michelagnolo
> ...., with one hand taking hold of Giulio, and with the other of Giovanni
> Francesco, with his utmost might drew them towards Diego, and obliged them
> to kneel down; at the same time falling upon his knees himself, and calling to
> the company he exclaimed aloud, "See in what form angels descend from the
> clouds! .... " At these words the facetious creature lifted up his right hand,
> and gave him a papal benediction.[85]

In Reade, the men "received her with loud shouts and waving of
caps, and one enthusiast even went down on his knees upon the
boat's gunwale, and hailed her of origin divine. But his *chère amie*
[the phrase borrowed from Roscoe's translation] pulling his hair
for it—and the goddess giving him a little kick—contemporane-
ously, he lay supine." In the novel, furthermore, the wit of the
supposed lady is emphasized much. Thereafter, in Cellini, the
company read sonnets and then sat down to dinner. Diego was
between two of the women and, after a while, was found by them
to be a boy, though in a different way from Reade's method.

When the other women, becoming jealous, made derogatory
remarks about the supposed girl in *The Cloister and the Hearth*, she
answered them with spirited taunts. " 'Look here,' and she

[85] *Memoirs of Benvenuto Cellini, a Florentine Artist; Written by Himself*, trans. Thomas
Roscoe (London, 1850), pp. 60–64.

pointed rudely in one's face. 'This is the beauty that is to be bought in every shop. Here is cerussa, here is stibium, and here purpurissum.' " These cosmetics are taken from Coryate, who mentions their use by Venetian courtesans.[86] Continuing the derision, Gerard's lady reproached the women for wearing "wooden heeled chopines" to make themselves appear taller. Moryson speaks of these "choppines" as worn by the women of Venice.[87] Coryate mentions them also, though using a spelling further removed from Reade's, but he tells us they were of wood.[88] Then the disguised youth wound up his speech, "Aha, mesdames, well is it said of you, grande—di legni: grosse—di straci: rosse—di bettito: bianche—di calcina." This Italian proverb Reade drew from Moryson,[89] adding the dashes for emphasis himself. These sayings, we observe, have been worked into the dialogue most naturally.

All these borrowings Reade has made excellent use of. He does not inform us at the beginning that Gerard's lady was a boy. At first, indeed, we are quite in the dark; then, as time goes on, Perugino's continual staring with an unusual expression at the supposed girl, and her unfeminine retorts at the other women, begin to arouse suspicion, which turns into certainty at the end. The interlude of pricking the buffalo and the consequent witty remarks of the disguised youth create interest. Finally, the meeting with the Princess Claelia is dramatic and likewise provides important motivation for the plot.

The sight of Gerard still in Rome and the belief that he had divulged the whole affair to his frivolous associates made the princess resolve to punish him. She accordingly summoned an assassin to her palace and gave him her instructions. In the course of them she asked what his weapons were:

The bravo showed her a steel gauntlet. "We strike with such force we need must guard our hand. This is our mallet." He then undid his doublet, and gave her a glimpse of a coat of mail beneath, and finally laid his glittering stiletto on the table with a flourish.[90]

[86] I, 404. (Noted by Wheeler.)

[87] IV, 220. (Not noted by Wheeler.)   [89] IV, 220. (Noted by Wheeler.)

[88] I, 400. (Not noted by Wheeler.)   [90] Oxf., pp. 489–90; Ev., p. 497.

This is borrowed from the passage in Coryate from which Reade previously took the statement that an assassin was called a "brave man":

> There are certaine desperate and resolute villaines in Venice, called Braves, who at some unlawfull times do commit great villainy. They wander abroad very late in the night to and fro for their prey, like hungry Lyons, being armed with a privy coate of maile, a gauntlet upon their right hand, and a little sharpe dagger called a stiletto.[91]

The bargain was soon made, and the assassin went out to seek Gerard.

The next sentence in the Coryate passage about "Braves" just quoted is most important:

> They lurke commonly by the water side, and if at their time of the night, which is betwixt eleven of the clocke and two, they happen to meete any man that is worth the rifling, they will presently stabbe him, take away all about him that is of any worth, and when they have throughly pulled his plumes, they will throw him into one of the channels.

We have already seen that Reade derived the assassin's arms from this Elizabethan passage; this last statement of Coryate's, accordingly, though made about Venetian slayers hanging about the canals, surely suggested that the Roman assassin should carry out—or at least intend to carry out—a similar stabbing and throwing of the body into the water of the Tiber. Then it would seem Reade's invention supplied a neat twist: the assassin would prove to be the husband of the Roman matron whose life Gerard had saved and thus, of course, would be unable to kill the young man. Thereafter, to produce a still more striking scene, Reade would have the unhappy Gerard, catching sight of the skulking assassin, entreat death from his hands, and then, not gaining his petition, jump into the Tiber and actually be saved against his will by the very man sent out to kill him. In some such manner Reade's mind must have worked. The result, of course, was that he tied the event securely, by cause and effect, to the shipwreck and achieved a most unusual scene. Indeed, it was just the sort of which he was especially proud, and, lest the reader should overlook its unusualness, he spoke of it in the text of the novel as "an

---

[91] I, 413. (Nothing in the passage is noted by Wheeler.)

event . . . . , which, take it altogether, was perhaps without a parallel in the history of mankind, and may remain so to the end of time."[92]

The assassin, on rescuing Gerard from the river, took him to a Dominican convent. There, in a few days, the young Dutchman entered the church and took the name of Brother Clement. The Princess Claelia, meanwhile, believing Gerard to be dead, suddenly became conscience-stricken for having killed him and undertook a hard penance.

Back in the Low Countries, too, a significant event took place at this time. In the city of Rotterdam was born the son of Margaret and Gerard—the child who was to become the great Erasmus.

In the same year Philip, Duke of Burgundy, lay seriously ill, as we read in the novel.

> The duke's complaint, nameless then, is now diphtheria. It is, and was, a very weakening malady, and the duke was old; so altogether Dr. Remedy bled him.
> The duke turned very cold: wonderful!
> Then Dr. Remedy had recourse to the arcana of science.
> "Ho! This is grave. Flay me an ape incontinent, and clap him to the duke's breast!"[93]

The courtiers looked for an ape, but could find none among the strange beasts about the palace. Then the seneschal had a happy idea:

> "Here is *this*," said he, sotto voce. "Surely *this* will serve; 'tis altogether ape-like, doublet and hose apart."
> "Nay," said the chancellor, peevishly, "the Princess Marie would hang us. She doteth on *this*."
> Now *this* was our friend Giles, strutting, all unconscious, in cloth of gold.
> Then Dr. Remedy grew impatient, and bade flay a dog.
> "A dog is next best to an ape; only it must be a dog all of one colour."
> So they flayed a liver-coloured dog, and clapped it, yet palpitating, to their sovereign's breast: and he died.

In addition to showing once more Reade's antipathy to bleeding, this passage is interesting because it is developed from a brief

[92] Oxf., p. 495; Ev., p. 503.   [93] Oxf., pp. 504–5; Ev., p. 512.

suggestion in Ben Jonson's *Volpone*. Mosca tells another man that Volpone is very ill and has been inspected by the doctors:

> And since, to seem the more officious
> And flatt'ring of his health, there, they have had,
> At extreme fees, the college of physicians
> Consulting on him, how they might restore him;
> Where one would have a cataplasm of spices,
> Another a flay'd ape clapp'd to his breast,
> A third would have it a dog, a fourth an oil,
> With wild cats' skins. . . . .[94]

The borrowing here is sure because of the similarity in wording—"Flay me an ape, incontinent, and clap him to the duke's breast," as the novel runs. The practice is strange and thus appealing to the reader, and it is another bit of satire by Reade on the medical profession of that age. Then the novelist's fancy, set working, has the courtiers pick out Giles as a possible substitute—to be, however, quickly rejected. Finally, the physicians decided on a dog—the third suggestion in the *Volpone* lines—and Reade has them pedantically insist on "a dog all of one colour." The whole passage is carried out, finally, with lively dialogue.[95]

Reade, having related how Duke Philip died and having specified how many illegitimate children he left, now makes a strong contrast:

Holland rang with his death; and little dreamed that anything as famous was born in her territory that year. That judgment has been long reversed. Men gaze at the tailor's house, where the great birth of the fifteenth century [that of Erasmus] took place. In what house the good duke died "no one knows and no one cares," as the song says.

And why?

Dukes Philip the Good come and go, and leave mankind not a half-penny wiser, nor better, nor other, than they found it. But when, once in three hundred years, such a child is born to the world as Margaret's son, lo! a human torch lighted by fire from heaven; and "fiat lux" thunders from pole to pole.[96]

[94] *Volpone*, II, 3.

[95] I have found no sure borrowings from Barante about Philip's death. Indeed, Barante gives apoplexy, not diphtheria, as the cause. Nor have I found in Smet's *Chroniques de Flandre* any account of the sovereign's being descended from "the Kings of Troy."

[96] Oxf., pp. 505–6; Ev., pp. 513–14.

This contrast is marked by a strong irony toward Philip the Good and by a glorification of Erasmus. The juxtaposition of the two may well be derived from a passage in Gerard Brandt's *The History of the Reformation:*

About four years before the death of Kempes, on Simon and Jude's day, was born that great miracle of Wit and Learning, Desiderius Erasmus, at Rotterdam, (his name in our Mother Tongue was Gerrit Gerritson), who has so well shown us the way to a true Reformation, ... never suffering himself to be enslaved by disputable questions, nor by the ceremonies of either Party. We Hollanders can never sufficiently thank this Man; and for my own part, I think my self happy, that at this distance I can in some measure comprehend his virtues.

Philip Duke of Burgundy, surnamed the Good, who by the help of the (so called) Kabbeljaw Faction, had thrust himself, by force into the Inheritance of his Niece Jacoba, the lawful Countess of Holland, in her life-time, died in the same year.[97]

This passage not only glorifies Erasmus but takes the same ironic attitude to Philip that we find in Reade. Moreover, there is no particular reason why Reade should take so much pains with the account of Philip's death (Philip is of but little importance in the novel), or even why he should mention it at all. It seems probable, then, that he happened to see Brandt's passage and, being struck with it, wrote a similar one himself.

[97] Translated from the original Low Dutch (4 vols.; London, 1720–23), I, 29–30.

Chapter Eight

INTO THE CHURCH

WHEN Gerard had become Brother Clement, it was thought good by his superiors to test him in Rome before sending him to preach in other countries. Accordingly Jerome—the friar whom Clement had met in the shipwreck— took Clement in hand and conducted him to witness two executions.

Both executions are drawn from Montaigne's *Journey*, where they occur close together. Reade, however, has exchanged their order. The second execution in Montaigne runs as follows:

> I saw two brothers done to death, former servants of the Castellano's secretary, who had killed him by night a few days before in the city, within the very palace of the said Signor Giacomo Buoncompagno, the Pope's son. They pinched their flesh with red-hot pincers, and then cut off their fist, in front of the said palace; and after cutting they applied capons to their wounds, which they had killed and immediately laid open. They were despatched on a scaffold, clubbed with a big wooden mace, and then immediately had their throats cut.[1]

The first execution in *The Cloister and the Hearth* drawn from this account was of a servant who had killed his master, the governor of Rome.

> The criminal was brought to the house of the murdered man, and fastened for half an hour to its wall. After this foretaste of legal vengeance his left hand was struck off, like his victim's. A new fowl was cut open and fastened round the bleeding stump . . . . ; and the murderer, thus mutilated and bandaged, was hurried to the scaffold; and there a young friar was most earnest and affectionate in praying with him, and for him, and holding the crucifix close to his eyes.
>
> Presently the executioner pulled the friar roughly on one side, and in a moment felled the culprit with a heavy mallet, and falling on him, cut his throat from ear to ear.[2]

[1] *The Diary of Montaigne's Journey*, p. 129.   [2] Oxf., pp. 507–8; Ev., pp. 515–16.

180

In this account Reade has sensibly had one criminal instead of two, has described the execution rather more fully, and has introduced Clement as the accompanying friar. Clement swooned at the end.

Montaigne's other execution proceeds thus:

It happened that they were taking out of prison Catena, a famous robber and captain of banditti who had kept all Italy in terror, and of whom they related some atrocious murders. . . . . There are two of those [attendants], or monks, clothed and masked in the same way, who stand by the side of the criminal in the cart and exhort him; and one of them continually holds before his face, and makes him incessantly kiss, a tablet on which is the image of Our Lord. . . . . After he was strangled, they cut him into four quarters. . . . . M. de Montaigne noticed here, what he has said elsewhere, how much the people are terrified by the severities practised upon dead bodies: for the people here, who had shown no feeling at seeing him strangled, at every blow that was given to hew him in pieces burst out into piteous cries. As soon as they are dead, one or several Jesuits, or others, mount upon some raised place and shout at the people, one in this direction, another in that, and preach to them to make them relish that example.[3]

This account prompts the second test of Clement in Reade's novel:

A robber was brought to the scaffold; a monster of villany and cruelty, who had killed men in pure wantonness, after robbing them. Clement passed his last night in prison with him [an addition by Reade], accompanied him to the scaffold, and then prayed with him and for him so earnestly that the hardened ruffian shed tears and embraced him. Clement embraced him too, though his flesh quivered with repugnance [these additions show Clement's religious ardor]; and held the crucifix earnestly before his eyes. The man was garotted. . . . . He was no sooner dead than the hangman raised his hatchet and quartered the body on the spot. And, oh, mysterious heart of man! the people who had seen the living body robbed of life with indifference, almost with satisfaction, uttered a piteous cry at each stroke of the axe upon his corpse that could feel nought. Clement too shuddered then, but stood firm, like one of those rocks that vibrate but cannot be thrown down. But suddenly Jerome's voice sounded in his ear.

"Brother Clement, get thee on that cart and preach to the people. Nay, quickly! strike with all thy force on all this iron, while yet 'tis hot, and souls are to be saved."[4]

[3] Pp. 128–29.   [4] Oxf., p. 508; Ev., p. 516.

Clement had already acted better at this execution than at the former. He now obeyed Jerome and made his first attempt at preaching. Reade goes into much more detail here than does Montaigne with his "one or several Jesuits," because this is an important moment in Clement's life. We hear something of how he felt, of what he said, of how the people responded. When he finished, the austere Jerome remarked to him, "Give the glory to God, brother Clement; my opinion is thou art an orator born."

The third testing of Clement occurred at an ordeal by cold water. The culprit, Julio Antonelli, was accused of robbing a church, but there was grave doubt as to his guilt.

In this doubt Antonelli was permitted the trial by water, hot or cold. By the hot trial he must put his bare arm into boiling water, fourteen inches deep, and take out a pebble; by the cold trial his body must be let down into eight feet of water. The clergy, who thought him innocent, recommended the hot water trial, which, to those whom they favoured, was not so terrible as it sounded. But the poor wretch had not the nerve, and chose the cold ordeal. And this gave Jerome another opportunity of steeling Clement. Antonelli took the sacrament, and then was stripped naked on the banks of the Tiber, and tied hand and foot, to prevent those struggles by which a man, throwing his arms out of the water, sinks his body.

He was then let down gently into the stream, and floated a moment, with just his hair above water. A simultaneous roar from the crowd on each bank proclaimed him guilty. But the next moment the ropes, which happened to be new, got wet, and he settled down. Another roar proclaimed his innocence. They left him at the bottom of the river the appointed time, rather more than half a minute, then drew him up, gurgling, and gasping, and screaming for mercy; and, after the appointed prayers, dismissed him, cleared of the charge.[5]

The source of this episode, I believe, is the account of ordeals in Henry's *History of Great Britain*, a twelve-volume work in the *Century* list. It is longer and more detailed than the account in *The Cloister and the Hearth*, for Reade omits some of the particulars. After all, this proceeding is not strange, for though the ordeal provides medieval local color and the sympathetic Reade is interested in the sufferings of Antonelli, the significant point for the novel is the way Clement prayed during the test (omitted in my quotation) and his reactions afterward apropos of the pangs

[5] Oxf., pp. 509–10; Ev., pp. 517–18.

of the accused. Thus the details of the ordeal itself must not be too long drawn out.

Henry tells how the accused man, after fasting for three days, was warned not to receive the Eucharist in case he were guilty. "If the prisoner made no confession, the priest gave him the communion, saying, 'Let this body and blood of our Lord Jesus Christ be received by you as a probation this day.' " Then the party went to a pool, the victim was given a drink of holy water, and a long prayer was said over the pool.

> The prisoner was then stripped naked, his hands and legs made fast [Reade's "stripped naked on the banks of the Tiber, and tied hand and foot"] and a rope tied around his middle, with a knot upon it, at the distance of a yard and a half from his body, and thrown into the pool. If he floated (which was hardly to be imagined) he was taken out and declared guilty; if he sunk so deep as to bring the knot on the rope under the water, he was instantly pulled out, before he could receive any injury, and pronounced innocent.[6]

There are a fair number of similarities between Henry and Reade here: the taking of the sacrament, being "stripped naked" beside the water and having hands and feet tied, being let down some distance, and the guilt of innocence being determined by floating or sinking. For dramatic effect Reade has the man float first and then sink. Reade's specifying "the appointed time rather more than half a minute"—a touch not found in Henry—appears a not unnatural addition; the time is about as long as a man could well endure immersion. The most serious disagreement is that, in Henry, the accused must be let down "a yard and a half," until the knot is submerged, and in Reade he must be "let down into eight feet of water." In extenuation of this variation, we may say, perhaps, that Reade is taking points freely from Henry instead of copying him closely, and also that a body let down eight feet satisfies the requirement of a yard and a half and is more impressive.

After discussing the cold-water ordeal, Henry next turns to that employing hot water: "As soon as the water began to boil, a stone was suspended in it by a string, at the depth of one, two,

[6] Robert Henry, *The History of Great Britain* (12 vols.; London, 1805), III, 431–33.

or three palms, according to the nature of the accusation." The
prisoner "plunged his naked hand and arm into the water and
snatched out the stone."[7] These details agree with Reade's "he
must put his bare arm into boiling water, fourteen inches deep,
and take out a pebble." Thereafter Henry treats the hot-iron ordeal, and then tells at length how the ordeals of hot water or hot
iron did not cause much trouble to the people being tested, when
the church favored them (for instance, good ointments were
used, and the hand was not inspected for three days). "We meet
with no example of any champion of the church who suffered the
least injury from the touch of hot iron in this ordeal," says Henry; "but when any one was so fool-hardy as to appeal to it, or to
that of hot water, with a view to deprive the church of any of
her possessions, he never failed to burn his fingers, and lose his
cause."[8] This remark appears surely to be the source of Reade's
statement, "The clergy, who thought him innocent, recommended the hot water trial, which, to those whom they favoured, was
not so terrible as it sounded." Altogether, then, the Antonelli
episode in the English novel seems drawn undoubtedly from
Henry's description of medieval ordeals.

It so happened that one day Jerome took Clement to see Fra
Colonna. They found him inspecting his work, *The Dream of
Polifilo*. Fra Colonna observed that poets had long wasted their
time praising mortal women who were but "sirens at the windows, where our Roman women in particular have by lifelong
study learned the wily art to show their one good feature, though
but an ear or an eyelash, at a jalosy and hide all the rest; Magpies at the door, Capre n'i giardini, Angeli in Strada, Sante in
chiesa, Diavoli in casa."[9] This assertion is a compound of Moryson and Montaigne. The six things to which women are compared come from Fynes Moryson, who lists them in Italian in
the order: magpies, saints, goats, devils, angels, and sirens; and
then gives the English equivalents in the same order.[10] Reade
wisely puts sirens first, since he wishes to add a borrowing from

[7] *Ibid.*, p. 434.   [8] *Ibid.*, p. 437.   [9] Oxf., p. 510; Ev., p. 518.

[10] *An Itinerary Containing His Ten Yeeres Travell through the Twelve Dominions*, III,
459. (Noted by Wheeler.)

Montaigne to this appellation, and, if it were introduced in the middle of the list, it would break up the sequence. Again, "devils in the house" he puts last for a strong climax, but I see no reason for his using, to make up his series of six, two of the English and four of the Italian forms in Moryson. The insertion about sitting at windows is from Montaigne's remark about Roman women: "They know how to present themselves from their most agreeable side; they will show you only the upper part of the face, or the lower, or the side face, covering or displaying themselves in such a way that you will not see a single ugly one at a window."[11] However, Reade's "their one good feature, though but an ear or an eyelash" is stronger than Montaigne's general mention of parts of the face.

Colonna declared of his book: "Then come I and ransack the minstrels' lines for amorous turns . . . . ; and I lay you the whole bundle of spice at the feet of the only females worthy amorous incense; to wit, the Nine Muses." V. F. Marchese, from whom Reade got much information about Colonna, devotes seven pages to *The Dream of Polifilo* and says, in particular, "Hence, I conclude that the Polia who so fascinated Polifilo was no other than the study of antiquity, as the whole Art-Romance bears evidence of the love with which Colonna cultivated it."[12] This may be the source of the friar's remark in the novel.

Jerome harshly dubbed *Polifilo* an obscene book, but Colonna, stomaching the insult as best he might, "turned the conversation to a beautiful chrysolite the Cardinal Colonna had lent him; and, while Clement handled it, enlarged on its moral virtues: for he went the whole length of his age as a worshipper of jewels."[13] This interest of Fra Colonna's in jewels no doubt comes from Marchese's statement that

all these precious objects of art which he feigned [in his book] to have seen in a dream, are not inventions, but realities, which came under his notice when he

[11] *Journey*, p. 155.

[12] *Lives of the Most Eminent Painters, Sculptors, and Architects of the Order of S. Dominic*, general treatment: I, 287–94; quotation: I, 290.

[13] Oxf., p. 511; Ev., p. 519.

was travelling. Amongst these were marble monuments, coins, cameos, (for which name we are indebted to him), cornelians, and other precious stones, in which he was deeply skilled.[14]

Reade has Fra Colonna make some general observations about stones exercising good moral influences, and particularize about the temperance coming from Gerard's amethyst. He might have become interested in the question from Monteil, where an apothecary holds forth on the virtues derived from different jewels, including the amethyst's rendering people moderate in drinking.[15]

Jerome sneered at Fra Colonna's credulity with regard to precious stones and then went on to exhort him to abandon the study of heathen superstitions and read the lives of the saints instead. This aspersion at length drove the learned Colonna to revenge himself. "He flew out, and hurled a mountain of crude, miscellaneous lore upon Jerome." The theme of the tirade was that the ancients surpassed the moderns in every respect and that a large number of modern practices—especially those of the church—were derived from earlier heathen ones.

Colonna was both learned and excited, and accordingly his whole invective lasted for nine pages![16] It is indeed a great collection of miscellaneous information. Mr. Wheeler, in the notes to his edition of the novel, shows much learning as to the facts, accompanied by much quotation from authorities. My purpose, however, has been to discover where the novelist borrowed the various points and how he changed them. I had hoped in the books in the *Century* list to find two or three passages which furnished Reade with great groups of his statements, but this hope has not been realized. Whether he had two or three extensive sources or whether his various bits of information came from many different books, I do not know. If the latter was the case, the labor involved was so great that Reade probably had recourse to those investigators of whom we know he made use. Indeed, in no other part of the novel does one suspect their presence so

[14] I, 291.

[15] *Histoire des français des divers états*, II, 307–8. (Reade could, of course, have taken the derivation of "amethyst" from a dictionary.)

[16] Oxf., pp. 512–20; Ev., pp. 520–28.

strongly as in this very harangue of Colonna's. Since the purpose of this study, however, is chiefly to investigate sources from which we know Reade drew, I have not tried to do further work on the facts in Fra Colonna's tirade, and I shall merely mention those borrowings which I have encountered.

The friar's statement that the mariners in antiquity had worshiped Venus under the names of *stella maris* and *regina caelorum*, and that contemporary mariners did likewise, with the substitution of the Virgin, comes from Erasmus' colloquy, *The Shipwreck*.[17] Colonna's remark, "The 'Bocca della Verita' passes for a statue of the Virgin, and convicted a woman of perjury the other day; it is in reality an image of the goddess Rhea,"[18] is perhaps twisted from Moryson's "Not farre thence is a marble head, called 'Bocca della verita,' that is, the mouth of truth, of a woman (as I remember) falsifying her oath, and bewraied thereby; but others say it is the Idoll of Rhea."[19]

Again the friar remarked, "At the gate of San [*sic*] Croce our courtezans keep a feast on the 20th August. Ask them why! The little noodles can not tell you. On that very spot stood the Temple of Venus. Her building is gone; but her rite remains."[20] This is taken from Moryson: "At the gate of this Church (S. Croce in Gierusalem) they shew a place where the whores keepe a feast upon the twenty of August, and there of old was the Temple of Venus."[21] Again Colonna's "our very Devil is the god Pan: horns and hoofs and all; but blackened"[22] may perhaps come from *Mores Catholici*, which says:

Many sorcerers in different ages have agreed in confessing that, at the nocturnal sabbat, they used to adore the demon under the form of a goat. This, it will be said, was the caprice of their imagination: yet these men had never read Herodotus, who tells us that the God Pan, more ancient than the Gods of Greece was represented in that form.[23]

[17] Oxf., pp. 513–14; Ev., p. 522; Erasmus, *The Colloquies*, II, 10. (Noted by Wheeler.)

[18] Oxf., pp. 514–15; Ev., p. 523.

[19] I, 284. (Noted by Wheeler.)

[20] Oxf., p. 516; Ev., p. 524.

[21] I, 285–86. (Not noted by Wheeler.)

[22] Oxf., p. 517; Ev., p. 525.

[23] II, 735.

Fra Colonna, in the latter part of his talk, makes a good number of references to the lives of saints. These references and other similar ones elsewhere in the novel are usually so general that one can rarely determine the specific source from which they come.

Meantime, in far-away Holland, Margaret was enjoying her baby, and Gerard's mother Catherine took scarcely less delight in it. Margaret tried to wash away a little mole on the baby's finger, just as Catherine had previously made the same attempt with a mole on Gerard's finger. "It is strange," said she (Catherine), "how things come round and about. Life is but a whirligig. Leastways, we poor women, *our* lives are all cut upon one pattern."[24] Professor Sutcliffe informs me that "how things come round and about. Life is but a whirligig" was a saying of Reade's father.

Clement was first to be sent to the University of Basle to teach, since he was "well versed in languages, and in his worldly days had attended the lectures of Guarini the younger."[25] The *Compendium* mentions his hearing this scholar lecture. Since Clement was not needed at the university for a time, he wandered through Italy preaching. One experience which he had was the following:

A young man was tarantula bitten, or perhaps, like many more, fancied it. Fancy or reality, he had been for two days without sleep, and in most extraordinary convulsions, leaping, twisting, and beating the walls. The village musicians had only excited him worse with their music. Exhaustion and death followed the disease, when it gained such a head. Clement passed by and learned what was the matter. He sent for a psaltery, and tried the patient with soothing melodies; but, if the other tunes maddened him, Clement's seemed to crush him. He groaned and moaned under them, and grovelled on the floor. At last the friar observed that at intervals his lips kept going. He applied his ear, and found the patient was whispering a tune; and a very singular one, that had no existence. He learned this tune, and played it. The patient's face brightened amazingly. He marched about the room on the light fantastic toe enjoying it; and when Clement's fingers ached nearly off with playing it, he had the satisfaction of seeing the young man sink complacently to sleep to this lullaby, the strange creation of his own mind; for it seems he was no musician, and never composed a tune before or after. This sleep saved his life.[26]

[24] Oxf., p. 525; Ev., p. 532.

[25] Oxf., p. 526; Ev., p. 533.   [26] Oxf., pp. 527–28; Ev., p. 535.

There are two possible sources for this among the books on the *Century* list, but the better of the two is J. F. C. Hecker's *The Epidemics of the Middle Ages*. One of the great diseases which appeared in medieval Europe was the dancing mania, and this is the affliction of the young man. Hecker gives a long account, whereof I shall quote certain portions, mostly from his discussion of the Italian form of the malady: "Nobody had the least doubt that it was caused by the bite of the tarantula, a ground-spider common in Apulia; and the fear of this insect was so general, that its bite was in all probability much oftener imagined, or the sting of some other kind of insect mistaken for it, than actually received."[27] Reade says the youth was "bitten, or perhaps, *like many more, fancied it*." Again Hecker declares, "Some became morbidly exhilarated, so that they remained for a long while without sleep, laughing, dancing, and singing in a state of the greatest excitement."[28] The youth in Reade "had been for two days without sleep, and in most extraordinary convulsions, leaping, twisting, and beating the walls." The leaping and convulsions are found more in Hecker's account of the disease as it occurred in Germany.[29]

The attempts of the village musicians and Clement's first endeavors made the patient worse. In the same manner in Hecker, "If any particular melody was disliked by those affected, they indicated their displeasure by violent gestures expressive of aversion."[30] Conditions were better, however, if they liked a melody. As Hecker remarks, "This condition was, in many cases, united with so great a sensibility to music, that, at the very first tones of their favorite melodies, they sprang up, shouting for joy, and danced on without intermission, until they sank to the ground exhausted and almost lifeless."[31] Again in Hecker, "It was generally observable that country people who were rude, and ignorant of music, evinced on these occasions an unusual degree of grace, as if they had been well practised in elegant movements of the body."[32] In other words, a melody that the patient liked made him dance gracefully until he sank down exhausted. It is thus in

[27] Pp. 110–11.   [29] E.g., pp. 87–88.   [31] P. 112.
[28] P. 118.   [30] P. 123.   [32] P. 116.

Reade, but the novelist has invented one attractive detail: the favorite melody in this young man's case was one that he had composed himself in his sickness. In a word, he showed the same unwonted skill in music that, Hecker says, untaught country people did in dancing. Reade's patient, too, seems to have moved gracefully to the music, and the exhaustion after prolonged exercise takes the form of refreshing and preserving sleep.

The other possible source of this episode of Reade's is Nathaniel Wanley's *The Wonders of the Little World*.[33] To be sure, if there were no Hecker, we should hold that this was the source and that the other details were additions by Reade, but the presence in both Reade and Hecker of certain details not found in the brief Wanley account makes us prefer Hecker as the source. Wanley says nothing about the bite of the spider being imagined often, as both the others do. There is, moreover, no remark about the patients' growing worse when the wrong music was played. Nothing is said by Wanley, again, about the afflicted persons' dancing gracefully, and, finally, by the long dancing "the poyson is expel'd" in Wanley, a circumstance from which Reade would be less likely to take the resulting sleep than from Hecker's exhaustion.

The next episode, about the Englishman and the mulberry branch, is based on an experience of Moryson's near Florence. He related it as follows:

> By the way it hapened that I brake a bough of a mulbery tree, to shade me from the sunne, and falling into the company of an honest Gentleman, he told me I seemed a stranger, because I carried that bough, since those trees planted in the high waies, belonged to the Duke, who preserved them for silke-wormes, and had imposed a great penalty upon any that should breake a bough therof: so as if I passed with this bough through any village, I should be sure to be taken and kept prisoner, till I should pay a great fine: Whereupon I presently cast away this bough, with many thankes to him for his gentle warning.[34]

From this suggestion Reade has developed his scene.[35] What Moryson said might have happened in his own case has actually taken place in the novel. In other words, Clement met the vil-

---

[33] P. 497. Of course Reade may have had in mind both Hecker and Wanley.

[34] I, 316. (Noted by Wheeler.)   [35] Oxf., pp. 528–30; Ev., pp. 535–37.

A WINE PRESS

Jean Gutenberg, Premier Maître Imprimeur

191 INTO THE CHURCH

lagers haling along an Englishman who had walked into town with a mulberry branch torn from a tree, to shield his head from the sun. Clement mediated, using Latin as a means of communication. He explained the offense to the traveler and accompanied him before the magistrate. When the matter was settled, the Englishman regained his good humor and invited Clement to visit his house in England: "You shall end your days with me and my heirs if you will. Come now! What an Englishman says he means." The two men discussed the Lollards briefly and, on parting, exchanged their books of hours. The traveler's was in Latin and English; Clement's, in Latin and Italian. Hence each would learn a new foreign language, or, as the Englishman put it, "So shall I learn the Italian tongue without risk to my eternal weal. Near is my purse, but nearer is my soul." Thus has Reade worked up an attractive episode from a hint in Moryson, making the action interesting and adding, even more, the appeal of an attractive personality in the traveler.

The next experience of Clement's is a very pretty episode—that of his actually meeting Sweynheim and Pannartz.[36]

Clement found two tired wayfarers lying in the deep shade of a great chestnut-tree, one of a thick grove the road skirted. Near the men was a little cart, and in it a printing-press, rude and clumsy as a vine-press. A jaded mule was harnessed to the cart. . . . . He looked kindly down on them, and said, softly,—

"Sweynheim!"

The men started to their feet.

"Pannartz!"

They scuttled into the wood, and were seen no more.

Then gradually he dispelled their fear of his being a magician and explained how he knew their names.

"My children," said Clement, "I saw a Lactantius in Rome printed by Sweynheim and Pannartz, disciples of Fust."

"D'ye hear that, Pannartz? our work has gotten to Rome already."

"By your blue eyes and flaxen hair I wist ye were Germans: and the printing-press spoke for itself. Who then should ye be but Fust's disciples, Pannartz and Sweynheim?"

They were now all good friends. Clement relieved their wants with some money the Englishman had given him to use for char-

[36] Oxf., pp. 530–32; Ev., pp. 538–39.

ity, and he advised them to unharness their mule and let him roll—advice which they followed. The men were most grateful to Clement, and, in order to show their gratitude, they took the press out of the cart, and printing some sheets with type that was already set up, gave them to Clement.

"What are all these words really fast upon the paper?" said he. " Is it verily certain they will not go as swiftly as they came? And *you* took *me* for a magician! 'Tis 'Augustine de civitate Dei.' My sons, you carry here the very wings of knowledge. Oh, never abuse this great craft!"

We have already noticed, in discussing the appearance of a printed copy of Lactantius in Rome, that Reade drew the facts from Henry Hallam's *Introduction to the Literature of Europe*. On the same page with the previous information Hallam asserts, "In 1467, after printing Augustin de Civitate Dei, and Cicero de Oratore, the two Germans left Subiaco for Rome, where they sent forth not less than twenty-three editions of ancient Latin authors before the close of 1470."[37] This sentence provides the necessary facts about the Germans moving their printing to Rome and their having recently produced Augustine's work.

The idea of Clement's meeting the printers on the road, I believe, is derived from an illustration in a French book, *Jean Gutenberg premier maître imprimeur*. This is a French translation, published in Geneva in 1858 of a little German romantic tale by Franz Ferdinand Friedrich Dingelstedt. The tale is about the last years of the great printer. Perhaps I should add that there is also an English translation, published in London in 1860; but this has no illustrations. Moreover, we have seen that Reade draws from French books as readily as from English ones.[38] The illustration in the French version[39] is a full plate—reproduced in this book for comparison—depicting the episode, in the tale, of Gutenberg's seeing a wine press at work and suddenly getting the

[37] I, 99.

[38] In the *Century* list the book is called *John Guttenberg*. The English form John does not, I think, mean that Reade necessarily used the English version. The list is very hasty (note the spelling "Guttenberg" here), and English-speaking people think of the printer naturally as *John* Gutenberg.

[39] Opposite p. 30.

idea that the printing press should take a somewhat similar form. The wine press, it will be observed, is on a little wagon, which, in turn, stands in the middle of the road. Similarly, in *The Cloister and the Hearth*, while the printers were pausing for a rest, "near the men was a little cart, and in it a printing-press, rude and clumsy *as a vine-press*." In the illustration two peasants are operating the screw that brings down the press, and the horse appears glad to be unhitched. We have seen already how easily a hint started Reade's mind working, and, at times, a hint from a picture. This plate, joined (as it is, in the tale) with the idea of the printing press, made Reade conceive an episode where traveling printers—who, in this case of course, would be Sweynheim and Pannartz—would stop their wagon on the roadway and would there operate the press and do some printing. This theory most easily demonstrates how this rather unusual scene in the novel could come into being, and it is just the sort of mental process that is characteristic of Reade. In addition, there is one strong bit of verbal evidence—Reade's speaking of the press as "rude and clumsy as a vine-press." The idea once adopted, the novelist has developed it by means of details and living dialogue into the appealing incident which we have surveyed.

One small item is added from Moryson. After saying that mules and asses are the only means of transportation in Italy south of Lombardy, he asserts of the mule: "When his burthen is taken off at night, he tumbles and rubs his backe in the dust to coole it, and is thereby more refreshed from wearinesse, then a Horse can be with lying halfe the night."[40] From this statement is taken Clement's recommendation to unharness the mule. Upon this being done, as Reade says, "the animal immediately lay down and rolled on his back in the dust like a kitten," for he had "this art to refresh himself, which the nobler horse knoweth not."[41]

One day while Clement was traveling through Tuscany he encountered a group of pilgrims. One of them, a lady in a mask, approached him and washed his feet. Thereafter, in accordance

[40] IV, 84. (This Moryson borrowing is noted by Wheeler.)

[41] Oxf., p. 531; Ev., p. 539.

with the terms of her penance, she recounted her story; it was the Princess Claelia atoning for her killing of Gerard. Though she did not recognize Clement in his new role, he told her that Gerard had not betrayed to others the story of her love and that he had not perished. At this point she recognized him and was overcome with a surge of feeling. But Clement told her to abandon this penance and return to Rome. There, by marrying a godly husband, she herself would live a better life. The scene is most dramatic and moving, and in my opinion, is unsurpassed in *The Cloister and the Hearth.*

In the meantime, Margaret, back in Holland, was struggling to support herself and her dependents. She was tortured by not knowing what had happened to Gerard and tried, in vain, to elicit information from the old burgomaster, now a very sick man. Her aged father, disabled for some time, died; his last words, concerning Gerard, were, "I see him. I see him." Margaret, left alone, was courted by a well-intentioned young man, Luke Peterson by name.

After Brother Clement had reached Basle and taught there for a year, he started forth with Jerome to go to England. On the way both men preached frequently in the villages through which they passed. Clement, who always tried to fit his sermons to the needs of his hearers, produced a sensation by preaching against drunkenness in one village. Reade's account[42] is made up from bits taken from Moryson.

Drunkenness, we read in the novel, "was a besetting sin, and sacred from preaching in these parts; for the clergy themselves were infected with it, and popular prejudice protected it." This point comes from Moryson: "I say give me one Minister of Gods Word, who preacheth against excesse of drinking. My selfe have heard some hundreths of their Sermons, yet never heard any invective against this vice."[43] In fact, Moryson's wish that he might hear a clergyman who dared preach against this vice—which he considered deep-set in the Germans—probably suggested to Reade that Clement should be the man to do it.

[42] Oxf., pp. 557–58; Ev., pp. 565–66.   [43] IV, 41. (Not noted by Wheeler.)

Then, since Clement was attacking a deep-rooted failing that was usually not attacked, there was bound to be a sensation in the village and another interesting narrative in *The Cloister and the Hearth*.

Some of the remarks in Clement's sermon are from Moryson. His point that "a band of drunkards had roasted one of their own comrades alive at a neighbouring village" is from Moryson's "certaine Husbandmen being upon a wager to drinke twelve measures of wine . . . . did roast upon a spit one of their consorts, because he left them before the taske was performed."[44] Again, said Clement, "Your last prince . . . . is reported to have died of apoplexy, but well you know he died of drink." This remark is drawn from Moryson's statement, "A Physician, a familiar friend of mine, tolde mee that many Germans dying suddenly upon excesse of drinking, were ordinarily (for hiding of the shame) given out to die of the falling sickenesse."[45] Soon Clement, turning to another side of the question, asserted that, if the women drank as much as the men the town would be done for, and he asked how long the women would refrain from liquor when the men were such tipplers. "Already in Bohemia they drink along with the men. How shows a drunken woman? Would you love to see your wives drunken, your mothers drunken?" This appeal comes from Moryson's declaration that, although the women of Germany are most temperate, "yet the Weomen of Bohemia use as great (or little lesse) excesse in drinking, as Men."[46]

The result of the sermon was a great uproar. The men were indignant; but the women, though they pretended to be sympathetic toward the indignation of their male relatives, were secretly so much pleased with Clement that a crowd of almost a hundred wished him Godspeed on his journey, "filling his wallet with the best, and offering him the very roses off their heads."[47]

[44] IV, 36–37. (Not noted by Wheeler.)

[45] IV, 37. (Not noted by Wheeler.)

[46] IV, 41. (Not noted by Wheeler.)

[47] Note the reoccurrence of the rose wreath, mentioned before in the novel and coming from Moryson.

Chapter Nine

BACK IN HOLLAND

TRAVELING down the Rhine, Clement and Jerome finally came into Holland. Here, because of his ignorance of the language, Jerome was unable to preach, but Clement did so with much success. At the close of one sermon he saw a nun weeping. On attempting to comfort her afterward, he discovered the cause of her grief—the fact that a young nun from her convent had been lured away and was now residing at an inn, where she sold her favors to the richer customers. Clement, taking pity on the grief of all the nuns, determined to help them. The next day, assuming a layman's costume, he went to the inn, secured an interview with the girl under the pretense of desiring her love, and eventually prevailed upon her to return to the convent.[1]

Various writers[2] have discerned in this episode the influence of Erasmus' colloquy, *The Young Man and the Harlot*. The theme is the same—a very old one—and there is a borrowing of one detail. A closer similarity, however, indicates that Reade based his scene much more on some excerpts, occurring in Michel and Fournier in translation, from a play entitled *Abraham* by the medieval German nun Hrosvitha.[3] The girl was named Marie in the French translation of *Abraham* and Mary in the novel, and both were escaped nuns, whereas there is no indication that the girl in Erasmus had ever been in such a walk of life. The protagonist, in both play and novel, was a churchman, but apparently not so in the colloquy. Furthermore, in both *Abraham* and *The Cloister and the Hearth*, but not in Erasmus, he assumed the

[1] The episode occupies Oxf., pp. 564–70; Ev., pp. 572–78.

[2] Among them, Mr. Wheeler in his notes to the novel and, before him, the writer in *Notes and Queries* (10th ser., 1905), IV, 313.

[3] Michel and Fournier, *Le Livre d'or des métiers*, I, 200 ff. The original Latin text may be found in *Hrotsvithae opera*, ed. K. Strecker (Leipzig, 1906), pp. 169 ff.

disguise of a layman and first consulted the landlord of the inn as to the possibility of an interview with the girl. Thereafter, in the course of a conversation with her, the visitor removed his disguise and in the argument reminded her that, in order to save her, he had been compelled to do actions unsuitable for a church-man, such as entering an inn. Finally, in both play and novel, after the girl had decided to return to the convent, she desired to take her jewels with her to sell for the benefit of the poor but was persuaded by the churchman to abandon them. On the other hand, the only point which Reade's episode has in common with the Erasmus colloquy and not with *Abraham* is the visitor's ex-pressing to the girl a wish to have a place so secret that even God could not see them.[4] Thus it is evident that, in this episode, Reade drew most of his points from *Abraham* and added only one from Erasmus.[5]

Reade works up his borrowings in this scene most skilfully. He brings in the girl sooner than does the play and introduces a quick and telling exchange of speeches between Clement and the landlord. Again, whereas in *Abraham* the latter remains present for some time without much effect, Clement and the girl are left alone in the novel, and he starts her at once on the way to re-pentance by desiring a place where God cannot see them—the effective borrowing from Erasmus. He then shows her a golden chain from the convent, and she, thinking he has purloined it, recoils in horror. He takes this propitious moment to doff his disguise and appear as a friar. The chain, be it noted in passing, is a most successful dramatic touch here and elsewhere and is

[4] Erasmus, *The Colloquies*, II, 28–29. In an excerpt by Robert Greene (*Harleian Miscellany* [10 vols.; London, 1808–13], VIII, 401–2), and in a short passage of Coryate (*Crudities*, I, 408), a similar scene is described, with the desire for a place too secret for God to behold. But, in both, the girl, not the visitor, expresses the wish.

[5] These conclusions of mine as to the borrowings from Erasmus and Hrosvitha in this scene were published in my article, "Another Source for *The Cloister and the Hearth*," *PMLA* (1925), pp. 898–909. A later article by Oswald R. Kuehne, "Possi-ble Latin Sources for an Episode in Charles Reade, *The Cloister and the Hearth*," *Classical Weekly*, April 25, 1932, pp. 177–81, arrives independently at the same ideas as to Reade's borrowings in this episode from Erasmus and Hrosvitha, except, of course, that the author did not know of Michel and Fournier and Reade's frequent use thereof.

Reade's own invention. In the remainder of the scene, instead of talking theology at considerable length as in *Abraham*, the cleric appeals more to the girl's feelings. Finally, in taking her out of the inn, he is waylaid by the landlord and keeps the latter from forcibly detaining the girl only by threatening him with the curse of hell-fire. The whole episode, then, is an excellent example of Reade's infusing his own emotion into a scene and his developing it gradually to a powerful dramatic climax.

In the meantime, Margaret had sent out her youthful suitor to search for Gerard. Again, when one of her neighbors named Jorian became very sick and could not be cured by all the prescriptions of learned doctors, she gathered sweet feverfew from the sick man's own garden and, making a decoction thereof, fed it to him and thus cured him. He was very grateful to her, though somewhat sorry to be cured by so trivial a means. As his wife put it:

> Not but what he thinks you might have saved him with something more out o' the common than yon. "A man of my inches to be cured wi' feverfew," says he. "Why, if there is a sorry herb," says he. "Why, I was thinking o' pulling all mine up," says he. I up and told him remedies were none the better for being far-fetched; you and feverfew cured him, when the grand medicines came up faster than they went down.[6]

This happening may, perhaps, come from one of Erasmus' *Parabolae*, a work in the *Century* list. It runs, translated from the Latin:

> As the silly populace, with great labor and expense, seeks for remedies from the distant Indians and Aethiopians although in our very gardens grows what may cure us of our diseases; so with great effort do we seek abroad the safeguards of a happy life in authority, wealth, or pleasure, although the means of making ourselves happy comes from the soul.[7]

Jorian, in his superior attitude to feverfew because it grew in his own garden, was one of the silly populace.

Jerome now abandoned his companion and sailed for England. Clement, however, went to Sevenbergen, Margaret's village, and searched for her tombstone in the churchyard. Seeing an old man standing by the gate, he asked him whether he lived in the

---

[6] Oxf., pp. 572–74; Ev., pp. 580–82.

[7] Erasmus, *Opera omnia*, Vol. I, col. 605.

village long. The old fellow answered, "Four score and twelve years, man and boy." Clement then inquired where Margaret Brandt lay buried, but the old man replied she had left the town and gone to Rotterdam. Then the aged rustic continued musing, "Well, well, she was a May rose yon; dear heart, what a winsome smile she had."[8] There are two echoes of *Hamlet* in this passage: the old man's speech is like the gravedigger's reply to Hamlet, "I have been sexton here, man and boy, thirty years,"[9] and his description of Margaret is like Laertes' exclamation over Ophelia, "O rose of May!"[10] These verbal echoes, too, call our attention to the fact that the situation of Clement's seeking for Margaret is very like Hamlet's wandering through the churchyard and finding the fair Ophelia's grave; the Shakespearean scene was evidently haunting Reade.

Then one day Clement preached in the great church of St. Laurens in Rotterdam. The church was well filled, and the people followed his sermon with interest. Suddenly his eye lighted upon a figure that had appeared in a spot previously vacant. It was Margaret Brandt. Indeed she had come to church and had just now changed her seat to get a better place. For a moment Clement stopped his sermon in consternation; everybody stared; then, constraining himself, he proceeded. He believed the appearance was the spirit of Margaret; she herself had failed to recognize him, so changed was he. Then after the sermon he went into the churchyard and inquired of the sexton, Jorian, where Margaret was buried.[11] Here again the situation is like that in the graveyard scene in *Hamlet*. Jorian informed him that she was still alive, and told him enough other facts for him to see that his brothers and the burgomaster had concocted the crucial letter falsely. Clement next betook himself to the new shop that his two evil brothers were starting in Rotterdam and put upon them a terrible, yet eloquent, curse. Then he departed.

In Thomas Dudley Fosbroke's *British Monachism* occurs the following sentence: "Those [persons] who were restrained from committing sin by unwillingness that their Parish Priests should

[8] Oxf., p. 576; Ev., p. 584.   [10] IV, v, 154.

[9] V, i, 156–57.   [11] Oxf., pp. 585–87; Ev., pp. 592–94.

know it, encouraged themselves by saying, we will confess to some Friar passing this way, whom we have never seen before, and shall never see again."[12] This sentence, occurring in the chapter on *Friars* which Reade would have been likely to study, is, I think, probably the source of another incident in *The Cloister and the Hearth*.[13] Clement started to visit the burgomaster, intending by means of the deed which he carried and which showed that the old villain had wrongly kept the property of Margaret's father, to make him give the wealth up to Margaret. While eating his meal near the man's house he was summoned by a servant to come and confess the very person he intended to visit. The burgomaster was in a dying condition. He began his confession to Clement but spoke only of trivial sins. Clement, however, warned him not to conceal his greatest sin. The church knew many things. "You said 'I *will not confess to the curé, but to some friar* who knows not my misdeeds. [The italics are mine.] So will I cheat the Church on my death-bed, and die as I have lived." In this manner, by threats of hell instead of by showing the deed, Clement finally drove the avaricious old man to confess that he had defrauded Peter and Margaret of their property and to promise to restore it. The situation, we should note, is exactly that spoken of in the excerpt from Fosbroke—an evildoer choosing to recite his sins to a wandering friar who knew nothing about them—and the sentence I have quoted from Clement is not unlike the phrasing of Fosbroke's statement. This sort of hint, furthermore, is the type that we have often seen Reade taking and developing into a good scene.

The next day the burgomaster made restitution of the property to Margaret. At this time Giles, as court dwarf, was high in favor with the Princess Marie, especially since he had recently outwitted the court giant by two clever tricks. Because of her fondness for Giles the Princess promised to confer on his brother the position of Vicar of Gouda, but Gerard (or Clement) was not to be found. As a result of the curse it seemed, Sybrandt broke his back and became an invalid for life.

Now there was a hermit living in a cave near Tergou; he had

[12] P. 170.   [13] Oxf., pp. 595–98; Ev., pp. 602–5.

come there—none knew whence—as a successor to an earlier recluse, who had died recently. This new hermit—who later turned out to be Clement—occupies a great deal of space in the novel and occasions much discussion of anchorites. Reade evidently had studied assiduously upon the subject. At any rate he remarks in a passage quoted in the *Memoir*, "I have found such a wealth of material about hermits in Magdalen College Library that I have filled three more of those gigantic cards."[14] "Gigantic cards," one feels, however, are the sort of things that are not likely to be preserved for many years.

Margaret spied upon the anchorite. On the face of the rock containing the cave, as she observed, was carved the line, "*Felix qui in Domino nixus ab orbe fugit*," an inscription found by Moryson in a Leipzig cemetery.[15] The birds were flying freely about the cavern, for the hermit was their devoted friend. So tame were they, indeed, that, as one person said, "A neighbour o' mine saw his hand come out, and the birds sat thereon and pecked crumbs."[16] This familiarity with birds is drawn from *Mores Catholici*, where the author grows rhapsodical over the lives of recluses:

> The hermit is at peace with creatures, and with universal nature: these trees, these birds, these reptiles, are all companions to him; the freshness of the morning air, the fragrance of flowers and plants, the solemn obscurity of the pine forest, the beauty of animals, wild to other men, all seemed to be the hermit's own by a peculiar affinity of a supernatural alliance.

And once more, "On Montserrat the birds used to fly round the hermits, and feed out of their hands."[17] This probable influence is made sure by the fact that Reade, beyond all question, borrowed from another passage only three pages distant in *Mores Catholici*. Finally, Margaret had a good look at the hand of the hermit concealed in the cave as it reached out to give crumbs to the birds. She saw, by a mole, that it was her Gerard's hand.

[14] II, 104–5.

[15] Oxf., p. 613; Ev., p. 620; *An Itinerary Containing His Ten Yeeres Travell through the Twelve Dominions*, I, 14. (Noted by Wheeler.)

[16] Oxf., p. 615; Ev., p. 622. See also Oxf., pp. 614, 617, 632; Ev., pp. 621, 624, 639.

[17] III, 561, 565.

Reade, going back for a moment, tells how Clement had been called to shrive the previous hermit. The dying man confessed his sins to Clement and advised him to be the next tenant of the cell.[18] Upon the death of the recluse, Clement, after burying him close by and paying a visit on the burgomaster, took up his residence in the now unoccupied abode. This account of one hermit's succeeding another and something of the manner of their life is drawn from Monteil. A youth who had lost all his property in gambling was met by two good women. They took him up a hill:

Several years ago, they said to me, our old hermit died. Since then, the district has always needed its hermit. We've brought you here to take the place. You've lost everything; stay here; you'll lack nothing. . . . . The next day I found the tomb of brother Athanasius—that was the name of the former hermit —covered with wheat bread, a bowl of cream, and a basket of fruit. Several times each week, my provisions were renewed, and soon I found, hung up at my door, a cloak of new material and a pelisse of lamb's skin.[19]

Aside from Clement's succeeding a former anchorite, a similar attitude is evident on the part of the neighboring villagers in *The Cloister and the Hearth:* they felt a pride in the holiness of their hermit, they visited his cell for advice, and they brought him food—including at first such comparative luxuries as eggs and milk.[20] Moreover, one day he found by his cell "a new lambs-wool pelisse and cape."[21] This last, almost a literal translation of the concluding French words in the Monteil excerpt (*une cape d'étoffe neuve et un pelisson de peau d'agneau*), proves that Reade had this French passage in mind in describing Clement's early life.

Perhaps, too, Reade has drawn something from a remark in Du Cange's huge glossary, under the word *anachoretae*. Reade mentions this work in a footnote in his novel,[22] and, since he used it at least once, he would be likely to investigate what it said about the word for "anchorite":

Moreover, these [hermits] . . . . dwell alone in the desert and the waste places of the wilderness . . . . they lead a strange life, and, having hollowed

[18] Oxf., p. 621; Ev., p. 628.

[19] *Histoire des français des divers états*, II, 419.   [21] Oxf., p. 637; Ev., p. 643.

[20] Oxf., p. 613, 626; Ev., pp. 620, 633.   [22] Oxf., p. 623; Ev., p. 630.

out rocks into a habitation, they dwell in these caves under ground, shielding themselves from sun and storms; they feed on stale bread, without the addition of other victuals, taking pure draughts of water from springs. Their clothing is made of skins or of hair cloth.[23]

If Reade did note this page, he may have taken from it certain details such as the cave, the "cilice of hair,"[24] and Clement's "horror" at the country people's bringing him eggs and milk— "Know ye not the hermit's rule is bread, or herbs, and water?"[25]

In a footnote to a passage in which he calls St. Bavon, "a hermit, and an austere one, a cuirassier of the solitary cell,"[26] Reade makes the reference, already mentioned, to Du Cange—to be exact, to the word *loricatus*: Du Cange says this word is applied to "monks of more holy life, who, for mortification of the flesh, as they say, wear an iron breastplate continuously next the skin and lay it aside for no necessity."[27] As a result of this remark, probably, Reade declared that the earlier hermit "carried a steel corselet next his skin" and that Clement wore the same breastplate.[28]

In connection with Clement's life as an anchorite there are a good number of references to saints, most of them too general to be traced to any immediate source. For one long and detailed passage about pious anchorites, however, we can find a sure source. Reade's passage is as follows:

Then, his [Clement's] teacher, Jerome, had been three years an anchorite on the heights of Camaldoli, where for more than four centuries the Thebaid had been revived; and Jerome, cold and curt on most religious themes, was warm with enthusiasm on this. He had pored over the annals of St. John Baptist's abbey, round about which the hermits' caves were scattered, and told him the names of many a noble, and many a famous warrior, who had ended his days there a hermit, and of many a bishop and archbishop who had passed from the see to the hermitage, or from the hermitage to the see. Among the former the archbishop of Ravenna; among the latter Pope Victor the Ninth. . . . . And [he

[23] Carolus Dufresne, Dominus du Cange, *Glossarium ad scriptores mediae et infimae, latinitatis* (3 vols.; Frankfort, 1681), Vol. I, col. 177.

[24] Oxf., p. 623; Ev., p. 630.

[25] Oxf., p. 626; Ev., p. 633.   [26] Oxf., p. 623; Ev., p. 630.

[27] II, second half (it is renumbered). (Wheeler quotes this, but does not draw from it the hermit's or Clement's wearing a corselet.)

[28] Oxf., pp. 621, 642; Ev., pp. 628, 649.

told him] how seven times in the twenty-four hours, in thunder, rain, or snow, by daylight, twilight, moonlight, or torchlight, the solitaries flocked from distant points, over rugged precipitous ways, to worship in the convent church; at matins, at prime, tierce, sexte, nones, vespers, and complin. . . . . [Among the famous anchorites were] Moncata, Duke of Moncata and Cardova, and Hidalgo of Spain, who in the flower of his youth had retired thither from the pomps, vanities, and pleasures of the world; Father John Baptist of Novara, who had led armies to battle, but was now a private soldier of Christ; Cornelius, Samuel, and Sylvanus. This last, when the great Duchess de' Medici obtained the Pope's leave, hitherto refused, to visit Camaldoli, went down and met her at the first wooden cross, and there, surrounded as she was with courtiers and flatterers, remonstrated with her and persuaded her, and warned her, not to profane that holy mountain, where no woman for so many centuries had placed her foot; and she, awed by the place and the man, retreated with all her captains, soldiers, courtiers, and pages, from that one hoary hermit.[29]

This long account is based on a passage in *Mores Catholici* wherein the author quotes from the Spaniard Andreas Mugnotius. The Spaniard, describing "the desert and hermits of Camaldoli, on the Tuscan mountains," says rapturously:

O sacred desert, desert of deserts! more than five hundred years have elapsed from thy erection to these times [Reade, treating probably an earlier epoch, says "more than four centuries"], and with wondrous immutability, thou continuest to bear the fruits of immortal life. [Jerome's "enthusiasm" on the subject is modeled after that of the Spanish writer.] . . . . Two [saints], especially eminent, have of late been here,—two great lights of the desert, Samuel and Silvanus: the latter profound in sacred erudition, and both admirable in holiness; under whose discipline Ambrose Moncata, a youth of that most ancient and illustrious ducal family of Moncata and Cardona [in Reade, this becomes Cardova, probably because his penmanship was misread] of Spain, despising the pleasures and riches and honours of the world, in the flower of his age, has chosen this solitude as his place of rest. Here, too, Father John Baptist of Novara, who had formerly been an illustrious warrior amongst the nobles of the world, became a true soldier of Christ, and spends his life in the desert. Cornelius has past more than twenty years in solitude here. . . . . Seven times each day and night they meet together in the church, to offer prayers and hymns to God, with holy ceremonies and seraphic devotion. No showers, or snows, or wild tempest, or vehement cold can prevent them. . . . . Silvanus told me that Eleonora, the wife of Cosmo de Medicis, had obtained permission from Pius IV to see and behold the place; but that he had gone down to meet her as far as the first of the wooden crosses, and had prevailed upon her to abandon her resolution, and not transgress so ancient and venerable an institution. [Seeing the

[29] Oxf., p. 622; Ev., pp. 629–30.

dramatic power of the duchess' visit, Reade builds this last part out, contrasting "her captains, soldiers, courtiers, and pages" with "that one hoary hermit."][30]

With this main source for his passage, Reade combines bits from a different part of the same work, *Mores Catholici*.[31] Speaking of a group of the order of Camaldoli living near Paris, this work remarks, "They say matins at one in the morning, tierce before mass, sextes immediately before dinner, nones at two, vespers before supper, and complin on retiring to rest." Reade has drawn, from this list of six, the names of his services—which he has kept seven in number as the other passage in *Mores Catholici* specified. He has made the six into seven by splitting "matins at one in the morning" into two services: "matins" and "prime." *Mores Catholici* on the same page again declares: "Thus Ugolino, bishop of Ostia, cardinal, and afterwards Pope Gregory IX., withdrew into that [desert] of Camaldoli, on the Tuscan mountains." Here is where Reade found the example of the prelate who passed from "the hermitage to the see," a man whom he called by error "Pope Victor the Ninth." The error is a rather bad one, for there has been no Pope Victor IX. Reade's example of a man who "passed from the see to the hermitage" is "the archbishop of Ravenna." This comes from the same page of *Mores Catholici*, where, among several "solitary hermits" in Italy during the eleventh century, occurs "John Vincent, who had been archbishop of Ravenna." It should be noticed, however, that *Mores Catholici* does not say, as Reade does, that the former archbishop was a hermit at Camaldoli.[32]

Clement frequently reflected upon various saints who are mentioned very briefly by Reade. Two of them about whom Mr. Wheeler found it impossible to secure any information from the regular sources appear in books in the *Century* list. First, Reade's mention of "the earthly purgatory at Fribourg, where lived a nameless saint in a horrid cavern, his eyes chilled with perpetual

[30] III, 568.   [31] III, 545.

[32] Reade's inaccuracies and his mention of some obscure persons in this passage of the novel have, naturally enough, sadly perplexed his editor, Mr. Wheeler. But, though there are errors, the description certainly produces a colorful effect on the reader.

gloom, and his ears stunned with an eternal waterfall"[33] surely comes from two sentences in *Mores Catholici:* "Near Fribourg, in the rocks which overhang the river Sane, cut out of the cliff, a suite of solemn rooms, through which its dark waves resound loud roaring, so as to stun the ear, still recalls the hermit who once inhabited them. His hands had wrought them."[34] Obviously this effective picture touched Reade's imagination. Again, Reade speaks of "the living tombs, sealed with lead, of Thais and Christina."[35] Mr. Wheeler found the information about the celebrated Thais in her cell sealed with lead, but could learn nothing about a Christina's being thus imprisoned. Reade almost surely derived the fact from Fosbroke's *British Monachism*, which refers to

one Christina, as an Anchoress, in a cell . . . . she was so concealed by boarded contrivances, as to be invisible to any person, externally; and instead of a door, was a hard trunk of wood, which was too heavy to be moved by her. She lay upon the cold stone, condemned to sit immovably, be tortured, and remain in silence.[36]

Clement busied himself in various ways, especially in carving edifying maxims upon the rock. The quotation which he carved from Augustine—"*O anima Christiana*"—Reade found in Coryate, who saw it inscribed in the cathedral of Nevers.[37] One night, too, when Clement was singing the praises of God to his psaltery, he looked out of his cell "and there sat a great red wolf moaning melodiously with his nose high in the air." *Mores Catholici* informs us that hermits came to be on friendly terms with all animals, including even fierce ones.[38]

Clement was beset by visions of Margaret, but he regarded them as the work of fiends. To conquer such temptations "he found the deepest part of the stream that ran by his cell . . . . ; and, clearing the bottom of the large stones, made a hole where he could stand in water to the chin, and, fortified by so many examples, he sprang from his rude bed upon the next diabolical

---

[33] Oxf., p. 624; Ev., p. 631. [35] Oxf., p. 624; Ev., p. 631.

[34] III, 550. [36] P. 380.

[37] Oxf., p. 630; Ev., p. 637; Coryate, I, 199. (Noted by Wheeler.)

[38] Oxf., p. 632; Ev., p. 639; *Mores Catholici*, II, 563–66.

assault, and entered the icy water."[39] This circumstance seems to be derived from the experience of St. Bernard, which Reade may perhaps have come across in Mrs. Anna Murphy Jameson's *Legends of the Monastic Orders:*

> On one occasion he recollected himself at the moment when his eyes had rested with a feeling of pleasure on the face of a beautiful woman [i.e., he remembered having gazed at her thus], and, shocked at his own weakness, he rushed into a pool of water more than half-frozen, and stood there till feeling and life had nearly departed together.[40]

When the visions returned, moreover, Clement "rose hastily with a cry of dismay, and stripping to the skin climbed up to the brambles above his cave, and flung himself on them, and rolled on them writhing with the pain."[41] This incident seems prompted by the action of St. Benedict, who, upon recalling vividly the face of a beautiful woman he had seen, behaved thus. Reade may have seen the account in the same work of Mrs. Jameson or elsewhere.[42]

Finally, Margaret herself came to induce him to go to his new parish of Gouda, since the people had become weary of waiting for their vicar. Beset with the idea of temptation and of saving his soul, he rebuffed her, and she departed. He soon, nevertheless, detected an infant left in his cell. He talked to it and learned from its babblings that it was afraid of storks.[43] These birds may have been brought to Reade's attention by Moryson's mention of them in Holland.[44] Then Clement continued to fondle the child. Margaret very soon reappeared, however, and told him that the baby was their own. Then by mementoes of her that Clement still preserved she saw that he loved her devotedly. She told him of the death of his sister Kate, and, finally, by loving exhortation, she persuaded him to leave his hermit's life and go to his vicarage. And thus Brother Clement became Gerard, parson of Gouda.

Gerard was duly installed in his parsonage. As he said to some-

---

[39] Oxf., pp. 634–35; Ev., p. 641.

[40] (London, 1852), p. 140. (The parallel to St. Bernard is not noted by Wheeler.)

[41] Oxf., p. 636; Ev., pp. 642–43.

[42] P. 8. (Mr. Wheeler noted the parallel to St. Benedict.)

[43] Oxf., p. 644; Ev., pp. 650–51.   [44] IV, 54. (Noted by Wheeler.)

one who asked whether he was really vicar: "Certes: have I not been to the bishop and taken the oath, and rung the church bell, and touched the altar, the missal, and the holy cup, before the churchwardens? And they have handed me the parish seal; see here it is."[45] This remark is drawn from Monteil's account of how a clergyman, from assisting priest, was made chief priest of the parish:

I presented myself to the bishop, who had just named me to the parish of St. Martin. I was received most graciously, and I took my oath beneath his hand. I then hastened to betake myself to my parish. The nearest curé was delegated to conduct my investiture. He came the next day. I rang the bell, I touched the altar, the missal, and the chalice. I had delivered to me at the same time the seal of the parish church, which from that moment has been my seal, and thus I took possession.[46]

Gerard's being a hermit and later becoming vicar of Gouda are not in the *Compendium* at all, but are inventions of Reade's. The *Compendium*, however, does of course say that Gerard never lived with Margaret as his wife, afterward. The novel agrees in this respect, and adds the most effective circumstance that the two dwelt near each other and remained tenderly attached. After describing their relation in detail, Reade characteristically remarks in a footnote, "On a summary of all the essential features, the situation was, to the best of my belief, unique."[47]

The child of the two, in the novel, bore the name of Gerard, as both Knight and Jortin say was the case in reality.[48] The *Compendium* says the boy made little progress in his studies in early youth; in much the same manner Reade declares he was spoiled by his mother and his grandmother at first. At the age of nine, however, in both the *Compendium* and the novel, little Gerard was sent to school at Deventer.[49] The *Compendium* says his mother went with him; the novel says Margaret was accustomed to visit him for "weeks at a time."

The birds that used to consort with Gerard in his cave now

[45] Oxf., p. 662; Ev., p. 669. [46] II, 197. [47] Oxf., p. 666; Ev., p. 673.

[48] Oxf., p. 668; Ev., p. 675; Samuel Knight, *The Life of Erasmus*, p. 10; John Jortin, *The Life of Erasmus*, p. 3.

[49] Oxf., p. 668; Ev., p. 676.

came to his manse—we learn later that Margaret induced them thither. Moreover, Gerard

found a squirrel with a broken leg; he set it with infinite difficulty and patience: and during the cure showed it repositories of acorns, nuts, chestnuts, etc. And this squirrel got well and went off, but visited him in hard weather, and brought a mate, and next year little squirrels were found to have imbibed their parents' sentiments.[50]

This episode is drawn from two neighboring passages in *Mores Catholici*. Of St. Columban we read, "The little animal which men call squirrel used often to leap down from the high branches, jump on his neck, creep into his bosom, and eat out of his hand."[51] Again, we are told about a certain friar: "When at Cortona he found a bird in the woods with its legs broken; and he contrived with quills to bind them up, and then covered them with some of his juniper oil, which he used as a medicine for sick persons; and when he had restored the poor bird to soundness, he set it free again."[52]

Margaret helped Gerard faithfully in the duties of his parish. On one occasion a woman of the district who suspected them of illicit relations saw them in earnest conversation and whipped behind a tree in order to eavesdrop:

It was winter; there had been one of those tremendous floods followed by a sharp frost, and Gerard in despair as to where he could lodge forty or fifty houseless folk out of the piercing cold. And now it was, "Oh dear, dear Margaret, what shall I do? The manse is full of them, and a sharp frost coming on this night."

Margaret reflected. . . . .

"You must lodge them in the church," said Margaret, quietly.

"In the church? Profanation."

"No: charity profanes nothing; not even a church: soils nought; not even a church. To-day is but Tuesday. Go save their lives; for a bitter night is coming. Take thy stove into the church: and there house them."[53]

The eavesdropper "glided home remorseful."

This situation is worked up from a passage in Monteil:

This year, there was so much cold weather and misery that I lodged poor people in the church; there they were warmed and fed; outside, they would

[50] Oxf., p. 673; Ev., p. 680.   [52] III, 566.

[51] III, 565.   [53] Oxf., pp. 674–75; Ev., p. 682.

have perished. It is generally known that it is allowable, on the appearance of enemies or undisciplined soldiery, to take food and furniture into churches. I agree that the law does not mention human beings, but surely it cannot think that they are less valuable.[54]

In 1481 Denys suddenly reappeared. Ten years previously he had seen service in England. At that earlier time, "1471, the Duchess of Burgundy with the open dissent, but secret connivance of the duke, raised forces to enable her dethroned brother, Edward the Fourth of England, to invade that kingdom; our old friend Denys thus enlisted."[55] Now in 1481, no longer fit for service, he journeyed through Gouda. Gerard, passing a public house, heard his voice.

> To the company he appeared to be bragging and boasting; but in reality he was giving a true relation of Edward the Fourth's invasion of an armed kingdom with 2,000 men, and his march through the country with armies capable of swallowing him, looking on, his battles at Tewkesbury and Barnet, and reoccupation of his capital and kingdom in three months after landing at the Humber with a mixed handful of Dutch, English, and Burgundians.[56]

Denys also proclaimed "the English King the first captain of the age."

Though it is hard to be absolutely sure of such borrowings, these bits of history certainly seem to come from Sharon Turner. At any rate, he is closer to Reade than any of the other volumes in the *Century* list. Sharon Turner relates that the Duchess of Burgundy "supplied her brother with such resources as she could command. The Duke of Burgundy being deterred, by his managing policy, from any avowed support, carried his duplicity . . . . so far as to declare publicly, that he would give the King no assistance. . . . . But he privately sent him 50,000 florins" and supplied ships to transport his men to England.[57] Edward had collected two thousand men by March 2, 1471. After crossing the water, moreover, he disembarked "at Ravenspur, on the Humber." Then he began his march. "Tho various bodies of armed men, six or seven thousand in number, were in different places

[54] II, 198.   [55] Oxf., p. 666; Ev., p. 673.   [56] Oxf., p. 676; Ev., p. 683.

[57] *The History of England: From the Earliest Period to the Death of Elizabeth* (12 vols.; London, 1839), VI, 278.

assembled against him, ... yet none moved to attack him."[58]
Several other armies let Edward march on thus, unattacked, to
London. Then, after an account of the battles of Barnet and
Tewkesbury, Turner declares: "It is probable, that the calcula-
tions of the Lancastrians would have been verified by the issue,
if Edward had not been the ablest captain at that time existing"
—a point which the historian develops and which Denys echoes
in calling him "the first captain of the age."[59] The only difference
between Turner and Reade is that the former said Edward's men
were English whereas the latter said they were "Dutch, English,
and Burgundians." This change by Reade may be due to care-
lessness, to drawing from some other authority (Monstrelet, for
instance, says the men were "English, Easterlings, Flemings,
Picards, and other nations"),[60] or to a desire to make the army of
a sort that Denys would naturally join.

Gerard was delighted to meet his old comrade Denys again,
and he accommodated him in an almshouse recently constructed
"for decayed true men in their old age." There Denys's "natural
gaiety returned, and he resumed his consigne after eight years'
disuse."

Little Gerard made good progress at the school at Deventer.
Indeed, Margaret, "flushed with pride," reported his success to
Gerard:

> "A great scholar, one Zinthius, came to see the school and judge the scholars,
> and didn't our Gerard stand up, and not a line in Horace or Terence could
> Zinthius cite, but the boy would follow him with the rest. 'Why, 'tis a prodigy,'
> says that great scholar; and there was his poor mother stood by and heard it.
> And he took our Gerard in his arms, and kissed him; and what think you he
> said?"
>
> "Nay, I know not."
>
> " 'Holland will hear of thee one day: and not Holland only, but all the
> world.' "[61]

[58] *Ibid.*, pp. 280–82.

[59] *Ibid.*, p. 302.

[60] *The Chronicles of Enguerrand de Monstrelet*, trans. Johnes (2 vols.; London, 1840),
II, 396.

[61] Oxf., p. 680; Ev., p. 687.

The *Compendium* spoke of the scholar Zinthius as a good influence in the school. Moreover, Knight, in his biography of Erasmus, declares:

One Zinthius . . . . is said, upon observing the prodigious Parts and Industry of the young Erasmus, to have foretold what afterwards came to pass, that he would sometime prove the Envy and wonder of all Germany: he might have added of the whole World. One thing is especially remarked of him, that he had so prodigious a Memory, that he was able to say all Terence and Horace by heart.[62]

Reade has enlivened this account by having Erasmus able to carry on any quotation begun by Zinthius, and has sweetened the whole by showing Margaret's pride in her son.

One day Gerard heard that the plague had been brought to Deventer by two sailors. He went thither to take away his son but found that Margaret had already sent the boy to a safe place. In addition, he made the tragic discovery that Margaret herself had caught the plague. The *Compendium* tells that Margaret died of this disease when it was raging in Deventer, but indicates that Gerard was not with her at the end. Obviously Reade makes the change to gain more pathos. For *The Cloister and the Hearth*, Reade has drawn some details about this pestilence from J. F. C. Hecker's *Epidemics of the Middle Ages*. Speaking of the form common in Florence, Hecker states, "It commenced here, not as in the East, with bleeding at the nose, a sure sign of inevitable death," but with tumors.[63] Similarly, Margaret, a physician's daughter, remarked, "My nose hath bled; none ever yet survived to whom that came along with the plague."[64] And, once more, Margaret told Gerard, "I shall not be spotted or loathsome, my poor darling; God is good and spares thee that."[65] This is from Hecker's sentence about the Florentine variety of the disease: "Black or blue spots came out on the arms or thighs, or on other parts, either single and large, or small and thickly studded."[66] In other words, Margaret had the eastern form of the disease, not that which attacked Florence. Margaret likewise gave directions as to what was to be done with her body: "Also my very clothes are

[62] P. 7.
[63] P. 5.
[64] Oxf., p. 682; Ev., p. 689.
[65] Oxf., p. 683; Ev., p. 690.
[66] P. 5.

tainted, and shall to earth with me. . . . . Wherefore lap me in lead, the way I am; and bury me deep."[67] This point of view is in harmony with Hecker's declaration, "The plague spread itself with the greater fury, as it communicated from the sick to the healthy, like fire among dry and oily fuels, and even contact with the clothes and other articles which had been used by the infected, seemed to induce the disease."[68] Margaret soon died, in loving conversation with Gerard, and her body was interred at Gouda.

Gerard, broken in spirit, entered a Dominican convent within a fortnight. The prior, he found, was his old friend Jerome. Jerome told him he ought to continue to live, but Gerard replied that he could no longer go on with existence now that Margaret was dead. A few days later, lying on ashes strewn in the shape of a cross on the floor, Gerard breathed his last. He was buried beside Margaret.

Upon finishing his long novel, *The Cloister and the Hearth,* Reade expressed his feelings in a letter:

You will be glad to learn that last night at nine o'clock amidst the cheers of my relations, I wrote the last page of this tremendous work, which in all probability will impoverish me for some time to come. No matter! It is done! And I breathe again. Strange to say, the last fifteen pages went smooth as oil; and I don't know whether it is parental vanity, but I think they will live.[69]

[67] Oxf., p. 685; Ev., p. 692. An entry in one of the Reade notebooks owned by Mr. Parrish refers to the *Times,* December 26, 1861, and runs: " 'Lapped in lead.' This expression seems to be borne out by discovery of a singular coffin in Worcester Cathedral." The entry shows Reade's interest in the process, even after finishing the novel.

[68] P. 5. Hecker says that most people died within three days.

[69] Malcolm Elwin, *Charles Reade: A Biography,* p. 156.

Chapter Ten

BORROWING AND ART

NOW that we have finished our study of the whole novel, it is pertinent to return to Reade's list in the *Century* once more and see from just how many of the works there listed he actually borrowed. There were seventy-four entries on the list. I shall go over the books according to the classes marked off in my introduction and mention those from which Reade drew surely and those from which he may have drawn. Books of the latter group are followed by a question mark.

I. ERASMUS AND HIS WORKS—5 entries

    Drawn from: *The Colloquies*
               Parabolae[?]
               Jortin
               Knight

II. LITERARY WORKS—8 entries

    Drawn from: *The Foure PP*[?]
               Volpone
               Hugo, *Notre-Dame*
               Scott's novels[?]

III. BOOKS ON LITERATURE—2 entries

    Drawn from: Hallam, *Literature of Europe*

IV. THE FINE ARTS—15 entries

    Drawn from: Bryan, *Dictionary of Painters*
               Mrs. Jameson, *Legends of the Monastic Orders*[?]
               Labarte, *Handbook of the Arts*
               Marchese
               Merrifield
               Pugin and Smith, *Ecclesiastical Ornament*
               ·Vasari
               Wilars de Honecort, *Sketch-Book*

V. Ecclesiastical Works—9 entries

Drawn from: Brandt, *History of the Reformation*
Fosbroke, *British Monachism*
Fox, *Monks and Monasteries*
Mores Catholici

VI. Political History—8 entries

Drawn from: Barante[?]
Commines[?]
Froissart
Monstrelet[?]
Henry, *History of Great Britain*
Sharon Turner, *History of England*

VII. Social History—8 entries

Drawn from: Le Grand d'Aussy
Hecker, *Epidemics of the Middle Ages*
Lacroix and Seré
Liber vagatorum
Monteil
Michel and Fournier
Strutt's works

VIII. History or Biography in the Form of Fiction—2 entries

Drawn from: *Norica*
Gutenberg

IX. Travels and Geography—6 entries [of which I could not find one]

Drawn from: Coryate
Montaigne, *Journey*
Moryson

X. Letters and Discourses—4 entries

Drawn from: *The Paston Letters*[?]

XI. Collections and Indexes—7 entries

Drawn from: Hone, *Every-Day Book and Table-Book*
Southey, *Common-Place Book*
Wanley, *Wonders of the Little World*

Of the total number of seventy-four entries, then, I have noted borrowings from thirty-five and possible borrowings from eight more.[1]

[1] I have already indicated that readers desiring to know just what Reade drew from any of these works must look up the title of the work in the Index and then consult all the pages there mentioned.

Though, as I have before said, I did not make a systematic and thorough investigation beyond the *Century* list,[2] I detected borrowings from the following:

Archaeologia	Lanzi, *The History of Painting in Italy*[?]
Cellini	Milman, *History of Latin Christianity*
Du Cange	Reade's father
Gallenga [*pseudonym* Mariotti], *Italy*	Shakespeare
Harman, *Caveat*	Stow, *The Survey of London*[?]

A point with which we are strongly impressed is that Reade drew most unequal amounts even from those works from which he borrowed at all. From some he took only one small point; from others he helped himself time and again. The following (with the addition of the all-important *Compendium*) are the works from which he drew most, and the sort of material he took from each:

CORYATE: Details about foreign countries

ERASMUS, *Colloquies:* Several important large scenes

LACROIX AND SERÉ: Especially details of medieval life

MICHEL AND FOURNIER: Suggestions for scenes, especially during Gerard's wanderings

MONTAIGNE: Especially scenes in Rome

MONTEIL: An unusually large number of suggestions for scenes all through the novel

MORYSON: A very large number of details about foreign countries, and also numerous scenes

The two classes of works from which Reade drew most, then, are books on social history—especially modern works in French— and Renaissance books of travel.

Another notable point is that Reade did not borrow equally for all parts of his novel. The portions about Holland have comparatively few borrowings; those concerning other countries have many. This is natural enough. The scenes in Holland take place in a fairly limited area; they concern, aside from bits about the Duke of Burgundy, only a limited group of people; the action, in

---

[2] A list of books—aside from those in the *Century* list—which I examined without detecting any influence may be found in the Appendix.

general, is less extraordinary; the interest in the loves, the joys, the sorrows of Gerard and Margaret is all important. In other words, there is not much need for varied local color, and there is no great call for unusual episodes, since the interest in character and emotion occupies the reader. On the other hand, when Gerard is away from home he wanders over Germany, Burgundy, and Italy; and the persons presented are most varied: German peasants, Burgundian soldiers, Italian monks, a Roman princess, a pope. There is need for extended treatment of the local color of various places and people. Again, wandering implies adventure, and so there is a great call for all sorts of strange experiences. Thus Reade is, naturally, far more inclined to borrow when treating the foreign than the Dutch scenes of the novel.

Now for Reade's treatment of his sources, we may distinguish two chief sorts of borrowing—that of specific facts and that of ideas for scenes.

Reade frequently takes over specific facts, and at times great groups of such facts. Some of the outstanding examples are the account of the Duke of Burgundy's feast early in the novel, the descriptions of the various German inns, the narrative of the siege at which Denys was present, and the details as to German drinking. The chief purpose, of course, in these passages is to give the local color of the Middle Ages or of a particular country.

The borrowing of ideas for scenes is, perhaps, even more frequent in *The Cloister and the Hearth.* The degree of closeness with which Reade adheres to his original varies greatly. At times, as in the account of the German gentleman having his servants rob Gerard or in the famous shipwreck scene, he keeps his main course of events like those in his source. At other times he is much freer in his handling, sometimes going so far as to take only a hint from the source—a hint which stimulates his imagination to go on and develop the scene freely. For example, the small hint in Michel and Fournier about the landlord at an inn summoning rascals to kill his guests has been built out fully, with the addition of the "Abbot" and his ax, the killing of the first assassin, and "*La Mort*" inscribed on his forehead. A still more freely developed suggestion is the one about two resolute men being able to kill a bear by attacking him in turn. Here indeed, Reade's imagination, receiving a basic idea, created a most thrilling adventure.

In this connection, let me say, I hope no one has come to have a less high opinion of Charles Reade's abilities by perusing this book. Of the two types of borrowing which I have just discussed the first is essential to a historical novelist. The manner of life in a past epoch is different from that today. The novelist cannot invent; he must have recourse to books. The second kind of borrowing—that of ideas for scenes—though of course not necessary like the first, has long been known as characteristic of Reade. His great system of notebooks served, among other things, to record those taking incidents and happy ideas for plots which he met in his reading of books or newspapers and felt might be useful to him in his writing.

Reade's handling of both sorts of borrowing is very able. At times he condenses. A good example is the description of Cologne with which Gerard entertains Denys. If we compare it with the original in Coryate, we see that Reade has cut it down enormously, keeping the essential points and increasing their force by the saving of words. Though this is an extreme example, it is usually true that Reade's drawing from a source, unless he adds new material, takes less space than did that of the original author. What he leaves out, moreover, are the useless repetitions or the weaker details that would injure his account.

On the other hand, Reade is quite capable of increasing the bulk of an incident, but this is by adding specific details, and especially dialogue, in order to make it more vivid. Thus the account of the drunken nobleman lying on the ground and watched by his servant occupies perhaps ten lines in Moryson. Reade adds the effective touch of the horse, indicates Gerard's surprise and the servants' character by extensive dialogue, and supplies a lively conclusion. The result is that he fills a page and a half; but it is space well spent, for he has fully realized the possibilities that were inherent, but not developed, in Moryson's short narrative.

Another very notable trait of Reade's handling of borrowings is his habit of drawing from more than one source for an episode and mingling the elements taken. This procedure has happened time and again. Thus the narrative about Gerard's acting the part of Count Detstein comes from two different portions of the same author—Monteil: one about changing places with a nobleman and riding thus for a long time; the other about changing clothes with another young spark. Reade combines the two borrowings into one incident and thus sharpens it, for it is certainly more striking, if Gerard is going to act the role of a count, to have him wear the gentleman's clothes too. More frequently, however, the borrowings which are combined come from different sources. Thus the exorcism is mostly from Montaigne, but with something from Moryson; the reclaiming of the nun from her infamy is mostly from a Hrosvitha passage quoted in Michel and Fournier, but with a touch of Erasmus; the boat party on the Tiber with the disguised boy is a mixture of Cellini, Montaigne, Moryson, and Coryate. In all his mingling of borrowings, moreover, Reade is extremely successful; the resulting passage is the better for the additional element, and the fusion is so perfect that the uninformed reader would never suspect that there were several sources.

In handling his borrowings Reade usually changes the wording somewhat. He is frequently very colloquial—at times unpleasantly so. On the other hand, his diction has life; in fact, it sometimes uses a neat turn that is sure to catch the reader's attention. An example is the rendering of Montaigne's "roast fowls, reclothed with their natural feathers as when alive," by the happy phrasing, "roast pheasants dished up with all their feathers as if they had just flown out of a coppice instead of off the spit." Whatever his faults of diction, then, the novelist's rendering of his sources is in language that is likely to hold one's attention.

Reade likewise often changes the order of things in his borrowings, with good results. Thus in the purely descriptive account of the wearing of rose garlands by the German women, Reade gives Moryson's details with close adherence, but he alters

Moryson's order, making it more logical; as a result the passage in the novel is easier and more graceful reading. Again in the famous shipwreck scene, though the novelist had a very well-written source in Erasmus' colloquy, he considerably improves the order of the different happenings.

Another quality that Reade shows in his handling of borrowings is the ability to heighten scenes. He is quite aware that, as an episode progresses, it should grow in tensity until the climax is reached. Thus the scene with the old German doctor, after giving a good account of the man's character and of medieval medicine, becomes more tense with the arrival of Denys, who opposes the physician's views. The opposition grows more forceful. Gerard sides against bleeding. The old doctor rages, and, as a climax, is knocked over by Gerard onto his own pan of burning coals.

Allied to this quality is the emotional dramatic power achieved in many scenes which are worked up by Reade from a borrowing. The adventure in the inn where Denys and Gerard are almost murdered is one of the most thrilling in English fiction. The miscreants talking below, the huge voice of the "Abbot," the terrified whispers of the probable victims above, their despairing plans how to make their strength count to the utmost, provide enormous suspense. Of another type is that most dramatic scene at another inn where Gerard reclaims the nun. The action gradually becomes more tense, as we have just noticed is the case with Reade's scenes. Gerard finally makes the girl consent to return to the convent. On the way out the pair meet the landlord. He attempts, with the help of his servants, to detain them, and it is only by means of the threat of hell-fire that Gerard makes him desist. The episode is extremely powerful and, like many of the novelist's scenes, would be excellent for acting.

Reade was, then, not only most extensive in his borrowings but most wise in his handling of them. From trivial details to ideas for large scenes, he made the best use of the elements he took. He revealed a fertile imagination in the way he built them out; he showed his art in what he omitted or in the changes he made in the order; he displayed in the liveliness of handling and readiness of emotion the touch of a great master of narrative.

Appendix

Besides the books in the *Century* list, I read, skimmed, or inspected, as seemed desirable, certain other works for possible influences on *The Cloister and the Hearth*. Most of them were mentioned in the Reade notebooks owned by Mr. Parrish. Those books from which I detected some borrowing are discussed in the body of this study, and their titles appear in my Bibliography. Those from which I detected no borrowing are the following:

AUBREY, JOHN. *Lives of Eminent Men.* 2 vols. London, 1813.

AWDELEY, JOHN. *The Fraternitye of Vacabondes.* Ed. E. VILES and F. J. FURNIVALL. London, 1869.

Cabinet des fées, Le, ou collection choisie des contes des fées, et autres contes merveilleux. 41 vols. Geneva and Paris, 1787–89.

CAMDEN, WILLIAM. *Britain*, Trans. PHILEMON HOLLAND. London, 1610.

CRAIK, DINAH MARIA MULOCK. *A Woman's Thoughts about Women.* New York, 1864.

Dialect of Craven, The, in the West-Riding of the County of York. 2 vols. London, 1828.

DÜRER, ALBRECHT. *Records of Journeys to Venice and the Low Countries.* Ed. ROGER FRY. Boston, 1913.

GOULART, SIMON. *Thrésor d'histoires admirables et memorables de nostre temps.* 4 vols. Geneva, 1620.

GRAEVIUS, JOHANNES GEORGIUS. *Thesaurus antiquitatum Romanorum.* 12 vols. Utrecht, 1694–99.

———. *Thesaurus antiquitatum et historiarum Italiae.* 9 vols. Leiden, 1704–23.

———. *Thesaurus antiquitatum et historiarum Siciliae.* 15 vols. Leiden, 1723–25.

GRONOVIUS, JACOBUS. *Thesaurus Graecarum antiquitatum.* 12 vols. Venice, 1732–37.

JAMIESON, JOHN. *An Etymological Dictionary of the Scottish Language.* 2 vols. Edinburgh, 1808.

JONES, OWEN. *The Grammar of Ornament.* London, n.d., but Preface is dated 1856.

Miscellanea curiosa. 3 vols. London, 1705–7.

RICHARDSON, M. A. *The Local Historian's Table Book of Remarkable Occurrences.* 8 vols. Newcastle-upon-Tyne, 1841–46.

Vidocq, Memoirs of. Written by himself and translated from the French. 4 vols. London, 1829.

Vitae virorum illustrium. Basel, 1563.

Voyages imaginaires, songes, visions, et romans cabalistiques. Ed. C. G. T. Garnier. 39 vols. Amsterdam and Paris, 1787–89.

Here, for want of a better place, I should like to mention the interesting article entitled "Erasmus and *The Cloister and the Hearth*," by E. C. Peixotto, in *Scribner's Magazine,* January, 1905, pages 116–22. The article discusses the author's visit to towns in Holland mentioned in Reade's novel and gives pictures of various buildings there.

Bibliography

This contains all the books mentioned in the *Century* list and all other works used.

Antiquarian Repertory, The. Chiefly compiled by FRANCIS GROSE, THOMAS ASTLE, *et al.* 4 vols. London, 1807–9.

Archaeologia: Or Miscellaneous Tracts Relating to Antiquity, Vol. XXXVIII. London: Society of Antiquaries of London, 1860.

Archaeological Journal, Vols. I–XVIII. London: British Archaeological Association.

AUSSY, LE GRAND D'. *Histoire de la vie privée des françois, depuis l'origine de la nation jusqu' à nos jours.* 3 vols. Paris, 1815.

BARANTE, A. G. P. B. DE. *Histoire des Ducs de Bourgogne de la maison de Valois.* 12 vols. Paris, 1839.

BAYLE, PIERRE. *Dictionaire historique et critique.* 4 vols. Rotterdam, 1720.

BLOXAM, MATTHEW HOLBECHE. *Fragmenta sepulchralia.* No place and date.

———. *The Principles of Gothic Ecclesiastical Architecture.* London, 1849.

BOWER, ARCHIBALD. *The History of the Popes from the Foundation of the See of Rome to the Present Time.* 7 vols. London, 1750–66.

BRANDT, GERARD. *The History of the Reformation and Other Ecclesiastical Transactions in and about the Low Countries, from the Beginning of the Eighth Century down to the Famous Synod of Dort, Inclusive.* Translated from the Low-Dutch. 4 vols. London, 1720–23.

BRYAN, MICHAEL. *A Biographical and Critical Dictionary of Painters and Engravers.* London, 1849.

Cellini, Memoirs of Benvenuto. Trans. THOMAS ROSCOE. London, 1850.

Chroniques de Flandre, Recueil des. 4 vols. Brussels: J. J. de Smet, 1837–65. (Vol. IV is after Reade's work.)

COLEMAN, JOHN. *Charles Reade as I Knew Him.* London, 1903.

Commines, Memoirs of Philip de. Ed. ANDREW R. SCOBLE. 2 vols. London, 1896.

CORYAT(E), THOMAS. *Crudities.* 2 vols. Glasgow, 1905.

DINGELSTEDT, FRANZ FERDINAND FRIEDRICH. *Jean Gutenberg premier maître imprimeur.* Trans. G. REVILLIOD. Geneva, 1858.

Dodsley's Plays: A Select Collection of Old Plays. 3d ed. 12 vols. London, 1825–27.

DU CANGE, CAROLUS DUFRESNE, DOMINUS. *Glossarium ad scriptores mediae et infimae Latinitatis.* 3 vols. Frankfort, 1681.

ELWIN, MALCOLM. *Charles Reade: A Biography.* London, 1931.

Epistolae obscurorum virorum. Latin text with an English rendering by F. G. STOKES. New Haven, 1925.

ERASMUS, DESIDERIUS. *Colloquia*. Leiden, 1636.

————. *The Colloquies*. Trans. N. BAILEY. Ed. E. JOHNSON. 3 vols. London, 1900.

————. *Opera omnia*. 10 vols. Leiden, 1703–6. (*The Parabolae* are in Vol. I, cols. 557–624.)

————. *Opus epistolarum Des. Erasmi Roterodami*. Ed. P. S. ALLEN. 8 vols. Oxford, 1906–34.

FIELDS, ANNIE. "An Acquaintance with Charles Reade," *Century Magazine*, XXIX (November, 1884), 67–79.

FOSBROKE, THOMAS DUDLEY. *British Monachism: Or Manners and Customs of the Monks and Nuns of England*. London, 1843.

FOX, SAMUEL. *Monks and Monasteries: Being an Account of English Monachism*. London, 1845.

FROISSART, SIR JOHN. *Chronicles of England, France, Spain, and the Adjoining Countries*. Trans. THOMAS JOHNES. 2 vols. London, 1855.

GALLENGA, ANTONIO (pseud. L. MARIOTTI). *Italy*. 2 vols. London, 1841.

Gentleman's Magazine. Indexes I–IV (1731–1818); indexes to individual volumes to 1861.

Gutenberg. *See* DINGELSTEDT.

HAGEN, AUGUST. *Norica, or Tales of Nürnberg*. Translated. London, 1851.

HALLAM, HENRY. *Introduction to the Literature of Europe in the Fifteenth, Sixteenth, and Seventeenth Centuries*. 2 vols. New York, 1868.

————. *View of the State of Europe during the Middle Ages*. New York, 1870.

Harleian Miscellany, The. 10 vols. London, 1808–13.

HARMAN, THOMAS. *A Caveat or Warening for Commen Cursetors*. Ed. E. VILES and F. J. FURNIVALL. London, 1869.

HECKER, J. F. C. *The Epidemics of the Middle Ages*. Trans. B. G. BABINGTON. London, 1844.

HENRY VIII. *State Papers Published under the Authority of His Majesty's Commission*, Vol. I: *Correspondence between Henry VIII and Wolsey*. London, 1830.

HENRY, ROBERT. *The History of Great Britain*. 12 vols. London, 1805.

HEYWOOD, JOHN. *The Foure PP*. In JOHN MATTHEWS MANLY, *Specimens of the Pre-Shaksperean Drama*, I, 483–522. 2 vols. Boston, 1897.

HONE, WILLIAM. *Ancient Mysteries Described, Especially the English Miracle Plays*. London, 1823.

————. *The Every-Day Book and Table Book*. 3 vols. London, 1835. (A combination of *The Every-Day Book* and *The Table Book*.)

————. *The Year Book of Daily Recreation and Information*. London, 1841.

HUGO, VICTOR. *Notre-Dame de Paris*. (In French.) 2 vols. Paris: Marpon and Flammarion, n.d.

————. *Notre-Dame de Paris*. (In English.) 2 vols. Boston: Estes and Lauriat, n.d.

HUMPHREYS, HENRY NOEL. *The Illuminated Books of the Middle Ages*. London, 1849.

———. *Illuminated Illustrations of Froissart. Selected from the MS in the Bibliothèque Royale, Paris*. London, 1845.

———. *Illuminated Illustrations of Froissart. Selected from the MS in the British Museum*. London, 1844.

———. *The Origin and Progress of the Art of Writing*. London, 1855.

———. *A Record of the Black Prince*. London.

———. *Stories by an Archaeologist and His Friends*. 2 vols. London, 1856.

———. *Ten Centuries of Art*. London, 1852.

JAMESON, ANNA MURPHY. *Legends of the Monastic Orders*. London, 1852.

———. *Sacred and Legendary Art*. 2 vols. London, 1857.

JONSON, BEN. *Works*. London: Routledge, n.d.

JORTIN, JOHN. *The Life of Erasmus*. 3 vols. London, 1808.

KNIGHT, SAMUEL. *The Life of Erasmus*. Cambridge, 1726.

KUEHNE, OSWALD R. "Possible Latin Sources for an Episode in Charles Reade's *The Cloister and the Hearth*," *Classical Weekly*, XXV, 177 ff.

LABARTE, JULES. *Handbook of the Arts of the Middle Ages and Renaissance*. Translated from the French. London, 1855.

LACROIX, PAUL, and SERÉ, FERDINAND. *Le Moyen Age et la Renaissance*. 5 vols. Paris, 1851.

LANZI, LUIGI. *The History of Painting in Italy*. Trans. THOMAS ROSCOE. 3 vols. London, 1852–54.

LELAND, JOHN. *The Itinerary*, 9 vols. Oxford, 1744.

Liber vagatorum. Trans. and ed. J. C. HOTTEN. London, 1860. Under the title *The Book of Vagabonds and Beggars*.

LUTHER, MARTIN. *The Table Talk or Familiar Discourse*. Trans. WILLIAM HAZLITT. London, 1848.

MAITLAND, S. R. *The Dark Ages*. London, 1844.

MARCHESE, VINCENZO FORTUNATO. *Lives of the Most Eminent Painters, Sculptors, and Architects of the Order of S. Dominic*. Trans. C. P. MEEHAN. 2 vols. Dublin, 1852.

MARIOTTI, L. *See* GALLENGA.

MERRIFIELD, MARY PHILADELPHIA. *The Art of Fresco Painting*. London, 1846.

———. *Original Treatises, Dating from the XIIth to the XVIIIth Centuries on the Arts of Painting, etc.* 2 vols. London, 1849.

MICHEL, FRANCISQUE and FOURNIER, EDOUARD, *Le Livre d'or des métiers: histoire des hôtelleries, cabarets, hôtels garnis, restaurants et cafés, etc.* 2 vols. Paris, 1851.

MILMAN, HENRY HART. *History of Latin Christianity*. 8 vols. New York, 1860–61.

MONSTRELET, ENGUERRAND DE. *Chronicles*. Trans. THOMAS JOHNES. 2 vols. London, 1840.

MONTAIGNE, MICHEL EYQUEM DE. *The Diary of Montaigne's Journey to Italy in 1580 and 1581.* Trans. E. J. TRECHMANN. London, 1929.

———. *Journal du voyage en Italie.* 2 vols. Rome, 1774.

MONTEIL, AMANS ALEXIS. *Histoire des français des divers états.* 5 vols. Paris, 1853.

Monumenta Franciscana. Ed. J. S. BREWER. Vol. I: London, 1858; Vol. II: London, 1882 (after Reade's novel).

Monuments français inédits pour servir à l'histoire des arts depuis le VI⁰ siècle jusqu'au commencement du XVII⁰. Text by ANDRE POTTIER. 2 vols. Paris, 1839.

Mores Catholici: Or Ages of Faith. Anon. KENELM HENRY DIGBY. 3 vols. London, 1845, 1846, 1847.

MORYSON, FYNES. *An Itinerary Containing His Ten Yeeres Travell through the Twelve Dominions of Germany, Bohmerland, Sweitzerland, Netherland, Denmarke, Poland, Italy, Turky, France, England, Scotland, and Ireland.* 4 vols. Glasgow, 1907–8.

MOSHEIM, JOHANN LORENZ VON. *An Ecclesiastical History.* Trans. ARCHIBALD MACLAINE. 2 vols. London, 1838.

MÜNSTER, SEBASTIAN. *Cosmographia universalis.* Basel, 1554.

NEWCOME, PETER. *The History of the Ancient and Royal Foundation, Called the Abbey of St. Alban.* London, 1795.

Norica. See HAGEN.

Notes and Queries, XI (7th ser., 1891), 348–49, 398–99, 438, 496; XII, 56; IV (10th ser.), 313.

Paston Letters: Original Letters Written during the Reigns of Henry VI, Edward IV, and Richard III. Ed. JOHN FENN. London, Vols. I–II (1787); Vols. III–IV (1789); Vol. V (1823).

PUGIN, A. WELBY. *Contrasts.* London, 1841.

———. *Glossary of Ecclesiastical Ornament and Costume.* Rev. BERNARD SMITH. London, 1868.

RANKE, LEOPOLD, *The Popes of Rome.* Trans. SARAH AUSTIN. 3 vols. London, 1866.

READE, CHARLES. *The Cloister and the Hearth: A Tale of the Middle Ages.* Everyman ed. London and New York, 1906.

———. *The Cloister and the Hearth: A Tale of the Middle Ages.* Oxford ed., Ed. with Introduction and notes by C. B. WHEELER. London, 1915.

———. *A Good Fight.* Introduction by ANDREW LANG. London, 1910.

———. *White Lies.* Boston, 1869.

READE, CHARLES L. and COMPTON. *Charles Reade Dramatist, Novelist, Journalist: A Memoir Compiled Chiefly from His Literary Remains.* 2 vols. London, 1887.

SCOTT, WALTER. *The Abbot.* London and Edinburgh, 1893.

———. *The Monastery.* London and Edinburgh, 1893.

———. *Quentin Durward.* London and Edinburgh, 1894

SHAKESPEARE, WILLIAM. *Works.* Ed. WILLIAM ALDIS WRIGHT. (The Cambridge Shakespeare.) 9 vols. 1902–5.

SHAW, HENRY. *Dresses and Decorations of the Middle Ages.* 2 vols. London, 1843.

SOMMERARD, ALEXANDRE DU. *Les Arts au Moyen Age*. 2 vols. of text and 3 of plates. Paris, 1838.

SOUTHEY, ROBERT. *Common-Place Book*. 1st, 2d, 3d ser. London, 1850. (Reade apparently did not consult the 4th ser.)

STOW, JOHN. *The Survey of London*. London, 1633.

STRUTT, JOSEPH. *A Compleat View of the Manners, Customs, Arms, Habits, etc., of the Inhabitants of England*. 3 vols. London, 1775–76.

———. *A Complete View of the Dress and Habits of the People of England*. 2 vols. London, 1842.

———. *The Regal and Ecclesiastical Antiquities of England*. London, 1777.

———. *The Sports and Pastimes of the People of England*. London, 1801.

———. *A Supplement to the Regal and Ecclesiastical Antiquities, etc., of the English*. London, 1792.

SUTCLIFFE, EMERSON GRANT. "Charles Reade's Notebooks," *Studies in Philology*, XXVII, 64–109.

TURNER, ALBERT MORTON. "Another Source for *The Cloister and the Hearth*," *PMLA*, XL, 898–909.

———. "Charles Reade and Montaigne," *Modern Philology*, XXX, 297–308.

TURNER, SHARON. *The History of England: From the Earliest Period to the Death of Elizabeth*. 12 vols. London, 1839.

TURNER, WILLIAM. *A Compleat History of the Most Remarkable Providences*. London, 1697.

VASARI, GIORGIO. *Lives of the Most Eminent Painters, Sculptors, and Architects*. Trans. MRS. JONATHAN FOSTER. 5 vols. London, 1850–52.

WANLEY, NATHANIEL. *The Wonders of the Little World*. London, 1678.

WARTON, THOMAS. *The History of English Poetry*. 3 vols. London, 1840.

Wilars de Honecort, Facsimile of the Sketch-Book of. Trans. and ed. ROBERT WILLIS. London, 1859.

INDEX OF SOURCES USED BY READE FOR
THE CLOISTER AND THE HEARTH
(With the pages in this book on which borrowings from them are discussed)

⟦ PRINTED
IN U·S·A· ⟧